The Bow Group

A
HISTORY

THE BOW GROUP

A HISTORY

JAMES BARR

Politico's PUBLISHING

First published in Great Britain 2001

Published by Politico's Publishing
8 Artillery Row
Westminster
London
SW1P 1RZ

Tel 020 7931 0090
Fax 020 7828 8111
Email publishing@politicos.co.uk
Website http://www.politicos.co.uk/publishing

First published in hardback 2001

A catalogue record for this book is available from the British Library.

ISBN 1 84275 001 1

Printed and bound in Great Britain by MPG Books, Bodmin Cornwall.

Contents

Foreword

French President Jacques Chirac was one of Tony Blair's first high profile visitors to New Labour Britain. How best to introduce the great man to Cool Britannia? At what symbolic showplace could he most strikingly be entertained? For old Bow Groupers like myself, there was more than a little irony in the answer.

For the choice fell upon Canary Wharf, the heart of London Docklands' Enterprise Zone. Twenty years earlier when I had first unveiled the Enterprise Zone idea at a special Bow Group meeting, in The Waterman's Arms in the rusting wilderness of the then Isle of Dogs Old Labour had denounced the entire concept. Yet now the erstwhile 'Capitalist Valhalla' had become a shop window for 'Cool Britannia'. In face of this conversion, small wonder that Paul Johnson was reclassifying Tony Blair – even before his arrival in Downing Street – as a 'One Nation Conservative', with 'Bow Group, written all over him'.

For Johnson this was the secret of New Labour's success – in presenting themselves as a 'safe and better alternative' to the ailing Tory government. But it was even more remarkable, as James Barr points out in this stimulating history, as a tribute to the success of those who had, for almost half a century, been managing and shaping the reputation of the Bow Group. In Barr's words, it was 'a galling indication of the continuing power of the Group's brand . . . exactly what Blair needed to inspire Tory voters to trust him'.

And what had been the original inspiration for the Bow Group 'brand'? Above all, I believe, the founders' reaction against the stifling intellectual atmosphere that had dominated our student years – the years of the post-war Attlee government. This had been created, as we perceived, by the Socialist thinkers of half a century before: by the Webbs and the Coles, by Wells, Shaw, Laski, Dalton and the rest; and the universities, as we perceived, were still breeding fresh Fabians aplenty. But by 1951 we, like many of our countrymen, had no appetite for more of the same. So we had turned to the Conservative Party, the only possibly credible alternative in sight – but still, as it seemed, strikingly short of intellectual ammunition for the years ahead. Hence our first (immodestly) proclaimed objective: 'to combat the influence of the Fabian Society'.

And how exactly was this to be done? In truth, we had very little idea – save that this small band of Right-thinking graduates (all with other jobs to do or other professions to follow) should start thinking, talking, researching, pamphleteering together about some of the key issues of the day. The Group's first pamphlet, by Anthony McCowan, tackled, as Barr remarks, 'an entirely original subject for research', *Coloured Peoples in Britain* (then no more than 35,000 in number). It received an enthusastic (if surprised) welcome from press and politicians alike.

This is not the place to trace (as James Barr does so well) just how the Group succeeded (for the most part) in building upon that success. Three illustrations must suffice.

First, in 1957, came the launch – by none other than the Prime Minister, Harold Macmillan – of the Group's quarterly magazine, *Crossbow*. Less than a year later the journal's first two editors, Colin Jones and Timothy Raison, along with Christopher Chataway and Trevor Philpott, persuaded HMG and then the UN to take up *Crossbow*'s proposal for a World Refugee Year (and later received the Nansen Medal for this imaginative work).

The second notable achievement was the part played by the Group (on this topic under James Lemkin's very 'plugged-in' leadership) in pressing the case for early (though still prudent) decolonisation. This enthusiasm for 'the wind of change' in Africa for a time threatened the credibility of the Group's 'no corporate view' policy. This had been specifically endorsed by the refusal, in 1956, either to condemn or to approve Anthony Eden's Suez venture. But if this 'anticolonialism' gave the Group a Leftish flavour, it was not inconsistent with *Crossbow*'s editorial aim to take 'a realistic view of Britain's position in the world'. So too was the Group's willingness – established after hot debate – to publish powerful material on both sides of the developing European debate.

And the third striking feature of the first decade was the extent to which any 'Leftish' image was offset by the decisively 'free market' balance of the Group's domestic output. My own contribution to our tenth anniversary booklet, *Principles in Practice*, has been recently described by Nicholas Timmins as having 'summed up much of what was to become the radical right's agenda during the 1980s'. At the time of publication, way back in 1961, *The Times* was even persuaded 'that the reactionary Bow Group are almost in charge of Conservative policy'.

This was hyperbole, of course. But clearly the Group had 'arrived'. On the Right hand, we had provoked the formation of the Monday Club (now almost defunct); and on the Left, the Fabian Society was flatteringly urged by its then secretary, Shirley Williams, to set about 'combating the influence of the Bow Group'. It was, says Barr, 'the range, and heretical quality, of the Group's work which had caused aggravation and recognition in equal measure'. And, inspired as we were by a wide range of gurus – from Iain Macleod and Edward Boyle to Enoch Powell and Keith Joseph – we had helped to change the image of 'the stupid party', to make it, in my phrase, 'fit for *Guardian* and *Observer* readers to live in'. The Group has been one of the intellectual magnets that has (often, if not always) helped to identify the Conservative party as one possible roosting place for (above all young) people who are prepared to think radically about the society in which they live. And just as it has promoted the party's electability, so it has – let's acknowledge it – helped too the electability of some of its own members. (There have also been times when it may have been having the opposite effect!)

So what of the future? The great news is that the Group continues not only to exist but also to flourish – and in a form still readily recognisable by an antique like myself. The median number for membership (and probably for general circulation of publications) remains at about 1,000 – with *Crossbow* still appearing regularly (more or less) and a full programme of meetings and ongoing research. And there is one yardstick of continuity, also fulfilled, which is more important than any of those: the nature and quality of contemporary publications. That judgment is based on my view of one of the most recent pamphlets, *The Worst Parent in Britain*, by Rachael Bolland and Mark Nicholson. For it is manifestly 'the product of independent research and analysis by two young graduates drawing on their own professional experience, as respectively a Senior Children's Nurse and an accountant with one of the 'big five'. They reach measured conclusions which command respect and the pamphlet has been well received.

So the Group continues to meet the needs of a political market (even sometimes to make it) – for idea generators as well as for ideas which can help to inform political opinion and, hopefully, to improve society.

Even so, the world is very different from that in which the Group was born. It has survived (occasional) conflicts, even famines, of leadership – as indeed has the Tory party itself. Money raising has been a recurrent problem. But, more important than any of that, there have been major changes in the ambient political environment.

The last two decades have witnessed not one but two political revolutions in this country. Neither of them is complete. Nor has either of them been perfectly conducted. But both were necessary. The more recent of these – the Blair constitutional revolution, in the form of devolution and Lords' reform – has been waiting to happen for a long time. So too had the preceding Thatcher economic revolution, which has replaced Attlee/Butskellism with what the French call 'Thatcher/Blairisme' – essentially the commitment to a market-led society. The first 30 years of the Bow Group's life was taken up with preparing the way for this and the last 20 with its implementation. Together we have indeed succeeded (as Keith Joseph was one of the first to commend) in redefining the common ground of British politics. This is the process which I tried to describe to two successive Bow Group fringe meetings at Blackpool and Bournemouth in 1989 and 90. Only in respect of European policy has my forecast been (dramatically) unfulfilled – so far! We may be sure that on that topic the debate will be self-sustaining for the foreseeable future. Nobody can imagine the degree of self-restraint that has persuaded me to refrain from addressing the case in this foreword.

So, Europe apart, we live – very like the people of the United States and of other mature democracies – in a country where most discussion is now about the methods and not the objectives of government. Changes, sometimes quite radical, remain necessary, of course, – but these are

generally deliverable only over a period of time. So revolutions are out –
even, *pace* Smith Square, 'commonsense' revolutions. And, as I suspect
most people feel, a good thing too.

But if that sea-change in the political scene poses problems of adjust-
ment for the Group, they are multiplied a thousand fold by the second
transformation that has been occurring in parallel. Our peoples may have
been led – knowingly or not – to understand, even to accept, that
political miracles are unnecessary as well as impossible. Yet in the rest of
their lives they find themselves confronted with a bewildering and
high-speed diversity of challenges. These are often the result of techno-
logical advance. Fiercely competitive media coverage then reflects and
stimulates a demand for almost instantaneous change – to which politicians are only too ready to respond. A 'disaster' is reported and 'requires
a response'. Competing sound-bites are produced and expectations
raised. Often there follow new 'task forces' – worse still new laws. But in
the result little, if anything, actually happens – apart from a further loss
of public confidence in the political system.

This is the challengingly difficult political environment into which
organisations like the Bow Group now have to launch their political
advice. And there are many more comparable (and competing) voices
today, from commercial, as well as academic and political, think tanks.
So the temptation to go for headline impact is very real – but, I believe,
resistible. For it is my conviction that there is out there a growing
constituency, which is looking for serious and more thoughtful contributions to political debate. In the United States, for example, neither
Senator Bill Bradley nor John McCain succeeded in winning nomination
as their party's candidate in the 2000 presidential election. But their input
throughout was designed to, and did, raise the debate to a much more
thoughtful level.

In Britain too there are some signs that the message is beginning to
get through. It was a key point in Francis Maude's speech to the Bow
Group in October 2000. And even Tony Blair has seemed to be trying to
steer Prime Minister's Questions into a more grown-up and less knock-
about occasion. The tenacious loyalty to current affairs programmes of
radio (but not TV) audiences may tell something of the same story. Can

the Bow Group make fresh headway by achieving a restrained and moderate but acceptably modern style, which can reach real people by breaking through the sound-bite ceiling? Not, I suspect, without a matching recognition by today's hugely powerful media of the need to restrain their own impatience and cynicism. But somebody has to make a start somewhere.

Forty years ago the *Sunday Mail* dubbed the Group 'the most remarkable and the most influential group of young people in Britain at present' – perhaps because, in the words of another journal, 'their first intent' was 'to be good researchers and not good politicians'. It is difficult to imagine similarly respectful comment from today's *Mail on Sunday*. Can today's Bow Groupers – let alone today's editors – rise to the corresponding, though more difficult, challenges of the 21st century?

And if any are looking for a really man-size target on which to start this work, they need look no further than an item which has been at the top of the research stockpile for at least 40 years: how, *without relying upon higher taxes to bridge the gap*, to increase Britain's total spending on health care by the 50 per cent necessary to bring it up to same share of GDP as is achieved in virtually every other mature democratic economy? Other countries have been able to persuade their citizens that private spending to that extent on health care is not unacceptable in a prosperous society. Why should the United Kingdom, which has enjoyed a huge increase in leisure spending during the last half century, find it apparently impossible to contemplate the possibility?

This question was one to which I directed attention in my *Principles in Practice* essay in 1961. It was at the heart of a paper on public spending which, as Chancellor of the Exchequer, I circulated to Cabinet just 21 years later. But that item disappeared from the national agenda a week later, when the Prime Minister assured the Conservative Party conference that the National Health Service was 'safe in our hands'. And 'safe' certainly, but sadly underfunded, it has remained from that day to this. Now even Tony Blair is reported to be 'looking at' the question in this way.

Will tomorrow's Bow Group be equipped and ready to do more than that? This perceptive history offers some pointers to the likely answer to that question. But it is one for decision by today's Group leaders – and not by a voice from the past.

GEOFFREY HOWE
January 2001

The Rt Hon. Lord Howe of Aberavon – Chancellor of the Exchequer 1979–83, Foreign Secretary 1983–9 and Deputy Prime Minister 1989–90 – was Chaiman of the Bow Group 1955-6 and editor of Crossbow *1960–2.*

Acknowledgements

Without the help of several people I doubt whether I could have written this book or that it would have been published. My mother, Valerie Barr, valiantly sorted and sifted the Bow Group's untidy collection of yellowing newspaper cuttings. Nicholas Perry lent me his file of notes and photocopies of the Group's early 'Confidential File', which formed the basis of his trail-breaking but ultimately abortive attempt to write a history of the Group. Without access to his notes the first three chapters of this book would have been much less detailed. My editor Nicholas Edgar, whose idea it was that the Group should mark its 50th anniversary with a history, has patiently waited for two years to see the finished work, when we had originally agreed a timescale of six months. The team at Politico's, Iain Dale, Sean Magee and John Berry, offered expertise mixed with humour and a sense of fun which made the final stages of the process of writing a pleasure.

I am grateful to the past and present members of the Group who spoke or wrote to me about their involvement: the Rt Hon. Sir Peter Emery MP; Pamela Thomas; James Lemkin; Russell Lewis; Alan Bennett; the Rt Hon. Lord Biffen of Tanat; the Rt Hon. Lord Howell of Guildford; the Rt Hon. Lord Brittan of Spennithorne; Henry Bosch; the Rt Hon. Sir Timothy Sainsbury; the Rt Hon. Michael Howard MP; Simon Jenkins; the Rt Hon. Sir Peter Lloyd MP; Nigel Waterson MP; Anthony Nelson; Patricia Hodgson; Douglas French; the Rt Hon. Sir John Nott; Michael Stephen; Nirj Deva MEP; David Shaw; Michael Lingens; Lynda MacKenzie; Stuart Jackson; Terry Bowers; Cheryl Gillan MP; Marie-Louise Rossi; David Harvey; Nick Hawkins MP; Katherine Bowes; David Campbell Bannerman; Jeremy Bradshaw; Fiona Buxton; Guy Strafford; and Maurice Button. I would particularly like to thank the Rt Hon. Peter Lilley MP for an illuminating insight into his involvement in the Group in the 1970s. Fred Kellogg, of the Ripon Society, provided me with an American view of the Group's 1982 Trans-Atlantic Conference. The Rt Hon. Lord Howe of Aberavon permitted me to read through and quote from his private papers, as did the Rt Hon. Lord

Jenkin of Roding. Mrs Mary Griffiths kindly gave the Group a selection of papers and photographs belonging to her late husband, Bruce Griffiths, which form a vital record of the embryonic days of the Group. Dr Nigel Ashford willingly sent me relevant excerpts from his doctoral thesis on the Conservative Party and Europe. Professor Tom Nossiter commented shrewdly from an academic perspective on drafts. Carol Moon, until recently the Bow Group's administrator, gave me a guided tour of the Group's archives and tolerated my frequent requests for information in the early stages of my research. I am also grateful to Irene Harris, Carol's successor at the Group, for her help in the final stages, and to Gilvrie Lock and George Perry for their memories of the October 1967 *Crossbow* cover. Finally I am grateful to James Walsh of the Conservative Policy Forum for granting me permission to quote from the Conservative Party Archive and to Jill Spellman the Party's archivist for helping me during my visit to Oxford.

My parents, Valerie and Stuart, have endured and encouraged throughout an exciting couple of years. It is to them that I dedicate this book.

A.J.B.
ajbarr@compuserve.com

Kennington, December 2000

Timeline

1962   *The New Africa* published; the Monday Club set up to counter the Bow Group's apparent influence on the Government

1963   Membership reaches a peak of 927 and begins to decline, spring

–   Committee convened to consider Group's role in Opposition, summer

–   Group creates new role of 'Political Officer' in Council, September

–   Group moves to larger offices at 240 High Holborn, November

1964   New Political Officer, Henry Bosch creates Standing Committees

–   Labour narrowly wins General Election

1965   'Are we Losing our Way?' *Crossbow* editorial published, June

–   Alec Douglas-Home resigns, July

1966   Former MP Julian Critchley becomes Chairman, spring

–   General Election returns 17 Group members

–   Membership reaches a low of 708, autumn

1967   Party Conference *Crossbow* cover girl gains widespread coverage; edited by Leon Brittan

1968   Membership rises; Group recruits 1000th member, November

1969   Financial problems force Group to relax membership rules

1970   General Election returns 39 Group members; nine members become ministers in Heath Government

1971   Anonymous letter 'Crisis at the Bow Group' signals 'Peasants' Revolt'; zenith of Group's membership (1,170)

–   Chairman, Norman Lamont, addresses pro-EEC rally in Trafalgar Square

1972   50% rise in subscription cost; 200 members leave

–   Edward Heath at Annual Dinner; has to leave to deal
        with NUM dispute, February

–   Paris Bow Group created, December

1972–3 Bonn, Brussels Bow Groups initiated; Group links up
        with European Movement for sponsorship

1973   *Crossbow* editorial 'We're In, Now What?' signals
        change on Europe.

–   *Crossbow*: Selsdon Man – 'nothing of him remains'.

–   *Alternative Manifesto* published for Party Conference

1974   General Election returns 46 Bow Group members as
        MPs

1974   Oxford Spring Conference becomes monetarist post-
        mortem on Heath Government; Peter Lilley stands for a
        second term as Chairman

–   *Crossbow* editorial written by Peter Lloyd tells Heath to
        resign

1975   Margaret Thatcher becomes Party Leader, March

–   Group starts scheme to pair member MPs with
        researchers; Group closely involved in Keith Joseph's
        rethink of Party policy

1976   Thatcher speaks at 25th Anniversary dinner

–   Rocketing rent and shortage of members precipitate
        financial crisis; slide halted by upturn in Party fortunes
        leading to membership increase

1978   Howe launches 'New Enterprise Zones' in Docklands,
        June

1979   Group canvasses for Nicholas Scott MP; Conservative
        General Election victory returns 63 members, May

1980   Group becomes platform for 'wet' and 'dry' split

1980   Spring trip to South Africa attracts controversy

–   Conference speaker Norman St John Stevas:
          monetarism 'not enough'

1981   Recession hits Group's activities; appeal raises just
          £2,000

–   *Crossbow* savages Sir Keith Joseph's record as 'weak',
          May

–   Roy Jenkins speaks to Group, October

1982   1st Trans-Atlantic Conference in USA coincides with
          Falklands Crisis

1983   Group members meet General Pinochet in Chile

–   Heseltine launches *Playing at Peace* to open anti-CND
          campaign, March

–   General Election returns 92 Group members: 1 in 4 of
          Parliamentary Party

–   Chairman David Shaw reverses deficit: £5,000 in
          surplus by year end

1984   Thatcher slaps down Group's 'Open Letter' criticisms

1985–6   Group discovers the value of Defence Procurement
          conferences

1986   Conservative Party accepts Bow Group loan of £15,000

1987   3rd successive Conservative election victory: 100 Bow
          Group MPs

1988   Geoffrey Howe returns to Docklands to take credit for
          transformation, June

1989   240 High Holborn caught in property boom.
          Refurbishment leads to sharp rent increase

–   Group forced to move to smaller premises at 92 Bishops
          Bridge Road, autumn

–   Howe urges Party to 'think afresh' at Group's
          Conference fringe event

1990	Howe warns of missing the EMU train in Conference fringe speech
1991	Bow Group 40th Anniversary appeal raises £50,000
1992	Nick Hawkins becomes first MP Chairman of the Group
1993	Lamont on Conference fringe: 'Recovery is when the Chancellor loses his job'
1994 –	Commercial conference success divides Group Frank Johnson: Blair a 'A One Nation, Bow Group Conservative'
1997	William Hague: Bow Group has important role in Party's 'intellectual renaissance'
1998	Group moves to 1A Heath Hurst Road, Hampstead
1999	www.bowgroup.org launched on the internet. Michael Portillo speaks on education at Party Conference
2000	Francis Maude addresses Group Conference fringe meeting on honesty in politics
2001	50th Anniversary

Introduction

How have this country's avid Tory apprentices spent the time between their days in the Union at university and their arrival in the House of Commons? Few political biographies, and even fewer autobiographies, shed much light on this question. The early years, as they are almost inevitably called, are condensed, as teleology takes over and the impact of decisions made in later life naturally assumes a greater importance. So we rarely find out how our Members of Parliament arrive in positions of relative power. This book focuses on these early years, not just of a single politician, but of two generations of young and intensely ambitious Tories.

It is a truism that the Conservative Party has been one of the world's most successful political organisations, and its interest for historians has been in analysing the factors which explain the electoral magic. Philosophy, the policy-making process, local organisation have all been investigated. But although young Conservatives, whether as a first meeting ground for a generation of middle-aged, middle-class parents today or a rich vein of satire for Harry Enfield, with his 'Tory Boy', remain strangely resonant long after they have waned as a political force in the UK, young people's involvement in the Conservative Party, crucial to its future, has been largely overlooked.

The Young Conservatives produced a league of future Tory voters, some activists and a few politicians who rose through its ranks. But they seemed too pedestrian an organisation for a series of precocious, extremely ambitious young graduates who had no interest in licking envelopes for party mailings and, deprived of the Oxford or Cambridge Unions, or their university Conservative Associations, decided to recreate these enclosed hierarchies in the new and open landscape of young working life. This was the purpose of the Bow Group, which in the words of one of its Chairmen, speaking in the 1970s, 'shops at the intellectual Biba, while the rest of the Party gets its theoretical underwear from British Home Stores'. Knowingly elitist, the Group was a hothouse for a self-selecting group of self-important young graduates and their chosen friends and acquaintances, aloof from the Young Conservatives. But, even though the Group was viewed with distrust from Conservative Central Office, this informal organisation which latched itself on to the Party could not be ignored. In time the Group became a quasi-institutional part of the Party, its 'Open University' or, with the law and the City, one of three 'classical recruiting grounds' for new Conservative MPs. This was a remarkable rise to prominence, given that it gained this reputation publishing pamphlets by unknown young men and women at a time when the Fabian Society, by contrast, maintained a steady flow of pamphlets written by well-known Socialist academics and politicians.

Yet the Group's purpose, to elevate young people into national politics and the limelight, is precisely the attraction which has sustained it longer than any similar grouping. The Group offered an exclusive chance for the bright and determined to side-step the world of constituency work and worm their way into the field of vision of politicians who were, for most of the Group's history, running the nation. The people who embarked on this short-cut to publicity and their impact, both on the Group of which they were members and on the wider political world, are the subjects of this book. This is a new look at Conservative politics: not from the perspective of the people in power, but from the point of view of young people at the foot of the ladder, trying to clamber up it into Parliament.

The Bow Group

A
HISTORY

One

'A MOST INTERESTING EXPERIMENT': THE BOW GROUP IN THE EARLY 1950S

They founded the Bow Group to counter the Tories' image as the 'stupid party'. Nowhere was that image stronger than in the universities, from which they had only recently graduated. The Left was intellectual, exciting and eclectic; the Right was hobbled by constant reference to an image of pre-war Conservative Government as 'a paradise for profiteers and hell for everyone else'.[1] J. M. Keynes' political economics dominated both Conservative and Labour thinking, but it was the Left which harnessed his message more effectively, and portrayed nationalisation as picking up where the wartime communal spirit left off.

Taking advantage of the social upheaval caused by war, Labour's young stars propelled themselves into power. The epitome of this phenomenon, Harold Wilson, entered the Cabinet as President of the Board of Trade in 1947, aged 31; he had been a lecturer in Economics at New College, Oxford less than ten years before. It was impossible not to notice the meteoric rise of young men like Wilson or his contemporary Richard Crossman. The ideology which they proposed, which was learnt directly from Harold Laski and G. D. H. Cole, permeated the universities almost by default. Outside, the amply funded Fabian Society, founded in 1884, provided a symposium for the Socialists and remained an important influence on the Labour Party. Clement Attlee provided a vivid example of the Fabians' significance when he described the day he became Prime Minister in 1945. 'We went to a Victory Rally at Westminster Hall where I announced that I had been charged with the task of forming a Government, looked in at a Fabian Society gathering and then returned to Stanmore after an exciting day.'² By contrast, the Conservative Party in the 1940s had no intellectual grouping occupying an equivalent semi-detached position. Even Lord Woolton, the man who was to revolutionise the Conservative Party's organisation, had been a Fabian in his youth.³ Significantly, Woolton was to become an enthusiastic 'patron saint' of the Bow Group who was able to help particularly with fundraising.⁴

Not that it was an unexciting time to be a Conservative either. As early as 1947 there were signs that the nationalisation programme was faltering as the Labour Cabinet split on the policy. The Labour Government's weaknesses began to come under examination in universities from enthusiastic and spontaneously formed Conservative research groups, especially in Cambridge.⁵ Yet, as the future MP Peter Emery observed, few Conservative undergraduates coming down from university would bother to join their local constituency associations.⁶ In the excitement stakes, licking envelopes could hardly contest with Union politics. Nor were there opportunities to continue research; Rab Butler had designed the Pink Papers to convey simple messages with clarity to the wider population, but many graduates preferred to explore rather than promulgate. Another founder of the Group, Bruce Griffiths, explained: 'We needed to harness the intellectual abilities of those who had had a good time in Conservative right wing politics in the universities.'⁷ But as yet no graduate Conservative organisation existed for the intellectual groundswell of Conservative reaction that was 'too old for the Oxford Union and too young for the House of Commons'.⁸ Given this observation, it was not surprising that Emery, an ex-Librarian of the Oxford Union, provided part of the initial impetus and, ultimately, the connection which gave the Bow Group its name.

If the Group was born in Bow, it was conceived – almost exactly nine months earlier – at the Federation of University Conservative and Unionist Associations' conference in the early summer of 1950. As students, many of the young graduates who would found the Bow Group attended the annual meetings of this body, with its unfortunate acronym, usually held at High Leigh, a hotel in Hoddesdon in Hertfordshire. Emery recalled a great deal of chatter, but little action on the subject of what would happen after the students had graduated and found work. He advocated 'the establishment in London of an institution, which offering the social amenities of a club to members drawn from the Universities, will focus and centre graduate and undergraduate thought, acting as a stimulus to the Conservative Party and providing an effective counter to "intellectual" Socialism and the Fabian Society'. Large and influential within the universities, the Fabian Society was an obvious target for attack.

What is notable is that Emery's group was defined primarily in terms of its opposition to Socialism, not the support of Conservative principles; its declared aim to 'ginger' up the Conservative Party with new ideas was a secondary purpose. The motion was passed and Emery and Bruce Griffiths, the outgoing Vice-Chairman of FUCUA, were left to develop the broad structure and purpose of the proposed club, meeting several times at Griffiths' Chelsea flat at 332 Kings Road. It was a slightly comic pairing. Griffiths, who had also been the President of the London University Conservatives, was a thin, sparkling-eyed man with a detached, academic air, who contrasted with the bluff, more worldly figure of Emery. They were strongly encouraged by Conservative Central Office, where the General Director believed it was 'a very ingenious suggestion for achieving a double object' – new thinking and maintaining a connection with undergraduate Tories after they had left university.9 As the FUCUA liaison officer at Conservative Central Office, 'Ba' Turner became the main point of contact for the Group. She was ideally suited to keeping students in order, having finished the war as a colonel in the War Office before joining CCO in 1947. Even before Emery's and Griffiths' putative group had met, they tossed a coin for its Chairmanship. Griffiths won. His first act as Chairman was to instruct Emery to write the rules of the group.10 He appears to have finalised the agenda for the first meeting in the Conservative Club in St James's.11 On a piece of Club writing paper, Griffiths outlined a fifty-strong group, with a graduate and professional membership, maximum age 35, endorsed by the patronage of a number of senior members.12 On a second piece of paper he added the names of 12 potential members, most of whom appear to have been London University contemporaries.13

The brief minutes of the first meeting grandiosely describe 'a provi-sional meeting of the Steering Committee in Mr Denzil Freeth's rooms on Monday 27th November [1950] at 8.30 pm'.[14] Freeth lived in Battersea, and the more prosaic reality was that Freeth, Griffiths, Willie Bankes, Dennis Walters, Anthony McCowan, Beryl Cooper and Emery sat perched around the edge of Freeth's bed.[15] So insalubrious seemed the surroundings that much of the discussion revolved around whether it was really acceptable to continue to meet in a man's bedsit when there was a lady present.[16]

Fortunately, the discussion over whether Denzil Freeth's bed was a suitable meeting-place was already in the process of being resolved. No sooner did the group's framework exist on Conservative Club writing paper than it was drawn into the East London political scene whence it drew its name. The reason for this was that Peter Emery had accepted the job of Secretary of the Poplar Conservative Association in the East End. Poplar's Chairman at the time was Colonel Cecil Joel, a significant but sensitively self-important personality in East London life.[17] Emery was nursing the Poplar association as part of his strategy to stand as the Tory candidate there at the next General Election; when Labour returned to the Commons with a much reduced majority following the February 1950 poll, a further election looked possible. Poplar's Conservative Association had its office next door to the town hall, in a dilapidated and gloomy house, 149 Bow Road, which it shared with Bow and Bromley Conservative Club. 'It was a billiards and drinking club,' recalled the first Treasurer of the Group, James Lemkin, who was a solicitor.[18] Joel also ran the Political Committee of the Constitutional Club in Northumberland Avenue, and it was to him that the Group turned when Griffiths and Emery realised that the cost of Constitutional Club membership would be too high. The Club's Political Committee was unwilling to undercut its existing junior subscription rate for the benefit of the Bow Group.

Having ruefully accepted that many potential members would baulk at paying out for membership of the Constitutional Club, Emery, Griffiths and a number of other FUCUA members went to see Joel in Northumberland Avenue on 14 November 1950. Joel suggested the Bow and Bromley Conservative Club. In Emery's plans for a group of impecunious graduates he saw new life for the ailing East End club he ran. It was clearly in Emery's immediate political interest that the Group should meet in Poplar, and the delegation stoically accepted Joel's argument that, 'if constructive thought and research was their real aim, this could probably be undertaken with greater success in the atmosphere of Bow than in a West End club'.[19] Bow was not the end of the world; Joel reminded Griffiths that membership of the Bow Club none the less brought affiliation to the wider network of all 1,500 Constitutional Clubs in the UK.[20] Joel immediately instructed the Bow and Bromley Club's chairman Mr Giddings to offer his premises as a meeting place for the 'young gentlemen from the Universities'.

So, armed with directions from Turner and an invitation from the Bow Conservative Club, the Steering Committee's members met at Bow for the first time on 29 November 1950. Looking back, Joel saw this as the first meeting of the 'Bow Group'.[21] But it is hard to see that either Emery or Griffiths saw the arrangement as long-term, since it was obvious that they could exert little direct political influence in Westminster from a point a dozen or so stops eastbound on the District Line. Even on the night it met at 149 Bow Road, the Steering Committee pondered alternative accommodation; but it seems to have had no better offer. For the time being, Bow would have to do. At least, darkly Victorian though the Club's small board room was, it was not Denzil Freeth's bedroom.

The name for the group followed logically from the connection provided by Colonel Joel through Peter Emery. Although reluctant about the Bow Conservative Club, the Steering Committee settled on a name which closely associated themselves with the East End. The name 'The Bowmen' was considered, but in the end the 'Bow Group' was chosen, albeit 'provisionally'.[22] It was 'inverse snobbery', believes Bruce Griffiths' London University contemporary Neville Beale, who did not attend the Group's first meeting but subsequently joined.[23] The name – and the Group's proposed maximum age limit of 35 – symbolised the Group's divorce from the more traditional Tory milieu of St James's, in which comfortable surroundings Griffiths had done much of the planning.

Certainly by 10 January 1951, when Ba Turner wrote to Peter Emery to tell him that Cuthbert Alport had agreed to become 'Godfather' to the Bow Group, the name had stuck. Indeed, the approach to Alport, the Director of the Conservative Political Centre and one of 'Rab's boys' – the group of young Tories whom Butler had charged with turning round the Conservatives' image – was an early indication of the Group's flavour.

The first formal meeting of the Bow Group took place on 7 February 1951. Several friends were invited to be founder members, but more general notice of the meeting seems to have travelled on the Conservative grapevine. Many of those who attended arrived after the proceedings had begun. The minute book from the meeting, now missing, recorded the names of 38 founder members.[24] The list included Emery and Griffiths as well as Geoffrey Howe, William Rees-Mogg and Norman St John Stevas.[25] There was no election of officers because Bruce Griffiths and Emery had already secured the top jobs for themselves and Freeth, who was the first Bow Group member to join the Government, agreed to become the Group's first Librarian. The Group owned no books; the job of Librarian echoed the hierarchy of the Oxford Union, and the Librarian in time assumed responsibility for the Group's research efforts. All that was needed was a Treasurer; and for that task, Peter Emery collared James Lemkin on the door. It was proposed that the Group should form a link between the universities and the wider political world, creating alliances with young academics and offering speakers. Four senior members – all over 35 years old – were elected for three years: Ba Turner, Colonel Joel, Mr Giddings – and Cuthbert Alport MP. Alport briefly addressed the meeting before the Bow Group dispersed.

Much about the Group's exact role remained unclear. It was, as Emery's original FUCUA motion revealed, an association defined better in terms of what it opposed than what it stood for. Whereas Emery saw the Group as a political tool to aid his selection for Poplar, Griffiths had broadly proposed that the Group's purpose would be to research, discuss and then publish ideas, so the Steering Committee agreed that the Group's remit should 'be left fairly loose at first'.[26] Later the Group was more forthright about the political leeway that this pragmatic step gave them, pronouncing iconoclastically that: 'We have no orthodoxy and thus no heresies.'[27] The 'no corporate view' policy adopted by the Group flowed logically from this position, although it was not seriously tested until 1956, when the Group called a general meeting to debate whether its members should issue a single statement on the Suez Crisis.

In its earliest days, the Group's social purpose was as important as its political research role. Prominent on Griffiths' list of priorities for the new Group was the item 'Club dinners'. Of the initial £1 subscription, 12 shillings went straight to the Bow Conservative Club.[28] The Group was attractive for two reasons: it would provide an occasional forum in which recent graduates could conduct research and discuss issues separately from local Conservative Associations; but it also provided a completely independent vehicle through which the first members believed that they could draw attention to themselves within the Conservative Party. Arrogant though this may seem, there were good reasons for believing that the Group might be listened to. Sir Anthony Eden had urged FUCUA two summers before to help R. A. Butler create new impetus among the Tories, and Sir Edward Boyle had played some part in the discussions leading up to Emery's proposal at the FUCUA conference in the summer of 1950. Central Office certainly encouraged the Group behind the scenes: it was 'a most interesting experiment', its directing staff agreed.[29]

At this early stage the key achievements of the Group were its ability to capture some of the spontaneity of the university Conservative impulse and its survival. By 1950 there were many uncoordinated attempts at intellectual opposition involving a number of university Conservative Associations. Although the FUCUA resolution reflected the fact that few of these previous attempts had blossomed, it also gave a focus to the efforts which culminated in the emergence of the Bow Group in the winter of 1950–1. News of developments in London spread relatively fast. Patrick Jenkin, who had involved himself in Conservative research before he had finished his degree, remembers hearing about the Bow Group during his final year at Cambridge. 'We found that there was the Bow Group, which was founded to do the same thing – original research – and publish the results.' Jenkin thought that the Group offered the best opportunity to fight back against Socialism: 'it sounded so much more positive than the Young Conservatives – I never did become a Young Conservative.'[30]

Although the Group was founded by a London and an Oxford graduate, Cambridge University provided many of its early activists. One, Russell Lewis, remembers that one early Council meeting almost resembled a Cambridge University Conservative Association committee meeting after a few non-Cambridge members happened to leave early.[31] Close friendships, which had been forged at university, dominated both the decision-making and recruitment processes. As young barristers, Howe and Jenkin shared a flat in Hampstead. Geoffrey Howe and Dick Stone, both early Chairmen, had shared rooms in college at Cambridge.[32] When Geoffrey Howe married Elspeth Shand in August 1953, Stone was Howe's best man; in the company of the male-dominated Bow Group, to which she had already belonged, Elspeth Howe became known as 'the Bow Group wife'.[33] Consecutive Librarians Colin Jones and Russell Lewis took it in turn to store the Bow Group's paperwork and pamphlets under their beds in the flat they shared. Reflecting on the Group's crucial early years, today Lewis believes that the 'trust and like-mindedness' endowed by the Cambridge connection was an important factor in its survival.[34]

Branches of the Bow Group emerged elsewhere in a similar fashion. The Birmingham Bow Group was founded by Alan Bennett and Sydney Smith-Gavine early in 1953 when Smith-Gavine, who might otherwise have joined the London Bow Group, was offered a job by Bird's Custard in Birmingham. As a new arrival to the city he met Bennett at a meeting of the Edgbaston Young Conservatives, and proposed that the two of them begin a group linked to the London Bow Group. Aimée Chilton became the Birmingham Group's first Treasurer and Anthea Collins took on responsibility for the Group's research effort.[35] Of these four, only Smith-Gavine had not studied at the University of Birmingham. Sir Edward Boyle MP agreed to become the Birmingham Group's President, having been the first MP to address it in August 1953.[36] By 1960 the Group's membership had reached its zenith, of about 60.

Although not on the same scale, active Bow Groups existed in Edinburgh, Liverpool, Manchester, Newcastle and Yorkshire by the early 1960s. The drive to create these had begun in 1953, when the then Chairman James Lemkin wrote a round robin to active members of

FUCUA asking whether they would 'be able to further this great venture, the Bow Group'.37 In fact the branches were more often set up by a handful of graduates leaving London to pursue industrial careers, rather than by local people, though these sometimes joined the seedling organisation. A branch at Cambridge University 'acted primarily as a recruiting ground' for the London Bow Group, according to David Howell, while Oxford's group was not initially based upon the university at all, but depended on the enthusiasm of Liviu Alston, a scientist at nearby Harwell. Relations with Oxford University existed in the form of an alliance with the Blue Ribbon Club, which was founded by Michael Heseltine and Julian Critchley in October 1952 to organise slates for Oxford University Conservative Association elections and to offer a more intellectual programme of meetings and dinners than was arranged by OUCA.

The development of these offshoots bred constitutional complications, and periodically strained relations between the London and Birmingham groups resulted. Birmingham viewed the London Group's occasional offers of money with suspicion and generally preferred to remain financially independent. However, as Alan Bennett, the Birmingham Group's first Chairman, remembers, 'Right from the start we had adopted the title of Birmingham branch of the Bow Group, so our claims to independence were clearly of a qualified kind.'38

Meanwhile in London, despite the attraction of the Bow Bells – the pub across the road from the Constitutional Club at which Sir Edward Boyle had addressed the London Group at its first annual dinner – the Bow Group's relationship with the Bow Club quickly waned. As he had planned, Peter Emery fought and lost the 'hopeless' Poplar seat at the October 1951 General Election. His opponent, the Rt Hon. C. W. Key MP, was returned with a majority of 24,502. Relations between the local East End Conservatives and the bumptious young Bow Groupers were occasionally strained. This was not entirely surprising: it transpired that another of Colonel Joel's motives for inviting the Group to join the Bow Club was to create a blocking majority to prevent the existing membership from voting to sell off the Club for redevelopment.39 The Group also encountered friction at the Constitutional Club in central London, where the Group found itself prejudiced by Joel's own reputation for plain speaking among other members. The Group must have been regarded by some as an unwelcome intrusion: 'Women members of the Bow Group should appreciate that some of the elderly members are still distressed to see women on the premises,' warned an undated internal Bow Group memorandum from around this time. Female members of the Group, who could enter the Club only as guests of male Bow Groupers, 'must NEVER use the cloakroom at street level, as this is the gentlemen's cloakroom only, and the appearance of various shopping baskets here during recent meetings has given offence'.[40]

With complaints about the Group's behaviour becoming more frequent and the Constitutional Club transpiring to be an 'exceedingly expensive' venue,[41] the Political and Economic Planning Club increasingly played host to Bow Group meetings from 1952.[42] An elegant Georgian building in Queen Anne's Gate, close to Parliament, the PEP was well-enough known in its own right as a venue to attract high-calibre speakers to speak to the Bow Group off the record. At the Committee meeting of 18 November 1952, at the then chairman Robin Williams' flat in Victoria, it was suggested that the Group's 'links with the Bow Club are now so slender that they ought not to be recognised by a separate category of membership of the Bow Group'.[43] By then, it was noted, 'it was no longer true that the Group met in Poplar, nor helped to run the Association, nor did it do research there'. Few members of the Bow Group bothered to take out membership of the Bow Constitutional Club. Even the obstacle of Colonel Joel's sensibilities was not so great as to prevent a move. Long before Emery was invited back to the Poplar Conservative Association by Joel to speak, after his election as MP for Reading in 1959, the Group's relationship with Bow was itself history.

The Group's association with Bow did however produce one significant publication, *Coloured Peoples in Britain*, which appeared in July 1952 priced sixpence and studied the issue of racial integration in Britain, with reference to the Group members' experience in the East End. The author of the finished report, Anthony McCowan, proposed integrating immigrants through education, radio and television as well as greater social contact, calling on individual Conservatives to put theory into practice. 'We place the greatest emphasis on social contact and we call on all Conservatives to give the lead in this matter.' It was an entirely original subject for research and the publication attracted the interest of the Prime Minister's office, which asked for copies.[44] The Group publicly presented the pamphlet to Lord Munster, Under-Secretary of State for the Colonies, to draw attention to its work, and Ba Turner reported back to the General Director of CCO that 'the Colonial Office officials were extremely pleased with it.'[45] The press were similarly enthusiastic: 'the pamphlet itself sets an example of good will in the friendly and frank way that it presents its material,' said the *Economist*, a verdict which pleased the Group so much that it was quoted on all new promotional literature for some time after.[46] The first impression of 1,500 copies sold out; by the end of 1952, 1,300 of a further impression of 3,000 had been bought.[47]

But as a solution, *Coloured Peoples in Britain* was flawed by two key assumptions: that full employment would continue, and that the number of black immigrants would increase only marginally. 'We foresaw an increase,' wrote Anthony McCowan 12 years later, 'but nothing like the rate which actually occurred.' Periods of high unemployment returned and combined with the increased rate of immigration to generate exactly the friction which caused violence. In retrospect, McCowan realised he had been rather too optimistic.

Besides developing a Conservative approach to an untouched issue, what was interesting about the pamphlet was the process of research which it involved. A leaflet published by the Group in 1952 tersely described its method: 'The research is developed scientifically. The subject yields a number of questions and a form of enquiry. Each member of a group investigates a certain aspect of the subject. Over a period of months the Study group meets from time to time to assess the evidence, which has been gathered, to discuss the shape of the inquiry, perhaps to hear a talk by an expert.' Some research lasted up to a year before tentative conclusions were produced.[48] Interested volunteers were asked to contact the Research Secretary, then Patrick Jenkin.[49] The results were more promising than the dry prose might suggest. The mix of analytical and anecdotal evidence gave *Coloured Peoples in Britain* a vivid quality and the press was fascinated by the fact that the Bow Group's work was conducted entirely during leisure time and bore the signs of having been researched from first-hand experience. Subsequent pamphlets were not always as rigorous, as the emphasis moved from perfect analysis of a problem to eye-catching action which might solve it.

The discipline involved in its research earned the Group an attractive image of being both earnest and constructive. 'These young men start with the fewest preconceptions . . . Their first intent is to be good researchers not good politicians. If more of their elders now sitting in the Commons were guided by similar motives we should have debates governed less by dogmatic bombast and better legislation would result.'[50] In this way the Group's members took advantage of their youth to gain great respect. 'They are studious,' observed the journalist Anthony Sampson, '. . . carefully pedestrian – compared to the more equestrian postures of pre-war young Tories. They write long, well-printed pamphlets full of accurate figures and cautious suggestions, and they give sober parties in Kensington and Chelsea.'[51]

The process was not always as sedate as Sampson implies. Writing some time after the event, a convert to the Bow Group who had been a Fabian, Fred Tuckman, recalled the 'great anger' aroused by the publication of memoranda without the knowledge or agreement of the study group concerned with the particular subject. He remembered how the Group's publication *Taxes for Today* ignited a serious controversy between its authors Richard Kellett and Patrick Jenkin, both of whom were highly ambitious and neither of whom was willing to back down. Beneath the surface, Tuckman reveals a Group which was 'highly explosive with talent and ambition'.[52]

But first-hand experience was as important as ambition in determining members' choice of research. In opposition to the Conservative Government's manifesto commitment, and in a deliberate attempt to divorce the Bow Group from its roots, Colin Jones cleverly argued the case against the restitution of the University Parliamentary seats in the Group's second pamphlet. Perhaps he could sense that the pledge was unsustainable: three weeks after *The University Vote* was published,

Winston Churchill shelved the plan.[53] Jones' good timing drew publicity, if not influence, for the relatively unknown Bow Group. In the Birmingham Bow Group's first pamphlet, *The Non-Specialist Graduate in Industry*, Anthea Collins dealt with a practical issue which faced many Bow Groupers – especially those in Birmingham – who had left university often equipped only with an arts degree to join an industrial company. She advocated a more scientific approach to graduate selection and training, as well as suggesting a reduction in the number of places on arts degree courses. London remained vigilant over Birmingham's work. Whether or not the pamphlet would be published was decided at a meeting of representatives of both London and Birmingham Bow Groups in the Randolph Hotel in Oxford in early 1955.[54]

The Group was selective about the ideas it passed for further research, and it was selective about what it published. Emery, who was a member of the Publications Committee which was the final arbiter on the Group's output, remembers rejecting a number of draft pamphlets which were not good enough.[55] We shall never know for example what one member, Mrs Waterhouse, might have written on 'The Young Spinster in London' since her proposal for work on this topic was rejected by the Publications Committee in 1954. Other controversial subjects fared better. The Group's first pamphlet on an economic issue, Russell Lewis' *Industry and the Property Owning Democracy*, provoked opposition within the Group in arguing the need for a social market economy. It was finally published after Lewis had rewritten it for the third time. Once completed, however, it became one of the Group's landmark publications since it addressed the timeless theme of whether industry was better served by state or private ownership.[56] Writing in *Tribune*, the Labour MP Ian Mikardo attacked the Group for *Industry and the Property Owning Democracy*: 'the species [of Conservative] I can't abide by are the new young Tories who hide their acquisitiveness behind a fake facade of do-gooder's terminology. They are the phoneys who sickly o'er their reactionary resolution with the pale cast of public relations.'[57] As if in proof of the effectiveness of the Group's political style which he so disliked, Mikardo was unseated by a Bow Group member, Peter Emery, in the 1959 General Election.

The Bow Group's early work raised an important question: whether Conservatives should think. *The Daily Telegraph* journalist T. E. Utley was invited to address exactly this question at an early meeting of the Group. The outlook of traditional Conservatives, articulated by Lord Hailsham, was that 'the simplest among them prefer fox-hunting – the wisest, religion . . . The believer in the importance of politics first is not fit to be called a civilised being, let alone a Christian.'[58] Hailsham was attacked in a review of his book, *The Conservative Cause*, in the Group's journal *Crossbow* for substituting emotional appeal for political argument. This reflected the central tenet of Bow Group research – empirical analysis. 'However boring it may seem to Lord Hailsham,' the reviewer argued, 'the true Conservative approach to politics demands that this rhetoric be replaced by a factual analysis.'[59] This approach raised a second question: could empirical analysis, started from a Conservative viewpoint, ever produce radical solutions to the problems of 1950s Britain? Although the Group argued that it 'should not be afraid to come out with bold proposals on a number of apparently chronic problems', it was difficult to see how evidence-driven research could achieve these results.[60]

Despite its emphasis on research, the Group was hardly as unpolitical as its highly ambitious members made out. Pamphlets were deliberately timed to bring the Group into the political arena. One tactic used was to present a publication to the relevant Conservative minister – as *Coloured Peoples in Britain* was presented to Lord Munster. In time the approach became more sophisticated. The publication of *The Life-blood of Liberty*, Geoffrey Howe's and Tony Lines' proposal for local government reform, was timed to coincide with the Conservative Party Conference, where Lines had been drawn to propose a motion on local government designed to draw attention to the newly published Bow Group research. But the real coup was later recalled by Sir Robin Williams, Chairman of the Group at the time: 'We were just well enough known to get a Minister to launch a pamphlet.' As Minister of Housing and Local Government, Harold Macmillan was invited to open the discussion at the PEP on 30 September 1954. The launch of the pamphlet itself barely mattered in comparison to what followed. In a simple episode that Macmillan later entwined into his own easy-going image, he stayed after the meeting for dinner in the pub across the road from the PEP, the Adam and Eve. For some time the political discussion continued. Finally, Williams remembered, 'Upon leaving he told me that he liked our group and that I was to get in touch if we wanted help.'[61] Playing up its own influence on Macmillan, the Group led the *Western Mail* to believe that 'No ministerial pronouncement at next week's Party Conference is awaited with greater interest than that of Mr Harold Macmillan on local government reform.'[62] With hindsight, it is easy to see why this involvement with Macmillan was so crucial for the future of the Bow Group as an important influence on the Conservative Party.

Ministerial endorsement might in the long run win the Bow Group recognition. But day to day, care of the Group's small finances was vital to keep it alive. As Treasurer, Howe turned a deficit of £6 3s 2d into a surplus of £41 5s 9d. That both Geoffrey Howe and Sir Robin Williams had served as the Group's Treasurer in the year immediately preceding their chairmanships would seem to be a reflection of the priority of survival in the early days. Geoffrey Howe's drive was an undoubtedly important factor in the Group's success at this time. As a friend and Bow Group contemporary later observed, 'the whole of what he was doing was geared to making an impact in political circles.'[63] Many years later the Group's co-founder, Bruce Griffiths, recognised that Howe's determination was beneficial to the survival of the Group:

> So many things fade within two years unless you have someone to take over in the second and third . . . I am sure the thing would have died but for Geoffrey and some others like him – for example James Lemkin – who were good solid chaps. They really took it over. Geoffrey in particular had a more penetrating attitude to see what potentials there were for the future. The amount of work he put into it, getting it onto a firm, sensible business-like basis was very considerable and a very substantial achievement.[64]

At the end of Howe's term as Chairman one member of his Council remarked that because 'Mr Howe was such a strong Chairman, he had been almost fearful of attending Council Meetings'.[65]

Howe was also a prolific author, writing another pamphlet in 1956 proposing that rent control should be eliminated, *Houses to Let*, and *Work for Wales* in advance of the 1959 General Election, in which he stood as a candidate for his home town of Aberavon. But it was a team effort. At the memorial service in 1985 for his Bow Group contemporary Tom Hooson, Howe recalled:

> I shall never forget the enthusiasm that he brought to that task [co-writing *Work for Wales*]. And the eye for detail, often transmitted to me on scruffy, energetic scraps of paper. Of the 199 footnotes in that pamphlet Tom contributed almost all of them. And all the Welsh quotations. I remember how he was determined that we should finish the pamphlet by the end of a bank holiday weekend in 1959. And how he kept us working through the Monday night, so that when Elspeth emerged at 6am in the morning to begin heating the milk for our two-month old twins she was astonished – although not really surprised – to find Tom still on the premises, as fresh and energetic as ever.[66]

The stamina of those early members, who combined the self-imposed deadlines of the Bow Group with daytime careers and family commitments, is an important factor in any explanation of why the Group lasted past the critical first five years.

Another of Geoffrey Howe's guiding maxims was that the Bow Group should exist 'to make the Tory Party fit for *Observer* and *Guardian* readers to live in'.[67] To do so, the Group deliberately tried to develop its cultural image, with the strategy set out in an undated memorandum on future Bow Group weekends away: 'By trying to choose younger artists and avant-gardistes to speak, we shall fight the "artistic" view of the Tory Party as philistine (however true that view may be!) and at the same time fight that very philistinism which we know to exist within the Party.'[68] The Group's members became regular attendees at Swinton College in Yorkshire. The Earl of Swinton had given over part of his home as a Conservative training school: there were full-time research fellows and a comprehensive library. Scholarships were available to meet the costs of travel and accommodation.

Weekends at Swinton offered an opportunity to discuss ideas – and meet Conservative politicians. It was a pleasantly informal environment which fostered political relationships which might not have developed in Westminster. During the day the Bow Group members discussed matters of policy; the evenings were filled with speculation about political careers. Ron Needs remembered putting five shillings on James Lemkin becoming a junior minister, Fred Tuckman £1 on David Hennessy making the Cabinet inside 20 years – which he did, as Leader in the Lords from 1973 to 1974. Even at that early stage, various people thought that Howe would be Home Secretary, including Jenny Raven, the Group's administrative secretary[69]

Swinton College was popular not least because the College doubled as a marriage bureau, and liaisons flourished after the lectures were over. The authorities were keen to catch lovers out: Pamela Thomas believes there was a man wearing soft-soled shoes who crept around on a 'purity patrol' after dark.[70] Bow Groupers' singing around the piano until late into the night kept others awake. Throughout the 1950s and 1960s the College was crucial in providing a common experience. It was through contact at Swinton that the Group's chairman in 1965, Henry Bosch, was able to approach Edward Heath just after the latter had become Leader of the Opposition, to speak early the following year, with positive results.[71] And increasingly in the 1950s, Conservative politicians were keen to play on their association with young people to great electoral effect. The Bow Group was very well placed to benefit from this deliberate strategy.

NOTES

1   Attributed to Herbert Morrison.

2   Clement Attlee, *As it Happened*, London 1954, p. 148.

3   Robert Blake, *The Conservative Party from Peel to Major*, London 1997, p. 260.

4   Tom Hooson, Memoranda in the Bow Group's Confidential File, November 1960 and February 1961.

5   The Rt Hon. Lord Jenkin of Roding, interview, 2 March 1999.

6   The Rt Hon. Sir Peter Emery was MP for Reading 1959–66, Honiton March 1967–97 and has been MP for Devon East since 1997.

7   Judy Hillman and Peter Clarke, *Geoffrey Howe: A Quiet Revolutionary*, London 1988, pp. 33–4. Bruce Griffiths had read law at King's College London. He was President of London University Conservatives. As a barrister he participated with Geoffrey Howe in the Aberfan inquiry. He was made QC in 1970 and became a Circuit Judge in Wales in 1972. A keen supporter of the Welsh Arts Council, he died in 1998.

8   Richard Rose, 'The Bow Group and the Tory Image', *Guardian*, 7 February 1961.

9   Conservative Party Archive (CPA) CCO 3/2/62, General Director to Maxse, 21 November 1950.

10   The Rt Hon. Sir Peter Emery MP, interview, 6 May 1999.

11   The Carlton Club now occupies the building; at the time it had premises next door to the Royal Automobile Club on Pall Mall.

12   Bruce Griffiths, papers, No. 1.

13   Bruce Griffiths listed 'Basil Webb, Ralph Cusack, Bruce Griffiths, Dr Thorpe, Colin Craddock-Jones, Pam Thomas, Colin's Oppo. (Richard Westbury), Neville Beale, John Lester, Bill Morgan, Hesketh and George Theobald'. Bruce Griffiths, papers, No. 2.

14   Bruce Griffiths, papers, No. 4.

15   Freeth graduated from Cambridge where he had been President of the Cambridge Union and Chairman of the University Conservative Association. MP for Basingstoke 1955–64. Anthony McCowan had been President of Oxford University Conservative Association and was chairman of FUCUA in 1951. He was called to the bar and took silk in 1972. He was Senior Presiding Judge in England and Wales, 1991–95; a Lord Justice of Appeal, 1989–97. Dennis Walters served with the Italian Resistance during the Second World War, returning to full-time education in the UK at the Armistice in 1944. He became Chairman of FUCUA in 1950 and was elected MP for Westbury in 1964, retiring in 1992.

16   Peter Emery, 'Bow Group Dawn', *Crossbow*, Summer 1981, p. 6.

17   Colonel H. Cecil Joel, obituary, *East London Advertiser*, 7 July 1961.

18   James Lemkin, interview, 4 May 1999. James Lemkin founded the African news digest *Africa Confidential* in 1960. Having left the Conservative Party to contest Cheltenham for the Liberals in the 1964 election, he rejoined and became a Conservative member of the Greater London Authority 1970–1986. He was Conservative Chief Whip in the GLA from 1982 to 1986.

19   Conservative Party Archive (CPA) CCO 3/2/62, Turner to Maxse, 16 November 1950.

20   Bruce Griffiths, papers, No. 3.

21   Tom Hooson's correspondence file, Joel to Hooson, 25 May 1960. Bow Group archive.

22   CPA, CCO 3/2/62, 'Notes of the meeting held on 29 November 1950 for Colonel Joel's information'.

23   Neville Beale, conversation with the author, early 1999.

24   Nicholas Perry, 'Bow Road Revisited', *Crossbow*, Autumn 1988, p. 11.

25   Geoffrey Howe was MP for Bebington, 1964–66; for Reigate 1970–74; for Surrey East 1974–92. He was Solicitor General 1970–72, Minister for Trade Consumer Affairs 1972–74; Chancellor of the Exchequer 1979–83; Secretary of State for Foreign and Commonwealth Affairs 1983–89 and Deputy Prime Minister 1989–1990. William Rees-Mogg had been President of the Oxford Union before joining the *Financial Times* as a leader writer. During this time he contested Chester-Le-Street in 1956 and 1959. After a spell editing various sections of the *Sunday Times* he was appointed Editor of *The Times* in 1967, holding the post until 1981. He was chairman of the Arts Council of Great Britain 1982–89. Norman St John Stevas was President of the Cambridge Union and Secretary of the Oxford Union. He was MP for Chelmsford 1964–87, Minister of State for the Arts, 1973–74, Chancellor of the Duchy of Lancaster, Leader of the House of Commons and Minister for the Arts 1979–81.

26   Bruce Griffiths, papers, No. 1 titled 'Agenda', not dated, but written shortly before 29 November 1950 and probably annotated with the Steering Committee's conclusions that day.

27   Bow Group Council, Minutes, 18 November 1952.

28   £1 in 1951 is worth £16 today (1998 prices).

29   CPA, CCO 3/3/48, Watson to General Director, 16 January 1951.

30   Jenkin, interview, 2 March 1999.

31   Russell Lewis ran the European Commission's Press Office in London. He was later Director of the Conservative Political Centre, and afterwards the *Daily Mail*'s leader writer, 1976–91. Turning his attention to the EU in the 1990s, he directed the Maastricht Referendum Campaign, and then the organisation which grew out of that campaign, the European Foundation, 1993–7.

32   R. F. Stone was called to the bar in 1952. He became a QC in 1968.

33   The phrase of Sir John Foster, founder of Justice. Elspeth Howe has been Chairman of the Broadcasting Standards Council/Commission since 1993.

34   Russell Lewis, interview, 30 June 1999.

35   Anthea Tinker (née Collins) has since had a distinguished career in gerontology. She was Professor of Social Gerontology, King's College London, 1988–98.

36   Alan Bennett, letter to the author, 9 December 1999.

37   CPA, CCO 3/3/48, 10 June 1953.

38 Bennett, letter.

39 The Rt Hon. Lord Howe of Aberavon, interview, 8 December 1999.

40 Undated memorandum to all members of the Bow Group Committee and convenors of study groups, in Tom Hooson's correspondence file, Bow Group archive.

41 Bow Group Council, Minutes, 3 March 1952.

42 It did so until 1956, when the Bow Group minutes noted that the Club had gone into liquidation and that there would be no further meetings there.

43 Sir Robin Williams was called to the bar in 1954. As Chairman of the Anti-Common Market League from 1969 to 1984 he played a leading part in the 'No' Campaign in 1975.

44 Hillman and Clarke, *Geoffrey Howe*, p. 34.

45 CPA, CCO 3/4/32, Turner to General Director, 2 September 1952.

46 The *Economist*, 6 September 1952; CPA CCO 3/4/32, The Bow Group – Trust Fund Appeal, not dated but c.1953–54.

47 CPA CCO 3/4/32, The Bow Group – Annual Report for 1952.

48 Richard Rose, 'The Bow Group's Role in British Politics', *Western Political Quarterly*, Vol. XIV, No. 4, December 1961, p. 867.

49 Patrick Jenkin succeeded Winston Churchill as MP for Wanstead and Woodford, 1964–87. He was Chief Secretary to the Treasury 1972–74; Minister for Energy 1974; Secretary of State for Social Services 1979–81; for Industry 1981–83; and for the Environment 1983–85.

50 'Carteret Street Journal', *Truth*, 6 August 1954.

51 Anthony Sampson, *Anatomy of Britain*, London 1962, p. 88.

52 Fred Tuckman, Note in the Bow Group's Confidential File, probably written in mid-1959. Tuckman was MEP for Leicester 1979–89.

53 Colin Jones, *The University Vote*, Bow Group, October 1953.

54 The Rt Hon. Lord Jenkin of Roding, letter to the author, 22 March 2000.

55 Emery, interview.

56 Russell Lewis, *Industry and the Property Owning Democracy*, Bow Group, 1954. Lewis reviewed his efforts with the benefit of hindsight in 'Three Acres and a Cow', *Crossbow*, October–December 1964.

57 Ian Mikardo, 'When Watery Blues Get Down to Work', *Tribune*, 30 August 1954.

58 Quintin Hogg, *The Case for Conservatism*, London 1959, pp. 12–13.

59 Bryan Cartledge, 'The Wrong Speech', *Crossbow*, Autumn 1959, pp. 65–6.

60 Richard Rose, *The Bow Group's role in British Politics*, pp. 872–3.

61 Williams to Hooson, 24 November 1960. The incident was mentioned over three years later in *John Bull* magazine, 4 January 1958.

62 *Western Mail*, 1 October 1954.

63 The speaker was Ron Needs. Quoted in Hillman and Clarke, *Geoffrey Howe*, p. 51.

64 Hillman and Clarke, *Geoffrey Howe*, p. 34.

65 'The Bow Group in Parliament: 30 years on', *Crossbow*, October 1983.

66 Hillman and Clarke, *Geoffrey Howe*, p. 52.

67 Geoffrey Howe, *Conflict of Loyalty*, London 1994, p. 25.

68 The Rt Hon. Lord Howe of Aberavon, papers.

69 Hillman and Clarke, *Geoffrey Howe*, pp. 51–2.

70 Pamela Thomas, interview, 24 April 1999.

71 Correspondence between Heath and Bosch, 1 September, 11 October, 18 October 1965. Henry Bosch's correspondence file, Bow Group archive.

Two

CROSSBOW: THE MAKING OF A
BOW GROUP MAGAZINE

I t is unlikely that the Group could have considered publishing a
regular journal had it not been for an unexpected fillip to its
financial circumstances which encouraged it to expand its activities.
It was Patrick Jenkin who provided what would become a vital link with
a body willing to finance the Bow Group's ongoing work. That body was
the United Industrialists Association, one of a number of wealthy organisations whose aim was to promote free enterprise and combat further
nationalisation by funding a wide spectrum of groups which opposed
Socialism.

The Group's original contact with the UIA was made in 1954 when
Jenkin was a junior barrister in chambers with John Senter, a QC who
provided legal advice to the Conservative Party and also involved in the
Party's financing, services for which he was later knighted. When Jenkin
discovered that the UIA had given £1,000 to help the Inns of Court
Conservatives publish a pamphlet, he speculated that the Bow Group
might also benefit from the Association's assistance. Senter agreed to
introduce the Bow Group's Chairman at the time, Sir Robin Williams, to
Colonel Juan Hobbs. An ex-cavalry officer and the UIA's general
manager, Hobbs invited Williams to meet him at the UIA's office at 140
Park Lane in December 1954. To give Hobbs an impression of the Bow
Group, Williams took with him copies of the four pamphlets published
to date. He subsequently recorded that:

> Hobbs was not interested in *Coloured Peoples in Britain* nor in
> *The University Vote*. He was very interested in *Industry and the*

> *Property-Owning Democracy*. He wanted to know whether we
> could get it read by teachers. He seemed very anxious about the
> prevalence of left wing notions in that profession and was very
> anxious for the Bow Group to get amongst them in some way. [1]

Satisfied that the Group's philosophy fitted the UIA's agenda, Hobbs
promised Williams a cheque for £500 at the end of the meeting. 'We
should not just go out and have a big dinner,' Williams remembered
Hobbs warning.

This unexpected donation was enormously significant to the Bow
Group, representing two years' funding of the Group's small-scale activities. The influx of cash encouraged the London Group to offer to
sponsor – and thus control – the Birmingham Bow Group. The
Birmingham Group's first chairman, Alan Bennett, clearly remembers
the impact of the extra money: 'During 1954 and 1955 there were some
fairly tense discussions with London concerning the constitutional
position.'[2] Lewis provides a London view of what happened: 'We wanted
to expand the Birmingham Group and then open up other centres but
Birmingham weren't interested in growing. They wanted to stay a cosy
little coterie.'[3] Looking for alternative ways to spend its money, it is no
coincidence that, within six months of receiving the UIA's cheque, the
Group began to consider a quarterly publication.

There was a long gap between the first mention of plans for a journal
of the Bow Group, and the publication in autumn 1957 of the first issue
of *Crossbow*, as the Group's journal came to be called. A quarterly
journal was mooted at the Council meeting on 12 October 1955, and
about the same time a ten-page proposal was circulated to Council
members. This argued the case for a regular publication by the Group, to
provide a frequent outlet for the many topical ideas which did not lend
themselves to publication in pamphlet form. By this means, the author
argued, the Group could expand its influence, attract contributions from
existing members of the Group, and encourage outsiders to join. The
problem for the Bow Group by late 1955, which the report identified, was
that the Group's research activity was conducted by a relatively small
proportion of the membership. Moreover, as the Group's records show,

after the initially strong interest, the growth in numbers had tailed off. Although membership had increased a quarter over the previous year, the total remained small, at just over 200, and – worryingly – there had been no further increase for six months. A Bow Group journal would 'provide a more tangible evidence of activity both to members and to outsiders'.

What is also absolutely clear is that the Bow Group believed that the lure of publicity would attract the self-publicists: 'The only inducement we can offer them at present – if these inducements are any help in recruitment – is the opportunity to write pamphlets. But since these sell on average only 1,000 copies or so, this facility is bound to compare somewhat unfavourably with openings already available to them elsewhere. A regular publication would be a more powerful inducement.' The proposal argued for the publication to start in 1956, but this was an unrealistic target for such a big venture.[4]

A high-calibre quarterly political journal represented a considerable risk. Three years later the Fabian Society would be forced to suspend its quarterly, the *Fabian Journal*, after ten years of publication.[5] The publicity given to articles in other magazines, such as *Encounter* and *Socialist Commentary*, encouraged the Group, although there was little realistic comparison to be made between a wide-ranging magazine like *Encounter* and a specifically focused Conservative (or, for that matter, Socialist) journal.[6] The Bow Group's target market – intellectual Conservatives – was diffuse, and the potential for a wider readership was limited by political apathy and the party affiliation *Crossbow* would have. Producing and publishing a regular magazine was a professional occupation, yet the Bow Group was a voluntary organisation which had relied on part-time efforts for its achievements to date. Unperturbed, the author of the report called for a journal to be 'ambitiously handled' with a 'consistently high standard in content, style and layout' and a minimum of 2,000 subscribers. Though these aims were necessary, they represented significant demands, given that the editor of the journal would be able to devote only his spare time and energy to the project. Also, a regular publication would inevitably require the Group to form a continuous professional relationship with a publishing company, at substantial cost initially, even if the magazine were eventually to finance itself through advertising.

These complex preparations required substantial fund-raising, which took longer than planned, possibly as a result of the effect which the Suez Crisis had on the Government's fortunes in 1956. James Lemkin, the then Chairman, and Russell Lewis witnessed the Government's disarray over Suez at first hand. '[We] went to see Henry Brooke [the Minister of Housing and Local Government] at the House and asked him "What the hell's going on?" He looked at us blankly and said he didn't know,' remembers Lewis.7 It seems that this experience encouraged the Council to think that the Government's problems made the introduction of a journal of new ideas imperative as an antidote. But the shortage of funds, and the Council's underestimation of the size of the task it had set itself, delayed the launch of the magazine by 18 months.

Financing the first issues of the journal was the Bow Group Council's first priority. Members of the Group formed an obvious pool of potential subscribers, but, surprisingly, in 1955 two-thirds of them did not pay extra to receive the Bow Group's publications. Assuming that the successful launch of the journal would have the effect of increasing the volume of Bow Group publications, the Council decided to raise the subscription charge, incorporating the journal and an unspecified number of pamphlets into the benefits of annual membership and ending the separate subscription service. The cost was to be 25 shillings. Even from this basis, to double the readership of the Group's pamphlets was a colossal task. In a second, more detailed proposal for the Group's journal, Colin Jones, who was to edit the first two issues of *Crossbow*, suggested that 'We must have a minimum starting capital of £900, £600 by Christmas [1955] and a further £300 during the ensuing 12 months.' When this report was presented at a Council meeting, one of those present, Patrick Jenkin, ringed the figures on his copy in pencil, drawing a sad face and exclamation marks since he correctly believed that to find £600 (equivalent to £13,500 in 2000) in a little over three months was an impossible task. Jones' arithmetic is interesting: he estimated that each issue, with a run of 3,000 copies, would cost £250 to produce, and that the first eight issues – two years' worth – would sell on average half the copies at 2 shillings each. Presumably, he envisaged distributing the remainder freely among MPs and influential people within London.

A number of possible titles for the journal were debated. 'The Bow', 'Issues', 'The Empiricist', 'Forum' and 'New Commentary' – suggested as a possible way to outflank *Socialist Commentary* – were all discussed and discarded. Explaining the eventual choice, Geoffrey Howe wrote that 'We were not impressed by the frivolity of Bow-peep . . . nor the portentous simplicity of Bow. The alternative weapons, Crossbow and Longbow, eventually attracted us. With a growing reputation for objective accuracy in research we could hardly start now to "draw the longbow". Crossbow is usefully suggestive of the cross-benches – and therefore of our own complete independence.'[8] Armed with a dummy copy of the proposed 32-page *Crossbow* made up by the Conservative Party's typographer, Elwyn Blacker, the Council began its attempt to find financial backing for the project. Edward Hulton, owner of the Hulton Press, which published the *Picture Post*, offered £2,600 to pay for the journal in its early stages.[9] James Lemkin, who had been the Group's second Chairman, returned to the chair between 1956 and 1958, which was a measure of the importance of the project. He was a regular visitor at Hulton House, the most memorable feature of which in the late 1950s was its rather Orwellian closed circuit television system which kept Edward Hulton in touch with the Press's management throughout the building. He believes that it may have been Edward Heath, then the Chief Whip, who persuaded Edward Hulton to support the Bow Group.

Although immediate funding had now been secured, longer-term questions of editorial and financial strategy remained unresolved. The first Editor, Colin Jones, repeated almost verbatim in his first *Crossbow* editorial the aims he had set out in his earlier proposal. *Crossbow* was to stand 'back from the dust and hurly-burly of daily and weekly commentary in order to seek the longer view'. Nevertheless, there was a tension, which Jones recognised, between the Conservative perspective and the Group's intention to find radical solutions. 'It [*Crossbow*] will be radical and empirical rather than doctrinaire about issues that are still on the fringe of accepted doctrine, but it must avoid appearing to ignore the broad mass of conservatism that has been tried and tested and is still valid.'[10] The problem of this tension between conservatism and radicalism was complicated by the potential encroachment of *Crossbow*

– the journal of the Bow Group – on the 'no corporate view' policy adopted by the Group. But the Group was determined that *Crossbow* should take issue with 'certain landmarks too sacred to be disturbed, certain questions which it is not permitted to reason about', exactly as the *Edinburgh Review* had done 150 years earlier.[11]

It had always been the Bow Group's intention that the first edition of *Crossbow* should be controversial. 'It might be a good idea to invite and carry at least one article in each of the first issues deliberately designed to attract wide attention,' observed the anonymous author of the first proposal in 1955.[12] Just such a forceful article was solicited from Lord Altrincham on the reform of the House of Lords for the first edition. An old Etonian, Altrincham was the *enfant terrible* of the Conservative establishment. He had refused the offer of a seat in the Commons from Lord Woolton, the Conservative Party Chairman. He used his title but obstinately refused to sit in the House of Lords. He also had personal experience of running a political magazine, *The English and National Review*, which made him an attractive ally as the Bow Group tried to establish *Crossbow* as a serious publication. 'We were rather flattered to have a peer in the ranks,' says Russell Lewis today.[13] But best of all – as far as the Group was concerned – weeks earlier Altrincham had called for the abolition of the monarchy, an action for which Harold Macmillan had personally apologised to the Queen. So by September 1957, one month before *Crossbow* was launched, Altrincham was infamously outspoken. That was why the Group commissioned him to write for *Crossbow*. In 'A Prayer for the Lords' Altrincham attacked the peers' attendance allowance as 'too little for those who are really qualified to be legislators and too much for those who are not'. Instead, he argued – extending an olive branch to Harold Macmillan – the Prime Minister should advise the Queen on which of the hereditary peers to summon. The assault on Parliament in the first issue was reinforced by a short satirical portrait of stereotypical MPs on both sides of the House of Commons by B. A. Young.

Bound though the content was to attract significant publicity, the Bow Group's real coup was to attract the Prime Minister to launch *Crossbow* at the Constitutional Club on 1 October 1957. Those close to

Macmillan thought it unlikely he would refuse the invitation. Philip de Zulueta, who worked in Macmillan's private office, believed that the Prime Minister thought the Group was 'so worthy of support'.[14] In part, Macmillan's willingness to attend was an example of the relaxed image which he had begun to cultivate at his first encounter with the Group, almost exactly three years earlier. But, aside from congratulating the Group, his real purpose that evening was to defend the Government's management of the current sterling crisis and, in the middle of the Labour Party's annual conference, to grab the headlines by scotching any suggestions that he would call an early General Election. It was this announcement, rather than the launch of 'a new political quarterly', which interested the press. 'There ain't gonna be any election', ran the headline in the *Daily Mirror* the following day. As Tom Hooson, who worked for the Tories' advertising agency Colman Prentis Varley and was in charge of *Crossbow*'s publicity at the time, remembered: 'His [Macmillan's] speech eclipsed the event it was supposed to celebrate and was widely covered without *Crossbow* getting too much of a mention.'[15]

When rounding up his speech, Macmillan did return to the Bow Group and *Crossbow*.

> I was never able in my time to persuade any Prime Minister to participate in the launching ceremony of one of my projects. I must confess my eye did rest a moment on your definition of a Crossbow as 'a weapon of great force and precision discharged from the shoulder'. But at whom? I am not simple enough to expect that I shall not be – from time to time – one of its principal targets. Of this I am certain, if you bring lively and penetrating minds to bear upon our problems, and seek continually and earnestly to restate and reaffirm our Conservative faith in the light of the changing days in which we live, you will enrich both our Party and our Country. I wish your Group and your *Crossbow* every success.[16]

If Macmillan put the Bow Group in the shade at the launch, some of the interest in the occasion – which gave him the platform he wanted – was generated by the Group. Titbits fed to the press – the first of which appeared in the *Daily Record* – whetted the newspapers' appetite for an awkward clash between Macmillan and Altrincham. In a digest of the magazine's contents, 'Altrincham on the Lords', ominously needed no further explanation. *Crossbow* 'is not for people old in heart or set in ways', hinted Jones, who worked at the Economist Intelligence Unit by day, a fortnight before publication. With the Chairman, James Lemkin, absent, his immediate predecessor Geoffrey Howe seized the chance to speak for the Group on the night of the launch. Unwittingly, Howe reinforced the Group's claim that it had commissioned Altrincham prior to his rise to political infamy, by apologising for the inclusion of the article in the light of the 'subsequent' controversy involving the monarchy. 'We have been back room boys,' he said, referring to the description of Rab Butler's apostles; 'now we are seeking a wider publicity.'[17] Not all of it was favourable. *The Spectator*'s diarist Bernard Levin viewed Howe's performance differently, describing the future deputy Prime Minister as 'as impertinent a young whippersnapper as ever needed his breeks dusting'.[18] Three years later, Howe himself recalled of the evening: 'I tried rather ineptly to make it plain that the Bow Group was not the Altrincham Group.'[19] Lord Altrincham was notable for his absence – 'he thought it would be better if he didn't come along,' suggested Jones cheekily to the *Daily Sketch* on the night.

In general, *Crossbow* was met with curiosity. The choice of a rather ponderous weapon by the Group was a frequent subject of comment on newspaper letters pages and a source of amusement in diary columns during the weeks that followed. In fact the press associated *Crossbow* with Macmillan, rather than the Group, in subsequent days. Harold Wilson alluded to the weapon in the House of Commons when questioning the Chancellor of the Exchequer, Peter Thorneycroft, over his handling of the sterling crisis – one of many times when the Opposition used the Group to attack the Government. '. . . is it true, as one hears in the City, that the Chancellor is getting his advice privately from some outside sources, some of those discredited *laissez-faire* econo-mists whose notions are about as outmoded as the Prime Minister's crossbow is in this nuclear age? If there are to be these *éminences grises*, these economic Rasputins advising the Chancellor, I would be prepared to settle for the Parliamentary Secretary to the Ministry of Education [Sir Edward Boyle] once again.'[20] The publicity was enough to sell 8,600 copies of the first edition, a total which settled down to just under 2,000 for subsequent issues.

The Group's leaders set up a separate company, Bow Publications Ltd, to manage *Crossbow* as well as limit the possible damage should any libel writs start to fly. The Board of Bow Publications was chaired by whoever was the Bow Group's Chairman at the time. Directors included the MPs Sir Keith Joseph and Richard Hornby. They served as both political and financial guardian angels of the new publication: Joseph gave *Crossbow* £150 as a gift. Associated Electrical Industries and Guinness gave £100 each and ICI donated £40. But the precariousness of the finances becomes apparent from reading the early minutes of the company. Both Lemkin and Williams had promised £50 as security against the outlay the Board was making. Philip Goodhart, the MP for Beckenham, joined the board in August 1958 and guaranteed the next four issues for £50 each. He arrived at a time when all the decisions being made by the Board were hedged with the proviso, 'in the event of Issue No. 5 being published'.[21]

There is little doubt that Lord Altrincham was keen to influence the editorial content of *Crossbow*, and as the donor of £100 to the journal he ranked among the Group's substantial backers. He too accepted an invitation to join the board of Bow Publications Ltd, but his directorship of *Crossbow* was to be relatively short-lived, although Howe had clearly made amends for appearing to insult him at the launch of *Crossbow*.[22] Problems arose after Colin Jones had completed the opening two issues of *Crossbow* and it was time to choose his successor as Editor. There were three main potential candidates. Russell Lewis favoured the respected *Telegraph* journalist T. E. Utley, as a high-profile appointment which would benefit *Crossbow*. Altrincham favoured George Scott, who had editorial experience on the polemical magazine *Truth*. But a majority of the directors backed Tim Raison, a young journalist on the *New Scientist*. Though this appeared an unusual choice, because Raison had not long been a member of the Bow Group, the Group had very little money to pay either Scott or Utley, both of whom were better qualified, and Raison volunteered to juggle *Crossbow* and his ongoing job at the *New Scientist*. To the cash-strapped Bow Group, Raison perhaps appeared an attractive prospect, since his father was a senior manager at Hulton Press and might be able to exert more influence when Sir Edward Hulton's commitment expired in November 1959. There is a hint that some members of the Council pushed Raison forward: 'that Tim did it at all is to my mind little short of a bloody miracle,' revealed David Hennessy – later the Group's Chairman – in a letter to Geoffrey Howe.[23]

It was with Raison's inexperience in mind that Lewis drafted some guidelines for *Crossbow*'s new Editor. These set out the four tenets into which the journal's editorial policy had crystallised. *Crossbow* would promote support for a market economy and a multi-racial Commonwealth, a more democratic Conservative Party and 'a realistic appraisal of Britain's place in the world'. As Howe recalled in his memoirs, 'The last of these was intended to leave open the question of our attitude towards Europe; and the first two to combine One Nation social policies with economic liberalism. Nobody ever chafed at that balance.'[24] But Altrincham registered his opposition to Raison's appointment and failed to attend any further meetings of Bow Publications, finally tendering his resignation from the board on 18 September 1958.[25] Altrincham cited Raison's editing of one of his articles as a final straw, but his letter of resignation revealed his deeper discontent at being sidelined: 'My disappearance from the Board of *Crossbow* will make no more difference to what is decided on than my presence on it has made. On all major questions my advice has either not been sought, or, if sought, has been ignored.' The power to appoint the Editor of *Crossbow* was perhaps the most significant and most contentious privilege and power of the Chairman because, regardless of the 'no corporate view' caveat, *Crossbow* was the Bow Group's collective voice – even if it was a dissonant one.

The choice of Tim Raison was probably a good one, because it seems that Raison's personal connections with Hulton's did help *Crossbow*. Photographs from the *Picture Post*'s library illustrated the covers of the Spring and Summer 1958 editions of *Crossbow*. A picture of a refugee – a young Korean girl – covered the third issue of *Crossbow*, which introduced the idea of a World Refugee Year. This article was perhaps one of *Crossbow*'s most influential, and the theme was recognisably similar to other Bow Group social initiatives, such as visiting the elderly at Christmas and participating in sponsored walks to benefit the homeless. Raison later explained the origin of his idea:

> about two years before I had visited Israel and seen some of the refugees there, writing about them in *Picture Post*. They had left a deep impact on me. Now one day, talking to my wife, I came up with the idea that there should be a World Refugee Year, to tackle not only the Palestinian refugees, but the other groups as well.[26]

Highlighting International Geophysical Year, Christopher Chataway, Colin Jones and Trevor Philpott argued that 'on a much smaller outlay, World Refugee Year could yield incomparable dividends in human happiness.' They advocated bullying the British Government into accepting the idea, and set a start date no later than Christmas Day 1959.[27]

The three Bow Group members went to see David Ormsby-Gore, then Minister of State at the Foreign Office, to sell the idea to him. In fact they received support from all parts of the political spectrum for their idealism and imagination, and the Government felt compelled to act six months earlier than the article's authors had predicted. Chataway and Raison represented the Bow Group on the committee set up to co-ordinate British support for resettlement of European refugees from China, and aid for the Chinese in Hong Kong and Arab refugees in general. Looking back in the context of the 1980s, Raison believed that

> there was a great deal in common between the British response to WRY [World Refugee Year] and the Band Aid phenomenon. Both started in Britain and for both Britain remained the pacemaker. The scale of what was raised was not dissimilar. The WRY UK figure was between £8 and £9 million. Multiply that by just under eight times, for inflation, and you will end up with a figure near to the Bob Geldof contribution.

By the time the appeal ended on 31 May 1960, Britain had raised over four times the initial target. Macmillan paid tribute to the Group: 'We may feel justly proud of the handful of young men who started this great movement, and by their imagination and persistence imposed their ideas upon this country and the world.'[28] Chataway announced the final figure raised at a meeting at the Royal Albert Hall. He, Raison, Jones and Philpott received the Nansen Medal for their 'devotion and perseverance in the pursuance of this idea and . . . their success in gaining widespread acceptance of the purposes of World Refugee Year', from the United Nations High Commissioner for Refugees, Mr Auguste Lindt.[29] Feeling that his stint was complete, Raison resigned as Editor of *Crossbow* shortly afterwards.

The change in editorship in 1960 catalysed something of a revolution in *Crossbow*'s management. James Lemkin, who had overseen the development of *Crossbow* from the first idea, stepped down from the Board of Bow Publications, as did Russell Lewis and Sir Robin Williams, both past Chairmen of the Group. This might have appeared to mark the retirement of the Bow Group's first generation from involvement in *Crossbow*, had not Geoffrey Howe taken over the editorship in March 1960, backed by Hooson and Lewis. Howe accurately believed that *Crossbow* was the most powerful weapon in the Bow Group's armoury, and he wanted his finger on the trigger. Until his appointment, the Editor had simply attended the Board's meeting and the Chairman was firmly in control of the finances. The publication had a corporate feel, with those responsible barely credited inside the magazine. But when Howe became Editor, he ensured that his own name appeared much more prominently on the contents page and he negotiated the right to choose his own editorial team, including a deputy Editor, although he accepted the Board's advice by choosing the strongly anti-Common Market journalist Leonard Beaton, who worked on the *Guardian*. Other journalists on Howe's team included Richard Bing, Adam Fergusson, Judy Hillman, Godfrey Hodgson and David Howell. He also recalled Colin Jones to help. The new Board would meet to discuss the content of each new issue once every three months on a Sunday evening at the Chinese Lotus House on Edgware Road.[30]

The scene was set for a profound sea change: this new team favoured the appointment of Michael Heseltine as *Crossbow*'s Managing Director. Even in 1960, Heseltine's flamboyant image went before him. An increasingly well-known figure through exposure in the newspaper diary columns, Heseltine had ambitious plans for *Crossbow*, although it was just one of his growing number of business commitments. He believed it was possible to increase subscriptions threefold to 5,000, an incredible target given that most of the subscription growth at the time derived from word of mouth recommendation through university Conservative Associations, and commercial retail schemes through W. H. Smith and other booksellers had proved unsuccessful.

James Lemkin emerged as the main opponent to selecting Heseltine, but he had no alternative candidate in mind. 'I have heard that a good number of members of the Group Committee are very chary of giving him such a great deal of power and I am quite convinced that you should have some stronger members of the Board than you have at present,' he wrote to Tom Hooson.[31] He 'felt that the Managing Director of *Crossbow* should have a sound commercial background, but that primarily he should have a sincere approach to the Bow Group and *Crossbow*. *Crossbow* should continue as a research magazine and not become a commercially successful "glossy".'[32] With this last phrase, Lemkin was obliquely referring to *Man About Town*, a quarterly magazine which Heseltine had acquired with his business partner Clive Labovitch, hoping to turn it into a glossy magazine catering for the men's market – an idea ahead of its time.[33]

Since Howe favoured a redesign of *Crossbow*, describing the existing format as 'ephemeral, brash, amateur and ex-university', it was Heseltine's achievement with *Man About Town* that was precisely his attraction.[34] The Group was keen to dwell on this new connection, but David Howell insisted that a reference to Heseltine's background on *Man About Town* be omitted from the announcement of the change.[35] Still, most members of Howe's Editorial Board were happy to take on Heseltine and they approved his more radical approach not least because the Group was about to report on its progress to its sponsors and visible results were imperative.[36]

Heseltine was duly appointed and set about an overhaul of *Crossbow*. A number of new cover designs were considered, Elwyn Blacker volunteered to produce a new typographical layout, and both Heseltine and Howe agreed that the link between *Crossbow* and the Bow Group should be strengthened, in contrast to previous policy which had tended to downplay the connection. The most obvious indication of a change of management came with the use of Thomas Wolsey's uncompromisingly modernist crossbow design for the cover, and photographs of the authors. The crossbow design, which filled the cover, directly contradicted Howe's advice that 'a small crossbow motif is permissible provided that it is not so dominant as to suggest that we are a journal for archers, antiquarians or arms manufacturers.'37 That he was ignored was some indication that the *Man About Town* design team was proving to be as autonomous as Lemkin had feared, although the results were striking. Hooson was able to write to the sponsors about *Crossbow*, saying that 'the format is being improved and a new business team is vigorously at work selling advertising space and subscriptions.'38

Heseltine's experimentation with *Man About Town* was very much to *Crossbow*'s benefit, and the new look did not go unnoticed.

> There were some young Tories from Bow
> Who were serious, hard-working and slow
> Till some men about town
> Came hurrying down
> And declared that the Bow should be beau.39

Another, probably apocryphal, story about the Bow Group which included this pun was recounted by the journalist Anthony Sampson: 'There is a story of a girl who joined them, thinking they were the "Beau Group", and was disappointed to find them dull and not very sexy.' Heseltine's chic image failed, perhaps fortunately, to rub off on the Bow Group, although the Group played up the joke, calling *Crossbow*'s diary column 'Beau Giles'.40 But Heseltine himself believed that his membership of this select group had a certain cachet: 'I took my girlfriend and future wife, Anne Williams, on our third date, to listen to . . . Ted Heath,' he recalled.⁴¹ His ambitious plans for *Crossbow* meant that the Group would have to find significantly more money to keep the magazine in the style to which its readers would become accustomed.

Crossbow catalysed two important developments in the Group's activities. The journal generated significant interest and the Group's membership doubled from 300 to over 600 in the two years following the launch. The extra work created by this increase and the running of the magazine required full-time administrative support. Until 1957 the Group used 30 Pall Mall as its address for correspondence and the group's letterhead included a local 'TRAfalgar' telephone number, answered in the mornings only. Reality diverged from the stature the address implied; the Group's access to 30 Pall Mall seems to have amounted to little more than its letterbox. Then in 1957 the Group moved to an office at 22 St Giles High Street, at the same time employing a secretary, Jane St George, to run its expanding operations. From then on, the Bow Group usually held its meetings in the cramped space of this office. The move was a landmark moment, because it suggested both that the Group had passed from being a precarious to a permanent addition to the political scene; but it also marked another outlet for which the Group would have to find funds.

Publicity was an expensive aphrodisiac. Like many groups seeking to influence the political arena, the Bow Group tended to publish first and consider the financial consequences later. It was also presumed that political pamphlets could not be commercially viable. Although, as the Chairman James Lemkin stressed, all three of the pamphlets published in 1956 generated wide publicity, *Advertising on Trial* and *Race and Power* recorded a combined loss of £243 on sales of 1,563. These two publications had been made possible only by a donation of £250. Exceptionally, *Houses to Let*, in which Geoffrey Howe proposed the abolition of rent control because it distorted the market, registered a small profit of £40; but this was due to the fact that the Conservative Political Centre paid the majority of the costs because Duncan Sandys had suggested the project to the Group at its annual dinner in 1956. How to pay for further publications became a pressing question.

One source of finance for *Crossbow* came from advertising, but finding advertisers was a time-consuming task. The Group was encouraged to lose Lord Altrincham who, it turned out, was anathema to many advertisers, notably the millionaire Bernard Sunley, who owned Sunley Investments. Demands for more advertising became a regular feature of Council meetings, and Council members relied upon their political and business contacts to extract commitments. As a result, revenue from advertising almost doubled in the first three years of *Crossbow*'s existence, with Schweppes and ICI being regular advertisers. The sometimes controversial content of *Crossbow* made for tricky relations. 'There was an occasional *ex post* discovery that once again we had offended . . . we were always offending somebody,' says David Howell, who was the Group's Chairman and then Editor of *Crossbow* between 1962 and 1964.[42]

The defining characteristic of the Group's finances until the late 1950s was a reliance on personal connections to raise money. 'When I was Chairman, the Bow Group nearly went bust,' Russell Lewis admits. 'I went to see John Morrison, Chairman of the 1922 Committee, in whose constituency I had done a week's speaking tour with Norman St John Stevas while we were at Cambridge. He was a great help and so was Lord Grenfell.'[43] Much of *Crossbow*'s advertising was achieved through contacts, not the intrinsic merits of marketing through a journal with so low a circulation as *Crossbow*. Clearly, there were limits to how often the Group could call in favours from the people its members had helped, and by the late 1950s the Group was actively looking for a source of regular donations to pay for its expanding activities and outlay. After a gap of two years, the Group again looked to the UIA for support.

When Colonel Hobbs had met Sir Robin Williams late in 1954 he had implied that the UIA would be willing to give more money depending on what the Group had achieved in two to three years' time. Contact between the Group and the UIA had evidently ceased since, because the Bow Group was amazed when it received a second donation from the UIA out of the blue in 1957. It was not until after the financial crisis of the following year that contact was re-established, this time on a regular basis.

To some extent the Bow Group had not needed the UIA's help while it set up *Crossbow*, because the requirement had been not only financial but also technical support to maintain its journal. It was natural, therefore, that the then Chairman, James Lemkin, should have found support within the publishing industry. Sir Edward Hulton limited his commitment to eight issues – or two years. The need to secure longer-term support as well as the appetite for publicity led the Bow Group to commission a professional fundraiser, Tommy Frankland, with whom Lemkin shared a flat, to hunt for further funding. To avoid treading on too many political toes, Frankland first contacted the Conservative Party Chairman, Lord Woolton, who had agreed to become one of the Bow Group's unofficial 'patron saints' on the condition that 'Altrincham is not a force in it'.[44] Coincidentally Altrincham resigned 18 days later. Woolton agreed that the Group deserved support and suggested the UIA as a source of funding. Although Woolton was undoubtedly an enthusiastic supporter, his suggestion reflected the fact that others in the Conservative Party hierarchy were decidedly ambivalent about the Group, a sentiment which was not dispelled when the Group published a memorandum by Howe and David Hennessy which criticised the supine character of the Party Conference in 1959.

In particular, the Group's aloof attitude to other elements of the Conservative Party grated with Peter Walker, who had been chairman of the Young Conservatives, and Ted Brown, the Chairman of the National Executive in 1960. Like Walker, others were piqued by the Group's persistent publication of views supporting decolonisation in Africa. People like these were willing to amplify a rumour that the Bow Group was seen in the City as something of a nuisance and rather juvenile. James Lemkin and Tom Hooson had planned an approach to City firms, as Hobbs had suggested. But when Lemkin sent a draft begging letter to the Prime Minister for his approval, it came to Woolton's attention: apparently he noticed it on Macmillan's desk. The letter incensed Woolton because it mentioned that he was a key supporter of the Bow Group's activities. This was an endorsement from which, he believed, recipients of the letter might understandably infer official party support for what was in fact an independent venture. Woolton's opposition alone would have derailed the project, but the final seal of disapproval came from the Party Treasurer, Sir Henry Holland Martin, who was anxious lest a Bow Group appeal divert donations to the Party before the General Election.

In the light of this incident, Woolton reasoned that asking the UIA for money was better than permitting the Group to mount an independent appeal to the Tories' business supporters before the election. Woolton asked the UIA to give the Bow Group a donation of £2,000 a year for seven years, to cover the period up to the end of the following parliament. The UIA met Woolton partway, offering the Group £2,000 for two years. Significantly, it refused to commit itself beyond the 1959/60 financial year, when the General Election was expected.

The UIA stipulated that the money was to be used to finance a considerable expansion in the Group's activities up to and after the General Election, as befitted a campaigning organisation. The UIA expected to see growth in the Bow Group's membership and *Crossbow* sales, and in the number of its regional branches, research groups and pamphlets. Hobbs emphasised that the Council should not rely on the donations being renewed and suggested that the Group continue to investigate alternative sources of income, possibly from the City, which was beyond the UIA's sphere.

The United Industrialists Association was a mysterious organisation and Colonel Hobbs seems to have relished his own cryptic role. 'They're a pretty quiet bunch – don't talk to anybody much,' said a man in a nearby office when press interest in the UIA grew after Labour's Shadow Home Secretary, Patrick Gordon Walker, alleged, quite accurately, that it had funded the Conservative 1959 election campaign.[45] Gordon Walker described the UIA as 'a rather secret and sinister front organisation', and successive Bow Group Chairmen made considerable investigations to find out more about the UIA and the exact nature of its agenda. 'It was like dealing with SOE [Special Operations Executive],' jokes Lemkin today.[46] Hobbs' deliberate obfuscation was compounded by the fact that the UIA paid its donations to the Bow Group through a separate company, Industrial Co-operation Ltd, and demanded that they were kept 'strictly anonymous'. In about 1960 the Bow Group made investigations into Industrial Co-operation, discovering that it specialised in 'Merchanting, Brokerage, Lending with or without security . . .' and, rather less specifically, '. . . any other business'. Revealingly, one of the company's directors was Harry Renwick, the 24-year-old son of Sir Robert Renwick.

Sir Robert Renwick was a rich stockbroker who was closely involved in the electrical industry and later independent television. Closely connected with the Tories, he was believed to raise funds for them. An early sign of his interest in the Bow Group's work had come in the form of a £100 donation to *Crossbow*, made by his company Associated Electrical Industries soon after the Macmillan launch in 1957. Renwick's involvement with the UIA seems to have been a well-kept secret, and did not become clear to the Bow Group until he intervened directly when the Group proposed its City appeal in early 1961. He was, however, a well-known opponent of nationalisation: 'After the war very few Tories really believed in free enterprise,' he explained: 'my own industry was nationalised, so I wanted to try and get my own back.'[47] The UIA had the triple purpose of sponsoring any organisation which encouraged unfettered free enterprise, keeping the Labour Party out of office and using its funds to lever the Tories towards a stronger line in favour of the market economy.

When it was exposed in 1960, however, the UIA denied that it funded the Conservatives, and played down its own significance: 'Colonel Hobbs agreed that the Association received subscriptions from firms – "but not large ones. It's difficult to get even a pound or two".'[48] This does not tally at all with what Hobbs had told various members of the Group. Although he was always careful to say that the UIA's money was paid to promote 'free enterprise', Hobbs told Williams in 1954 that the UIA spent about £500,000 annually to combat nationalisation, adding that 'the biggest share of this goes of course to one organisation and you know who.'[49] Williams 'came away with the impression that at that time the UIA supported the CCO for about £300,000 annually, Aims of Industry for about £100,000 annually and a large number of other bodies for quite small amounts.' In today's terms these were colossal sums, and while the Conservative Party's financial records for the period remain secret, this remark gives some indication of the magnitude of the financial support which the Party enjoyed during this era. Never mind the country; the Conservative Party's coffers had never had it so good by 1959.[50]

As a result of both unwillingness within the Party to sanction independent fundraising and the willingness of the United Industrialists Association to continue its sponsorship, the Group became dependent on the UIA. The subsequent Conservative General Election victory did not affect this situation, although the UIA's reasons for funding the Group probably changed subtly. Before the election the UIA's motive had been to prevent a Labour Government; when the Conservatives were returned for the third successive parliament, the UIA saw in the Bow Group a suitable catalyst for its free enterprise agenda, which was closely connected to the Government. 'You've hit them hard and have become so important that they cannot ignore what you say,' Hobbs told Tom Hooson and David Howell over dinner on 31 January 1961. This was not just wishful thinking. By then Hooson, who worked as an advertising executive for Colman Prentis Varley, was known as one of the brightest young Conservatives.[51] At the Bow Group's tenth anniversary dinner later in the Spring, Hooson remembered Butler commenting that the current Conservative back bench was rather poor in quality: 'He surprised David Howell and myself over dinner by asking "Would either of you like a safe seat?".'

Not everyone had such a high opinion of the Group. One who was less impressed was Lord Balfour of Inchrye, whom the Group had libelled in one of its publications, *Wings over Westminster*. The Group had repeated a suggestion made in the House of Commons that Harold Balfour, as he then was, was involved in one of a number of companies suspected of collusion. 'I strongly advise you to hasten to get agreement,' warned Lord Woolton in a letter to Tom Hooson, the Group's Chairman, after Balfour had made his objection.[52] The Group's first line of defence was a grovelling letter to Balfour, written by Ron Needs. 'The funds of the Bow Group are very limited . . . Our reserves are only sufficient to carry us over from one appeal to another.'[53] But this was not enough. First Balfour wanted an apology in Crossbow. Then, after it was published, he decided that he also expected an apology in open court, which David Howell, as the Group's Librarian, had to attend. Howell remembers Balfour saying that he felt obliged to take legal action, but a further twist in the story was added by Colonel Hobbs' later disclosure that the UIA had leant on Lord Balfour: 'We help his [Balfour's] Empire Industry Association, and I told them that if his action costs us money, it would come out of our funds for them.'[54] There was an odd footnote to Balfour's behaviour. In 1972 he wrote to the Group to ask whether he could use the phrase *Wings over Westminster* – he had been Under Secretary of State for Air – as the title for his memoirs.[55]

The ease with which the Group had procured a donation from the UIA in 1958 and the name it was making for itself, made a second approach to the British United Industrialists (to which the UIA had changed its name by late 1959) attractive. Hooson wrote again to Colonel Hobbs in September 1960, updating him on the progress the Bow Group had made with the help of the donations made in the previous two years. It was an easy report to write. As Hobbs had required, the Bow Group had certainly expanded: membership had doubled to 800 and there were now not one but seven provincial branches. Of these, the Birmingham Bow Group was the largest with about 60 members, but there were also Groups in Cardiff, Edinburgh, Manchester, Merseyside, Newcastle and Yorkshire. In addition, the Group had strong connections with Oxford and Cambridge Universities' Conservative Associations. The Group could claim that its work had had a bearing on Government action on a number of occasions. In a letter to a journalist, Hooson cited *The University Vote, Houses to Let* and *Minds Matter*, as well as *Crossbow* articles calling for World Refugee Year and a Minister for Science as ideas which the Government had followed up.[56] The Group had also enjoyed unprecedented publicity for the memorandum it produced to coincide with Macmillan's tour of Africa at the beginning of 1960. Referring to *Crossbow*, Hooson ventured that 'probably no other journal gets so much editorial space'. Forthcoming pamphlets included work on the outlook for small business and Conservative principles, and the expansion in the number of research groups, from ten to 25, suggested more to come. Hooson concentrated on *Crossbow*, arguing that although it was the main cause of the increase in Bow Group member-ship, the journal's careful budgetary constraints meant that although 'Crossbow is now just self-sustaining on this basis,' the Group could not afford to publicise its efforts adequately without jeopardising its existence. 'The accent in budgeting is on survival not expansion,' moaned Hooson theatrically in his submission to Hobbs.[57]

Tom Hooson wanted to give the impression that, to push forward their own agenda, the British United Industrialists were left with no option but to increase the donation they gave the Bow Group. He managed to request a 75% rise in the annual donation, to fund two special projects to extend Crossbow's circulation, with a very deliberate choice of words ensuring at the same time that there was no suggestion that the Group was spending recklessly. 'We have ploughed our whole publicity budget into one issue in this financial year – the current issue,' explained Hooson. This issue was the first featuring the new crossbow cover design, and bore all the striking design hallmarks of the new partnership between Heseltine and Howe. In mid-November the BUI's directors agreed to the increase: 'I am glad to be able to enclose a cheque for £3,500 to assist the Bow Group in carrying on the most valuable work which they do in the interests of free enterprise.' There was no guarantee of further funds, warned Hobbs, but he hoped that the amount would enable the Group to expand its activities and hence its membership.

In 1961 Lord Woolton was once again instrumental in ensuring that the British United Industrialists maintained their sponsorship of the Bow Group. He wrote enthusiastically to Renwick in praise of the Group, but explained the possible danger of confusing the Conservative Party's and the Bow Group's separate fundraising efforts. Renwick recognised Woolton's cause for concern and telephoned Hooson, assuring him that the BUI could meet the Bow Group's requirements and offering a further £2,000 straight away. This raised a delicate problem, because Colonel Hobbs was the Group's normal point of contact with the BUI. Hooson was worried that this direct approach from Renwick could damage the image of indebtedness he had built up to flatter Hobbs, so he refused Renwick's offer, even though he was fully aware by then that Hobbs had little say in whether or not the BUI made the Group a donation. Clearly, however, Renwick instructed Hobbs of his position, since Hobbs' often cryptic and contradictory tone suddenly changed. A fortnight later, when Hooson introduced David Howell to Hobbs as his likely successor, Hobbs made it clear that his 'directors would not let the Bow Group die'.[58] Thanking him for dinner the following day, Hobbs confirmed the commitment: 'You can rest assured of the continued interest of our Organisations here in your work . . . do not cut down your existing activities because you feel that finance may be difficult.'[59]

This commitment secured the Bow Group's immediate future, and the episode put paid to its Council's earlier fears that it was regarded as 'rather pink' by Sir Robert Renwick. But it remained unclear whether the donations resulted mainly from Woolton's intervention or the intrinsic value of the Group's work. Hobbs' mention of the Group's work in the interests of 'free enterprise' supports the latter view. It seems that the BUI saw its funding of the Bow Group as of a piece with its support for other, smaller groups who were beginning to proselytise economic liberalism in the early 1960s, rather than as an extension of its support for the Tories. Tom Hooson understood this, and was careful to argue his requests for further funds on the basis that with the extra money the Council could expand the Group's activities. The BUI, perhaps encouraged by the Bow Group's precociousness, also had 'a gut feeling that these were the leaders of the future', believes Lemkin. It was for this reason, and the fact that the Bow Group existed to ginger up the Tory Party in government – which was by no means entirely committed to the market economy at this time – that the BUI continued to fund the Group.

The Bow Group's reliance on a single organisation for financial support begs the question whether the BUI was consequently able to call the Bow Group's political tune after 1958. One episode which appears to imply that BUI funding came with political strings attached was the Bow Group's publication of a pamphlet in support of Renwick's campaign for commercial television. *New Channels – A Report*, by Graham Norton, was published in 1962 as the Pilkington Committee revealed its conclusions. But those involved at the time strenuously deny that the donations made them indebted to the number of commercial interests represented by BUI. In the case of commercial television, widespread opposition from older Tories, the printed media and advertising made a heterodox argument which developed the idea of a market for television attractive to the Bow Group. There is evidence that the Group's leaders recognised the danger of becoming indebted to the BUI. Commenting on Hobbs' apparent attempts to keep the Group uncertain of the state of the BUI's favour, and his enthusiasm that the Group should research space enterprise and seek to influence Kenyan politics, Hooson feared that the Group was vulnerable, saying, 'Later chairmen may find that the idea of "using" the Bow Group may be rather attractive and we may face a serious problem.'[60] The Group did, however, invite the Conservatives' spokesman on space, Airey Neave, to speak on his brief later that year.[61]

In general, there was a remarkable confluence of the Bow Group's ideas and the BUI's agenda rather than a process of dictation from the sponsor to the Group. This goes some way to explaining Hobbs' occasional suggestions that, were there to be a realignment in British politics from which a 'Market' party emerged, supported by the Bow Group but not necessarily involving the Conservative Party, the BUI would continue to fund the Bow Group. At the time Tom Hooson suspected that Hobbs was trying to test the Group's fidelity to the Conservative cause and dismissed this possibility. But it is conceivable to see in retrospect that had the Liberals taken up the liberal market principles which Arthur Seldon, the Institute of Economic Affairs' founder, had developed, the BUI might have moved its allegiance elsewhere. As it was, it already gave the Liberals some money each year. In the event, it was the Conservatives, partly cajoled by the Bow Group, who remained most receptive to free market solutions, the strongest political party and thus the BUI's best lever. As the 1960s began, the BUI's money helped the Group to stabilise its finances. This security was reflected by changes in the Group's character and its activities during the next ten years.

NOTES

1   Williams to Hooson, 24 November 1960.

2   Bennett, letter to the author.

3   Lewis, interview.

4   Memorandum, 'A Regular Bow Group Publication', included among Patrick Jenkin's papers, was written for the committee meeting of the 5 – presumably of November, 1955.

5   Richard Rose, *The Bow Group's Role in British Politics*, p. 869.

6   In 1955 *Encounter* had just published Nancy Mitford's ideas about U and non-U vocabularies to great media interest.

7   Lewis, interview.

8   Letter to *New Statesman and Nation*, 26 October 1957.

9   Bow Publications Ltd, Meeting of the Directors, 25 January 1958.

10 Colin Jones, *Journal*, 1955 proposal for a Bow Group quarterly.

11 'A New Quarterly', *Crossbow*, Autumn 1957, p. 11.

12 'A Regular Bow Group Publication', p. 8.

13 Lewis, interview.

14 CPA, CCO 3/5/38, de Zulueta to Yonge, 9 July 1957.

15 Tom Hooson, 'Crosstalk', *Crossbow*, Summer 1980, p. 4. Tom Hooson became MP for Brecon and Radnor in 1979. He died in 1985.

16 There are at least two versions of this speech, which Howe helped to draft. This wording was quoted in the Chairman's Report for 1960.

17 'Premier's Host', *Western Mail*, Cardiff, 3 October 1957.

18 'Snowball Rolling', *Spectator*, 4 October 1957.

19 Howe to Hooson, 23 November 1960.

20 *Hansard*, 29 October 1957.

21 Philip Goodhart was MP for Beckenham, March 1957–1992.

22 Altrincham to Howe, 28 October 1957.

23 Howe, papers, not dated. After a career as a journalist Tim Raison was MP for Aylesbury 1970–92. He was a Minister of State in the Home and Foreign and Commonwealth Offices, 1979–86. David Hennessy inherited his father's title in 1962 and became Lord Windlesham. Leader of the House of Lords, 1973–74. Managing Director, Grampian Television 1967–70, 1975–81. Principal, Brasenose College, Oxford, 1989–.

24 Geoffrey Howe, *Conflict of Loyalty*, p. 31.

25 Minutes of the Meeting of *Crossbow* Directors, 10 November 1958.

26 Timothy Raison, The Chance of a New Life', *Crossbow*, Winter 1987, p. 3.

27 Christopher Chataway had already represented Great Britain at the Olympics of 1952 and 1956, and briefly held the 5,000 metres track world record in 1954. After

working as a television presenter for ITN and the BBC he was elected MP for Lewisham North, 1959–1966 and Chichester May, 1969–1974. His last office in Government was as Minister for Industrial Development.

28 *Daily Mail*, 31 May 1960.

29 Previous recipients of the Nansen Medal had been Mrs Eleanor Roosevelt, and Queen Juliana of the Netherlands.

30 Hillman and Clarke, *Geoffrey Howe*, p. 48. Len Beaton went on to be the *Guardian*'s Brussels correspondent and became an expert on defence, and particularly nuclear proliferation. Adam Fergusson had previously worked on the *Glasgow Herald*. He subsequently worked on *The Times* and was elected MEP for Strathclyde 1979–84. Godfrey Hodgson is Director of the Reuters Foundation today. Following a short stint at the Treasury, David Howell became a leader writer for the *Daily Telegraph*. He was MP for Guildford 1966–97. Secretary of State for Energy 1979–81; for Transport 1981–83. Chairman of the Foreign Affairs Select Committee 1987–97.

31 Lemkin to Hooson, 17 June 1960, in Hooson's correspondence file, Bow Group archive.

32 Meeting of the Directors, Bow Publications Ltd, 1 June 1960.

33 Michael Crick, *Michael Heseltine: A Biography*, London 1997, p. 95. Heseltine was MP for Tavistock 1966–74; for Henley, 1974–. He was Minister for Aerospace and Shipping 1972–74, Secretary of State for the Environment 1979–83 and 1990–92 and for Defence 1983–86. President of the Board of Trade 1992–95; Deputy Prime Minister 1995–97. He has balanced his political life with a substantial business interest, Haymarket Publications.

34 See for example, Howe's memorandum of 8 July 1960 to Hooson and Heseltine, which cites *Man About Town* as an example of best practice. Hooson correspondence file, Bow Group archive.

35 Memorandum, Howell to Hooson, 15 June 1960. Hooson correspondence file.

36 Memorandum, Howell to Hooson, 15 June 1960. Hooson correspondence file.

37 Note on Cover Design by Geoffrey Howe, 24 May 1960. Hooson correspondence file.

38 Hooson to Colonel J. B. Hobbs, 22 September 1960.

39 'Table Talk', *Observer*, 30 October 1960.

40 The 'Giles' referred to the Group's new address, 22 St Giles High Street.

41 Michael Heseltine, *Life in the Jungle*, London 2000, p. 48.

42 The Rt Hon. Lord Howell of Guildford, interview, 24 March 1999.

43 Lewis, interview.

44 CPA, CCO 3/5/38, Woolton to Poole, 1 September 1958. Altrincham's resignation from the board of Bow Publications occurred 18 days later.

45 'Nothing Sinister', *Daily Mail*, 22 July 1960.

46 Lemkin, interview.

47 Sampson, *Anatomy of Britain*, p. 606.

48 'Nothing Sinister', *Daily Mail*, 22 July 1960.

49 Williams to Hooson, 24 November 1960.

50 £500,000 in 1954 is worth about £7.5 million today. Richard Cockett, *Thinking the Unthinkable*, London 1995, pp. 72–4 suggests that the Economic League, the Progress Trust and the Institute for Economic Affairs from 1955 were other recipients of UIA funding. Aims of Industry had been involved in the campaign to prevent the nationalisation of the sugar industry in 1959. In its later guise, as the British United Industrialists, the UIA would help set up the National Association for Freedom, which became the Freedom Association.

51 *Evening Standard*, 8 February 1961. Colman Prentis Varley held the Conservative Party account.

52 Lord Woolton to Hooson, 21 April 1960.

53 Needs to Lord Balfour of Inchrye, 27 March 1960.

54 Memorandum, 'Dinner with Col. Hobbs – Tuesday, January 31', Bow Group Confidential File.

55 *Crossbow*, August 1972.

56 Hooson to Frank J. Melville, 24 February 1960, Hooson Correspondence File.

57 Tom Hooson, memorandum, 'Widening the Audience of Crossbow', September 1960, p. 1.

58 File Note: 'Dinner with Col. Hobbs – Tuesday, January 31', Bow Group Confidential File.

59 Hobbs to Hooson, 1 February 1961.

60 Supplementary notes by Tom Hooson, February 1961, Bow Group Confidential File.

61 27 June 1961.

Three

KITE FLYING: THE BOW GROUP IN THE EARLY 1960S

In an otherwise hostile article written around the time of the Bow Group's tenth anniversary in 1961, Henry Fairlie admitted that the Group had been 'the most surprising and successful political adventure since the war'.[1] The press was captivated by the image of a group of twenty-somethings who seemed to have the power to bend ministerial ears. 'The most remarkable and the most influential bunch of young people in Britain at present' was a typical comment on the Bow Group during 1961.[2] As if to mark a new chapter of its life, at the end of 1960 the Group moved out of its office at 22 St Giles High Street, where it had been since it had first published *Crossbow*, and into new premises at 60 Berners Street, off Oxford Street. Inside the Group, there were tell-tale signs that the Council recognised the Group's growing importance. In April 1961 the Council agreed that any earnings received by officers from broadcast appearances, published articles or speaking, would be paid to the Group whether or not they were invited in their Bow Group capacity.[3] Russell Lewis recalls that the Group had always joked that the definition of its success would be when an American political scientist made the Group the subject of his doctoral thesis. That moment came close as early as 1961, when an American academic at Manchester University, Richard Rose, had an article 'The Bow Group's Role in British Politics' published in an American academic journal, the *Western Political Quarterly*.

Rose's research had an unexpected spin-off. One of his Manchester pupils, Emil Frankel, was an American student who set up the Ripon Society on his return to the United States. Frankel met a number of members of the Group and there is no doubt that he drew on the model of the Group for the Ripon Society's own role and relationship with the Republican Party; indeed, for a time the Ripon Society was known as 'the American Bow Group'.4 It was not only the Americans who had something to learn from this development in British politics. Shortly after he had finished his term as Chairman, Tom Hooson left for the United States. From there he reported back that 'A talk I gave to a conference on citizenship sponsored by the Canadian Government has led to a curious result in Ontario; both the Conservatives and the Liberals have groups of graduates working to set up research societies patterned on the Bow Group.'5 The French too took interest; the Group was described in the French Parliament's magazine as a 'typically British creation, very flexible and not dogmatic, the Bow Groupers . . . have had the healthiest effect on the Conservative Party's mindset'.6 During the first half of the 1960s the Group became the subject of considerable interest, speculation – and, finally, opposition. This chapter focuses on how this happened.

The simplest reason for interest in the Bow Group was the political success of several of its early members. 57 Bow Group members stood in the 1959 General Election, of whom ten were returned to Parliament, six of them for the first time. They included the Group's co-founder, Peter Emery, who beat Ian Mikardo in Reading; Christopher Chataway and Julian Critchley both also won seats from Labour.7 Their youth and energy tended to counteract the impression generated by a slightly tired election manifesto. Moreover, the impression of the Bow Group as a highly intelligent and influential organisation was boosted before and after the election by the Government's studied association with young people in general and the Group especially. The personal electoral successes of its members appeared to be a manifestation of this. In an editorial on the Sunday after the Conservatives were returned to office, the *Observer*'s leader-writer remarked that 'The true interest of the Tory Party clearly lies in the continuation of that secret and unacknowledged alliance between the leadership and the younger progressives, such as the Bow Group, which Mr Macmillan himself has encouraged and which has been fruitful in bringing forward new ideas. If this happens, the country need not regret its choice.'8

With a majority of 102, the Government could afford to indulge its constructive critics. R.A. Butler, who continued to strengthen his links with the Bow Group, described the Bow Group at its annual dinner in 1960 as a beehive 'from which we obtain honey, as well as the occasional sting'.[9] It was one of a number of well-documented occasions on which Butler had developed his own belief that the Conservative Party should be permeable to young blood and new ideas from a broad base, rather than taking its beliefs as coming from above on tablets of stone.[10] Butler had already offered safe seats to the current Chairman Tom Hooson and his likely successor David Howell during the course of the evening. In fact Butler was engaged in a more delicate balancing act to involve as many people as possible in the policy-making process, as he made clear to colleagues within the Party:

> while some central control of writing must obviously be retained, as many people as possible in the Party should be brought in to the background work. He envisaged what he called the 'octopus plan', which could reach out to groups in the House, the Young Conservatives, the Inns of Court, the Bow Group, the Universities, Swinton etc. and collect their reports and ideas on specific and general subjects. Use would also be made through the CPC of the 'Two-Way Movement of ideas'. The idea was not to direct the work of these bodies, but rather to bring them into the study of various subjects, and probably involve people from these groups in the central and ad hoc policy committees that would be set up.[11]

As Bow Group members formed an elite common denominator of the House of Commons, the Society of Conservative Lawyers and the Young Conservatives, it was likely that they would play a prominent part in contributing to policy, under Butler's strategy, or testing ideas on behalf of ministers, whilst wearing one or other of their hats. The outward impression of this integration was that the Conservatives were open to radical ideas. 'Today's young people are more likely to be Conservative than Labour,' observed Mark Abrams reluctantly in *Socialist Commentary* as the 60s began.[12]

The accuracy with which the Bow Group seemed to predict Government policy lent substance to the aura of influence. This was partly because the mantra which informed the Bow Group's thinking since the first issue of *Crossbow*, 'a realistic view of Britain's position in the world', was in effect a pithy summary of Government policy after Suez. It underpinned the support within the Group – which was strong but by no means universal – for membership of the European Common Market. Occasionally the line between predicting and influencing policy was blurred, both by those supporters eager to attribute to the Group an importance it did not quite have, and by those seeking to portray the Group as a malignant, invisible hand behind policies they opposed. It is unlikely that this second group would have developed, had not the Group become closely involved in the controversy over African decolonisation at the end of the 1950s.

The Bow Group's interest in Africa was developed largely around the experience of one of its founder members, James Lemkin, a solicitor who later became the Tories' Chief Whip on the Greater London Council. His interest stemmed from shore leave in South and West Africa during his National Service with the Royal Navy. He began to develop a strong belief in decolonisation at this time and found that his views were taken seriously by the Conservative Commonwealth Council, which he joined after finishing his National Service.[13] He used his personal experience to illustrate one chapter of *Race and Power*, which was published by the Bow Group in hardback in 1956. In five essays, *Race and Power* analysed five East African colonies' futures under limited self-government. It hinted at the possibility of violence if the local inhabitants' demands for greater self-government were not met. According to Philip Murphy, a recent student of the British Government's handling of decolonisation, the essays were 'more candid about the problems faced by Britain in the colonies than was normal in Conservative Party publications'.[14] *Race and Power* marked the Bow Group out as an important agent in the debate on the future of Africa, so much so that the Minister for the Colonies, Alan Lennox-Boyd MP, persuaded James Lemkin to go on a Colonial Office-sponsored tour of the Central African Federation, to allay the doubts he had revealed in his essay.[15] But the tour had – if anything – the opposite effect. Lemkin returned to Africa on several further occasions and remained an important sceptical influence on Conservative thinking that British colonial rule in Africa remained viable. Under his chairmanship the Group devoted an entire term to discussion of colonial issues. Lemkin made an effort beyond the Group to create a cross-party coalition on decolonisation, and he organised a joint meeting with the Fabian Society on 20 May 1957 on 'a bi-partisan approach in Britain to African colonial problems'.[16]

Race and Power marked the start of a lengthy Bow Group vigil on the state of affairs in Africa. James Lemkin's personal influence can be detected in the Group's November 1957 publication *Crisis over Central Africa*, which supported the Federal Constitutional Amendment Bill, but urged the Government to seek assurances from the Central African Federation that the franchise would be amended to allow Africans a greater say in the political process. By early 1958 the Group's expertise on Africa, and its dominant support for decolonisation, had attracted the interest of Iain Macleod. Hoping for endorsement of his own beliefs and to test the temperature of opinion within the Conservative Party, Macleod suggested to the Party's Policy Studies Group that the Bow Group might be commissioned to write a study on Commonwealth and colonial policy, arguing that 'useful kites might be flown'.[17] Macmillan gave Macleod permission to go ahead with this plan in April 1958, but the Group only published a memorandum calling for a Commonwealth Commission to be set up to study the future of the Central African Federation in July 1959. The Monckton Commission which was subsequently set up by the Government accommodated this suggestion, its members including representatives from the Commonwealth.[18] During this time members of the Group who were exercised by the subject of Africa were in close contact with Iain Macleod, whose determination to be the last Colonial Secretary they strongly supported.[19]

The pace and tenor of events in Africa changed during 1959. In suppressing the Mau Mau revolt in Kenya earlier in the decade British forces had imprisoned 80,000 Kikuyu Africans, all but 1,000 of whom had been released by 1959. Due to the Mau Mau's own violent record, there had been no significant opposition to British tactics – until the

Hola Camp incident of 1959, when it transpired that 11 of the remaining detainees had been beaten to death in a British-run prison camp. According to Iain Macleod, the news of Hola shocked Macmillan. At the same time Britain faced crisis in the Central African Federation, which combined the predominantly native African Nyasaland and Northern Rhodesia with Southern Rhodesia, where Sir Roy Welensky defended the interests of the white population. Rumours in Nyasaland that the Congress Party, led by Dr Hastings Banda, planned a massacre of white Europeans, Asians and moderate Africans, led to swift repression. On 3 March 1959 British forces pre-emptively imprisoned the Congress Party's officials, including Banda; over 50 Africans were killed in the course of the operation. Although the Group did not comment on these debacles, an idea where some of the Bow Group's leading members stood on the wider issue can be gleaned from *Crossbow*'s publication shortly afterwards of an article by C. Braganza entitled 'Catharsis for Kenya', which called for Kenyan independence by 1964.[20]

With a General Election in the offing, Macmillan's Government was swift to cover up the details of what had happened at Hola and in the Central African Federation, both to avoid public reproach and to limit division inside the Parliamentary Party. Lord Devlin was appointed to lead the inquiry which was called after the Opposition refused to accept the explanation by the then Colonial Secretary, Alan Lennox-Boyd, of the need for a state of emergency. Devlin's report was published without a summary of its conclusions, which Macmillan deemed would be too damning by its brevity, and the Cabinet fed the Governor of Nyasaland, Sir Robert Armitage, a swift and effective rebuttal.[21] Shortly afterwards Lemkin, who was again touring the Federation, met Armitage, who told him what had actually happened.[22] So it would seem that members of the Bow Group had access to at least one first-hand account of what had happened in Central Africa. Straight after the General Election, members of the Group once again met with the new Colonial Secretary Iain Macleod to press him to bring about decolonisation.

Lemkin's inside information made him increasingly confident that the Group should comment as the situation grew more complex later in 1959. His motive was simple: at a Council meeting earlier in the year, he had commented that 'the be-all and end-all of the Group was political influence.' It is clear that he, with some other members of the Group, wanted to push the Government to introduce self-government as quickly as possible.[23] Accordingly they ensured that the Group came to be seen as an important forum for debate on the future of Africa by inviting the key participants in the debate to speak to the Group. Michael Blundell, a white Kenyan farmer who proposed more gradual reform than the Bow Group, had been horrified when he read Braganza's article on Kenya in *Crossbow*, saying that 'it was more like the work of Barbara Castle than that of a Tory-sponsored organisation.'[24] He jumped at the opportunity to put his views to the Group late in May 1959. The meeting ran on, and the Group fetched Iain Macleod, who had not met Blundell before, to join the debate.[25] A fortnight later, David Stirling, the co-founder of the SAS and a campaigner for the end of white minority rule, addressed the Group on 'A Proposal for Africa'. The Group also had an acrimonious meeting with Sir Roy Welensky at about this time. What was noticeable was that the supporters of the status quo in Africa, though they were well organised, were not in contact with influential Conservatives. Being so patently close to Iain Macleod, the Bow Group was the next best organisation for Africa's white politicians to meet, after they had travelled thousands of miles in the hope of putting their point of view. But none of those who opposed decolonisation appear to have had the faintest effect on the views of the small group of people within the Bow Group who drove the Group's publications on the subject. They decided to publish their thoughts as Macmillan left to tour Africa in person in January 1960. The anonymous memorandum, *Africa – New Year 1960*, called for the release of Dr Banda and independence for Kenya. At the same time, *Crossbow* awarded first prize in its essay competition 'Priorities for Tory Reform' to an essay on Africa, entitled 'One Man, One Vote'.[26]

As means of achieving the image of influence, the timing and tone of the memo were impeccable, with that day's *Evening Standard* cartoon – drawn by Vicky, who was also sympathetic to the arguments for decolonisation – depicting an arrow with 'Bow Group Memorandum' attached striking the wall behind the Prime Minister's head as he packed his bags for Ghana. But it would seem that the Group was asked to fire the arrow; or, at the very least, Macleod knew the Group well enough to not be surprised when it was fired. Enclosing a copy of *Africa – New Year 1960*, he wrote to Macmillan to say that 'Though I differ in some respects from the conclusions reached in the memorandum, particularly as regards Kenya, I understand the thinking behind it.'[27] Macleod organised a Kenya conference which lasted for six weeks from January 1960. In his inaugural speech he argued that majority rule would inevitably come to Kenya, though he was unwilling to restrict himself by setting a timetable. On 1 April 1960, Banda was released from prison; Kenyatta was released in late July, following a discussion in Cabinet in which no minister voiced opposition to the move. In fact it was both Kenyatta's and Banda's willingness to negotiate which made it impossible for the British Government to ignore them, although Macmillan privately feared 'another Congo' in an independent Kenya.

Nevertheless, to some onlookers, the coincidence of the memorandum and the abrupt change of heart which Macmillan seemed to signal in the two 'wind of change' speeches he gave on his tour, pointed to the direct involvement of the Bow Group in drafting the wording of the latter. This was not the case: it was David Hunt, the Assistant Under-Secretary at the Commonwealth Relations Office, who wrote Macmillan's speech.[28] Nevertheless, several members of the Conservative Party's National Executive were outraged by the Group's stance. Sir Toby Low, the Party Deputy Chairman and a member of the Executive who befriended the Group, was later credited with averting punitive action.[29] However, it is difficult to see what effective official action against the Group the National Executive might have taken, given the line taken by the Government, and it was possibly that sense of powerlessness – in contrast to the Bow Group's apparent influence – which exacerbated friction between other Tories and the Group.

The memo also divided the Group. Although it represented a summary of Lemkin's and others' thoughts on the African issue, other members of the Group were outraged because the media inferred from the memo's anonymity that the Group as a whole favoured decolonisation, when there were grounds to believe that Lemkin was wrong. One

potential weakness of his experience was that it was based on West
Africa, where Ghana had enjoyed a successful transition to independence
partly because there were enough well-educated Africans to administer
the new state. The situation in East Africa was different: here there was
a wide educational divide between the black and white populations, a
situation which some believed made the transition to democracy impossible. Consequently, there was uproar at the Group's Annual General
Meeting two months later; Lemkin was 'in the hot seat', Lewis
remembers. Both Lemkin and the outgoing Chairman, David Hennessy,
were forced to apologise, and the Council promised that a more formal
procedure for publishing memoranda would be followed in future,
involving wider consultation within the Group.[30] For the time being the
Group fell silent on Africa.

The Group's work on decolonisation raised a much wider question
with a direct domestic impact. Although some believed that the newly
democratised nations of Africa should receive support in the form of
some sort of post-Imperial trading preference, others recognised that the
end of Empire meant that it was time to forge a closer relationship with
Europe. The Group had first published on Europe as the Treaty of Rome
was signed in 1957. In *The Challenge from Europe* Russell Lewis
supported the case for joining the Market on the grounds that it would
free up capital and labour. Lewis believes that this pamphlet sealed him
a job as a Press Officer at the EEC's Community Information Office in
London. As a result of this job, when he wrote again on the subject in
Britain into Europe in 1962 he was obliged to use a fairly transparent
pseudonym, William Russell (his Christian names) to clear the project
with his employers.

The Group quickly developed a recognition of the constitutional
implications of membership, which were brilliantly spelled out in a brief
supplement to *Crossbow*, *The Rome Treaty and the Law*, published with
the July 1962 issue. This accepted at the outset that 'Accession to the
Rome Treaty will present us with problems of great constitutional importance.' Hugo Young has written that this study 'foreshadows with great
exactitude the effect the Treaty of Rome has had on British law'.[31] As a
result, perhaps Bow Group authors who supported British membership

tended to downplay the political implications of membership in relation
to the economic motives. In 'Integration or Isolation?', a landmark article
for *Crossbow* which was reported overseas,[32] Patrick Jenkin concluded a
broadly economic analysis of the benefits of membership with a stark
paragraph on the political consequences of staying out:

> We must recognise that unless we are prepared gradually to sink to
> the status of Europe's off-shore island, we must identify our
> interests with those of our nearest neighbours and form a single
> coherent unity which can stand on its own and compete with the
> other major powers. If this involves a surrender of sovereignty,
> then so be it. For that way, and that way alone, lies our future as a
> power capable of influencing world events.[33]

Interest in the Group's ideas about the development of the free
market flowed from the publicity generated by its statements on Africa.
After the Government had appeared to follow the Bow Group's line on
colonial policy, commentators began to take greater notice of the
Group's other pronouncements and speculate about whether they prefig-
ured other changes in Government policy. To very little interest, the
Group had set out its clearest statement yet of a credo supporting the
market economy in a *Crossbow* article, 'Notes towards a Tory
Manifesto', in the run-up to the 1959 election. 'The principles of the free
market are those which work most effectively and ensure the highest
standard of living for the whole population,' argued the anonymous
author.

In February 1961 the development of the free market theme in a
publication to mark its tenth anniversary, *Principles in Practice*, sparked
much greater interest. The book was a collection of essays which
addressed 'the question of where we should draw the limits of State
action'. Two essays stand out: Godfrey Hodgson's and Geoffrey Howe's.
Hodgson argued for the reintroduction of school fees: £3 a term for
primary schools, £5 at secondary level, and higher school meal and milk
charges to generate revenue of about £61 million on the basis that 'People
appreciate more what they have to pay for.' In practice the scheme was
hedged with an exemption for the poorest 10% of the population and an

additional reduction for a further 25%. Howe's essay was a broad statement of philosophy which he would bring into government just under 30 years later. 'Conservatives surely must strive for a large reduction, in the long run, of the public social services . . . Over the whole field of social policy our firm aim should be a reduction in the role of the State.' Radically, Howe advocated voucher schemes for health and education, a subject which the head of the Conservative Research Department, Brendon Sewill, had already touched on in *Crossbow* over four years earlier. In his comprehensive history of the welfare state, Nicholas Timmins has effectively summarised the significance of Howe's essay: 'in 15 pages in 1961, Howe summed up much of what was to become the radical right's agenda during the 1980s. At the time, however, what was most notable about the essay was how much it was the exception to the rule.'[34]

Timmins argues that 'The pamphlet failed to ignite any political storm or crusade . . . Not one of his [Howe's] more radical prescriptions crept into any of the four Conservative manifestos between 1964 and 1974.' Though the second point is evident, it is not true that the pamphlet went unnoticed, since it arrived during an already fierce debate on public spending. But the debate was largely confined to the Conservative Party, since the Liberal Party had rejected the calls of a number of Liberal academics to embrace market economics. Commentators widely expected Enoch Powell, then Minister for Health, to apply his well-known philosophical beliefs to the pragmatic question of NHS spending. Supporters of sustained public spending felt pressurised by increasing disillusion in the welfare state to the right and left of the political spectrum. As Chancellor, Gaitskell had already introduced charges in the National Health Service, and although Conservative Central Office had been quick to distance itself from the proposals made in *Principles in Practice*, *The Times* regarded the Bow Group's pamphlet as a means of softening public opinion. 'It is now clear that the reactionary Bow Group are almost in charge of Conservative policy and the Bow Group have suggested that there is no reason why one should not tax education if one taxes the Health Service.'[35] Such a statement would have been laughable had it not followed the Group's apparent influence over events in Africa. Conservatives themselves were frightened by the unashamed radicalism of *Principles in Practice*. Speaking to Oxford University Conservative Association, the MP Sir David Eccles denounced the proposals as 'bad Toryism'.[36]

At the time, *The Times* believed that the Group was driving Government policy; in retrospect, Timmins recognises that in economic policy terms the Group had virtually no impact at all until its members of the 1960s came to power in the 1980s. This paradox illustrates the complicated nature of the Bow Group's influence, derived in part from the press's very perception, exaggerated as it was, of that influence.

One episode in the early 1960s suggests that because the Group was believed by the press to be highly influential, ministers were forced to pay attention to what it had to say. The Bow Group was forced to recognise the consequences of the wider perception of its own political clout when the Minister for Defence, Harold Watkinson, reacted irritably to its pamphlet *Stability and Survival*, after a leak of its contents was published in the *Daily Mail* on 5 January 1961, a month ahead of publication. To attract interest, the Group's technique was to publish its members' analysis of a particular issue shortly before expected official reports. The Group tended to focus on areas where it was felt that a change of policy was possible. The future MP Peter Lloyd alluded to this technique almost ten years later, when he was the Group's Research Secretary: 'We shall generally want to produce our pamphlets before the Government view has crystallised on a subject where a new departure is in the air.'[37] When a report subsequently coincided with an opinion published by the Group, it thus tended to reinforce the impression that the Group enjoyed influence within the establishment, whether or not this was the case. *Stability and Survival* was published at a time when defence policy was under close examination, since the Government was about to publish a White Paper on defence. Under question was whether Britain needed an independent nuclear deterrent or a stronger conventional force to resist an invasion across northern Europe by Warsaw Pact troops.

When *Stability and Survival*'s main author, Julian Critchley, had arrived in the Commons, his father had advised him to specialise his knowledge.[38] Critchley chose defence: *Stability and Survival* was one of his early outings into the subject. He believed that the best way to

be noticed was to be radical. He advocated ending Britain's mainte-
nance of an independent nuclear deterrent as well as the use of
conscription to build a 200,000 strong army – some 35,000 stronger
than the White Paper would suggest. To make up the numbers,
Critchley argued for a return to conscription for social reasons,
suggesting that young men be selected at random to fill the ranks. 'We
were in the questioning mood,' recalled Howell. In a tense session
Howell, Critchley and Len Beaton finalised the pamphlet while staying
in a cottage on Lord Waldegrave's estate. The Group could not resist
releasing a sneak preview of the proposals in the *Daily Mail*, in
advance of the publication of the White Paper. The scoop landed the
then Chairman Tom Hooson in hot water.

Watkinson was not impressed when he read the *Daily Mail*'s preview
of the Bow Group's defence proposals on the Thursday morning. He had
already been aware that the Group were planning to publish on the
subject but, not having been sent a draft, he could only rely on the *Daily
Mail*'s interpretation, headlined 'Switch V-Force to Nato – Premier faces
shock Tory demand'. The pamphlet 'comes from the influential Bow
Group – the Tory Party's "young lions" whose views have often heralded
sweeping changes in Government policy'.[39]

Later in January Watkinson called Hooson to the Ministry of
Defence for a dressing-down. The exchange which followed illuminated
the position which the Government found itself in with the Bow Group
by 1961. 'My public relations people tell me that the foreign groups
regard the Bow Group as the Government's normal *ballon d'essai* . . .',
remarked Watkinson, '. . . and you will understand that when you are
advocating policies contrary to the Government's which affect the
alliance this is embarrassing.'[40] Hooson protested that not only was the
Bow Group independent, but the view expressed in the pamphlet was
that of the authors alone. Watkinson was somewhat mollified; at the
beginning of the meeting he had threatened to attack the Group in public
if its work undermined his own position. Hooson wrote the same day to
Sir Toby Low, the Party's Deputy Chairman, that 'I saw Mr Watkinson
this afternoon and assured him that the *Daily Mail* report last month
about our forthcoming defence pamphlet was very misleading.'[41]

None the less Critchley, the new MP for Rochester and Chatham, offered the Opposition an attractive target in the House of Commons. The Labour Party had perhaps become aware of the possibilities offered by the Bow Group during the debate on the Central African Federation. When the Group had sent the Shadow Colonial Secretary, Jim Callaghan, a copy of its memorandum *Crisis in Central Africa*, from which Callaghan then quoted figures to support his argument in an Opposition debate on Rhodesia and Nyasaland, to cheers from his own side.[42] In the debate on the Defence White Paper, the Labour MP for Islington North, G. W. Reynolds, almost immediately intervened during Watkinson's speech to ask him what part *Stability and Survival* played in Government defence thinking. 'Recent articles by the Bow Group show what a broad-minded party the Conservative Party is,' Watkinson replied.[43] Denis Healey inferred from Critchley's pamphlet that he had support from 'a large number of us on both sides of the House' for increased conventional defences, balanced by reduced reliance on the nuclear deterrent. The best way to conceal the wide divide on defence within Labour's ranks was to highlight a difference of opinion within the Conservative Party, which the Bow Group's *Stability and Survival* could be used to illustrate.[44] 'I am glad to say that I am able to welcome this criticism also [of the Blue Streak missile programme] from a group of Conservative thinkers – in the old days that used to be an oxymoron – in a recent pamphlet which the Bow Group has published,' Healey noted.[45] In the future, Watkinson advised Hooson, the Bow Group was welcome to speak to civil servants and use resources from the Ministry of Defence to help with its research. It was his oblique way of asking the Group to clear future publications with him. In a letter to Watkinson, Sir Toby Low had previously discouraged this course of action: 'it would, I think, be a mistake to lose the advantage that we gain by neither being responsible for them or closely related to them.'[46] The episode illustrated both the power of the Group and the enmity it could arouse: Peter Goldman, the Director of the CPC, called the pamphlet, which he had refused to publish, 'ill-written, ill-argued, ill-tempered and ill-timed'.[47]

The delivery system for Conservative political pamphlets had already increased the dislike of the Group's work in certain local Conservative

Associations which paid a subscription to the CPC for a quota of each pamphlet it published, including some more heterodox contributions by the Group. Although the Group published *Stability and Survival* itself, the trouble it caused offered an opportunity for those who resented the Group to complain to Conservative Central Office. Moreover, the media had begun to develop an image of the Bow Group as exclusive and powerful which, though it was undoubtedly intoxicating to members inside the Group, encouraged jealousy from several quarters outside. In February 1961 the BBC chose the Bow Group and not the Young Conservatives as one of the subjects for discussion in the first of a new series, *Gallery*, a magazine programme which covered politics. Through coverage in unlikely places like *Harper's Bazaar*, for which the Group was part of the 'whole mood of irreverence, vitality, scepticism, experiment, and tough-thinking that is transforming the arts and criticism', the Bow Group moulded itself a sophisticated and aloof image.[48] This spurred the Young Conservatives to set up their own policy committees; but the YCs were depicted in the newspapers as 'keeping up with the Bow Group' and increasingly marginal in political terms.[49] The heady effect of the publicity given to the Bow Group revealed itself in a misguided mailshot proposed in October 1960 to attract new *Crossbow* readers. The content came under discussion at the Bow Group's Council meeting where the chairman, Tom Hooson, registered his opposition. The letter went ahead nevertheless. It read:

> I am a member of the Bow Group; you are not. However, I'm giving you a chance to make up for this terrible inferiority by becoming a subscriber to *Crossbow*. This, of course, will never make you my equal, but it will certainly put you one up on *The Spectator – New Statesman – Observer* crowd – and think how satisfying that would be. I expect you already take *The Times* and therefore fondly imagine you are a Top Person. Take *Crossbow* and become a Summit Personality . . .[50]

Many did not see the joke, and the letter attracted outrage inside the Bow Group, let alone outside. Although tongue in cheek, it appeared to confirm the impression of the Group's petulant character, and exacerbated the divide between the Bow Group and the Young Conservatives, some of whose members received the mailshot.

Barely three weeks earlier, coverage of the annual Party Conference – at Scarborough in 1960 – had highlighted the growing tension between the two groups.[51] The Young Conservatives considered the Bow Group to blame. A later comment summarised YC feeling towards the Bow Group throughout this era: 'I would say that the YC movement might gain if there was a less clear distinction from the Bow Group but the initial gesture must come from the Bow Group which has made itself far too exclusive,' argued one Young Conservative.[52] But, infuriatingly for the YCs, the Bow Group continued to debate their future within the pages of *Crossbow*. If anything the Group was encouraged to overstep the mark by the unwillingness of local Party agents to criticise it openly. The Central Office co-ordinator of area agents told one that he would openly oppose the creation of a local Bow Group except for the fact that its members 'have received de facto recognition from the Prime Minister and other leaders'.[53] Macmillan's endorsement of the Group was probably crucial in ensuring that opposition to the Group's activities remained bottled up.

So throughout the 1960s, bashing the Young Conservatives was an evergreen activity of *Crossbow* Editors, who seemed to underestimate the ill-will such soul-searching provoked. The Young Conservatives were a theme to which Leon Brittan returned as *Crossbow* Editor in late 1967, using a cover shot of an anonymous and underdressed female 'Young Conservative' with an empty wine glass, to illustrate a report on 'What Young Conservatives are really like', which provoked amusement and uproar.[54] Nine years later still Julian Critchley, who was closely involved in the Group at the beginning of the 1960s, found room in an article to describe the Bow Group as being 'Conceived for the Young Conservative who could both read and write'.[55]

Nevertheless the Bow Group did the Conservatives' public image an important service during the early 1960s. They were an acceptable face of the hirsute, youthful radicalism which was caricatured by *Punch*: 'The Young Action Party, man, is the party of youth and action. This country has been run by a bunch of old squares. And what have they done except grow old?'[56] The Group played up to this image: 'The important thing', exhorted the anonymous author of *Crossbow*'s Bow Notebook in the Spring of 1961, 'is to shut our ears to Oxbridge bumbledom or the need for caution, state a target and get on with the job.'[57] This from an editorial panel, most of whom were the polished products of an Oxbridge education. Research into reforming the licensing laws reinforced the radical image the Group had acquired for itself. In 1960 the Group drew the ire of the redoubtable Welsh temperance lobby when, backed by copious research by Geoffrey Howe into the correlation between drunkenness and crime, it called for longer drinking hours in Wales as part of a more general relaxation of licensing laws, as well as a ten-minute period of drinking-up time after the bar had closed.[58] In *Scotland for the Tourist*, published in 1962, the Group offered ways in which Scotland might attract more tourists. The authors, Gerald Elliott and Cecily Giles, who were both members of the Edinburgh Bow Group, again argued that tight Sunday drinking laws were partly to blame for difficulties in expanding tourism. The Secretary of State for Scotland, Michael Noble, seemed to agree as he launched the pamphlet, saying that 'In Scotland there is a rather clear lack of what my daughters call "living it up".'

So while the Labour Youth Campaign preached a 'socialist revolution' in its magazine *Counterblast*, and tried, without success, to secure the playwright John Osborne's support, it was the Bow Group which felt compelled to defend itself against the charge of being 'angry young men'.[59] Within the Conservatives, the Bow Group stimulated the Young Scottish Unionists and the YCs to act. Outside, the Young Fabians, the Liberals' New Orbit and the Labour Youth Campaign all emerged to counter the Bow Group's monopoly on radical ideas. In a role-reversal that was a measure of the Group's success, Shirley Williams, at the time the Fabian Society's secretary, declared that the main task of the Fabian Society was to combat the influence of the Bow Group.

The corollary of the Bow Group's head start in this renaissance of young intellectual radicalism was that it found itself under attack from both left and right. Much energy was expended trying to tie down the Bow Group's exact political affiliation, which had been the subject of satire for as long as the Group had been in the public eye. The *New Statesman* offered a prize for the best verse definition of a member of the Group. Richard Rose, the political scientist who had written an academic article on the Group, subsequently described it as 'a purplish mixture of blue and red with a tincture of Liberal yellow'.[60] Following an attack on Gaitskell in *Tribune* at the beginning of 1960, the *Evening Standard* printed a cartoon depicting Anthony Crosland on the telephone to Gaitskell with the caption, 'On the other hand Hugh, we can probably depend on a message of support from the Bow Group.'[61] Gaitskell was personally attacked as a 'refugee from the Bow Group' at one particularly heated Labour students' meeting in Leeds.

Of greater concern on the Right was the benevolent attitude towards the Group held by the Left during this time. Writing in *Tribune*, Donald Soper admitted that 'these Tories strike me as being most knowledgeable and many of them possess an expertise which I envy.' Tony Benn regularly referred to the Group as evidence of a progressive tendency within the Conservative Party during his 1961 campaign to allow peers to renounce their titles to sit in the Commons. It was thus not surprising that Conservatives were often hostile towards the Bow Group: the *Daily Telegraph*'s columnist T. E. Utley described the Group's beliefs as 'hardly to be distinguished from radical liberalism and sometimes even from socialism'.[62] It took one further volley from the Bow Group – on the subject of Africa in 1962 – to translate this general feeling into a political act which would permanently change the way in which the Bow Group was viewed: the Monday Club's creation in January 1962.

The Bow Group's concern about Africa was reinvigorated when in October 1961 Macmillan replaced its chief ally on Africa, Iain Macleod, with Reginald Maudling, who was an unknown quantity. Macleod became Party Chairman and Leader of the House. Maudling was known to be acceptable to Welensky, and it seems that the Group believed it was necessary to press him to ignore the resistance to decolonisation of the Rhodesian Federal Government. *The New Africa* was written by the MPs Charles Longbottom, Chris Chataway and Julian Critchley, and David Howell and James Lemkin.[63] They picked up on the strategic issue which Macmillan had addressed in the 'wind of change' speech: 'whether the uncommitted people of Asia and Africa will swing to the East or to the West'. *The New Africa* argued that Soviet penetration of Africa was best countered by creating genuine independence, maintaining Commonwealth links and improving education. As it transpired, Maudling was just as keen an advocate of decolonisation as his predecessor had been, the only difference being that he was better able to maintain the confidence of both sides in the course of negotiations. Again the Bow Group's view chimed with that of the Party leadership. Earl Winterton, writing to the *Daily Telegraph*, accused the Bow Group of exerting hidden influence on the Government.[64] Macleod's influence was tangible: Longbottom was his Parliamentary Private Secretary. The growing number of 'Bow Group MPs' reinforced the general impression that the Group was able to pressurise the Government. In 1962, the most recent addition was John Biffen, who was Librarian of the Group at the time of his election.[65] *Crossbow* was at great pains to deny that his membership of the Bow Group implied any indebtedness or interest: 'Contrary to the reports of some political commentators he [Biffen] will not find himself joining some sort of party within a party when he gets to Westminster. Those Bow Groupers who are elected to Parliament regard their membership of the Group in precisely the same light as membership of any other club or organisation, not as something to influence their Parliamentary conduct.'[66]

Amid uncertainty about Maudling's policy Lord Salisbury, who had closely allied himself to Welensky, wrote to Macmillan on 3 January 1962 demanding that he scotch the rumours that Maudling was contemplating a constitution for Northern Rhodesia which would guarantee a largely black franchise. Realising that the Cabinet was set to change the franchise in Northern Rhodesia, Salisbury agreed to become a patron of the three-month old Monday Club, which had taken its name from Monday 3 February 1960, heartily regretted by its members because on this day Macmillan had made his 'wind of change' speech for the second time, to the South African Parliament. This was, of course an event with which the Bow Group remained strongly, albeit tenuously, associated. Writing in 1962, Anthony Howard recalled that memories of the Bow Group's role two years earlier were still strong: 'a genuine shriek of Tory pain did go up when in 1960 the Group called for both the release of Dr

Banda and independence for Kenya.'

It was ironic that, just as the Bow Group had been set up to combat the influence of the Fabian Society, the Monday Club was created to redress the perceived imbalance of views pressing on the Government, which manifested itself in the emerging Africa policy, and of which the rise of the Bow Group was a symptom, if not a cause. Africa was the subject of the Monday Club's first meeting late in 1961, but many joined the Club because they felt a general unease at the direction of Conservative policy. The Club's founder, the 24-year-old Chelsea Young Conservative Paul Bristol, remarked that 'we feel there is a general impression that younger Conservatives are all left-wing Bow Groupers, which is not so. The Monday Club aims to restore the balance.'[67] A member of staff from Conservative Central Office who attended a Monday Club event early in the autumn of 1961 reported that the Club had been founded by former members of the Bow Group 'who held extreme right wing views'.[68] Styling itself as a young people's organisation, the Club published its policy and aims in January 1962, just as the Bow Group released *The New Africa*. As the Bow Group quickly became aware, the Monday Club was 'quite active in recruiting members and holding meetings' and maintained a pitch of activity which was to impact on the Group later in the decade.[69] But even early on, the formation of the Club pushed the Bow Group on to the defensive. David Howell, then Bow Group Chairman, stated that the Monday Club 'in no way conflicted with the Bow Group and that there was no reason why people should not belong to both organisations'.[70] Eight days later Howell restated this position at the Group's Annual General Meeting, since it appeared that the Monday Club provided an alternative to those members who opposed the Group's line on Africa, and the Bow Group's Council was anxious not to lose members.

The formation of the Monday Club, which was unashamedly a pressure group, threw the issue of the Bow Group's own political purpose into sharp relief. By implication, the progressive pressure exerted by the Bow Group was causing an equal and opposite reaction on the other wing of the party. But 'pressure group' was a description the Bow Group's members had always strenuously denied by continual reference to its 'no corporate view' policy. To have admitted a campaign of concerted pressure would certainly have encouraged the unwelcome attentions of the party managers, a scenario the Group had managed to avoid largely because it did studiously maintain a policy of publishing contradictory material. The Group's publications on Africa bucked this trend. Though it is not clear that anyone expressed an interest in writing an opposite view, the Group did not publish a defence of colonial rule, nor even consider a slower handover of power to the local population than was advocated by Lemkin and others. This contrasts with the care the Group took to express both sides of the similarly polarised debate on Europe. But the attraction of earning news coverage for comment on controversial political issues meant that the Bow Group ran the risk of appearing to be a pressure group. George Gardiner recalled that 'What put me off both [the Bow Group and the Monday Club] was the habit of chairmen in those days of issuing *ex cathedra* statements with which all members became automatically associated whether they agreed or not.'[71] The Group's apparent influence made the issue of who controlled its output an increasingly hot topic. Membership of the exclusive circle which decided how the Group should respond to particular situations had, until 1960, been determined by its founders and their immediate successors; the election contest between David Hennessy and Colin Baillieu in 1962 marked an attempt to end this convenient arrangement.

It was no coincidence, then, that the Monday Club's angry birth coincided with a battle for the Chairmanship of the Bow Group, a contest afterwards described by one of the participants, Colin Baillieu, as 'vigorous'.[72] Anthony Howard, writing in the New Statesman, looked favourably upon Baillieu's candidature. Possibly quoting from his old university friend and member of the Group, Michael Heseltine, he reported that Baillieu was campaigning against 'what some members are believed to regard as the stuffy, worthy, smug image' which had developed in the Group.[73] 'We have wished the wind of change on others,' Baillieu said, 'It is now time to let it blow through our own organisation'. His choice of phrase implied that the Council's handling of the issue of Africa had inflamed his belief that the Group was being run by an impervious cabal.74 But David Howell, who had stood against Julian Sandys for the Chairmanship the previous year and won, plays down any principle which may have underpinned the election:

> It was the old familiar thing in any institution, the established succession versus outsiders saying 'wait a minute, why can't we bust in'. I was the established succession after Tom Hooson, who was after Geoffrey Howe and so on. It wasn't just on the nod because there were one or two outsiders – I don't mean that word rudely – but they were outsiders who thought they'd have a go, and Julian Sandys was one of them. 75

The dealings of Howell's predecessor, Tom Hooson, with Colonel Hobbs of the British United Industrialists revealed the almost hereditary process by which power was handed down from year to year. Having met Howell, Hobbs wrote to Hooson: 'I will look forward to keeping in touch with him when, as you anticipate, he takes over from you as Chairman.'76 The manner in which an opponent, the former Chairman David Hennessy, was quickly mobilised against Baillieu tends to strengthen the hereditary impression, though there is no question that Hennessy was a credible alternative. As Howell suggested, Baillieu was seen as an outsider, a fact which was perhaps reinforced by his opposition to British membership of the Common Market at a time when successive Chairmen of the Group had favoured European integration. Howell, as Chairman, had been one of a number of high-profile political and public figures who had agreed to endorse Britain's campaign for membership when this was announced in May 1961. That Howell was asked for his support as Chairman of the Bow Group is certainly a measure of the Group's significance by the early 1960s.

Although Colin Baillieu lost the election, his decision to stand was none the less an important milestone in the political development of the Group. Given the press interest in the election contest, it was clear that the close-knit hierarchy which had run the Group from its first days would in future have to be more accountable to a growing and increasingly disparate membership which was split on issues such as Africa and Europe. From being an extended group of friends, the Bow

Group evolved into a much broader political association. An early sign that the Group was expanding beyond the close social circle of its leading players came at the 1961 Annual General Meeting. In response to a question about membership policy, the Secretary Ron Needs said that any applicant who lived within 20 miles of London, but was not known personally to a member of the Group, was interviewed as a matter of course. Generally membership was largely in the gift of active members.

The branching out of the Group, and resulting recruitment in the regions, increased the pressure for a written policy. This was supplied in the Council meeting of 12 October 1962: 'the types of members wanted were people likely to contribute to research at University level although members did not necessarily have to be graduates.' The interview policy was stringently applied; but it was as demanding to existing members who had to conduct the interviews as it was to applicants, and the fervour with which the interview procedure was applied varied from year to year, waxing and waning according to concerns about the threat of 'entryism'.[77] In March 1964, faced with falling membership while needing to fund an increasing output of publications, the Secretary Tony Newton explained how difficult it was to arrange interview panels and recommended that the standards required 'should now be somewhat relaxed'. He duly reduced the interview panel to one senior and one junior member.[78] But there was always pressure for the Group to maintain a discriminating membership procedure to buttress the image that the Group was composed of only the best young Conservatives.

It is hard to disentangle the factors leading to this decline in the Group's membership. The rapid increase in the numbers stimulated by *Crossbow* and the resulting greater media coverage ended abruptly in early 1962. The Monday Club certainly presented a challenge to a complacent recruitment policy. But more general trends were at work. The Conservatives' misfortunes provided an unwelcome backdrop which did not encourage members to renew their subscriptions, and the Group faced accusations that it was partly responsible for the Tories' jaded image by the time of the October 1961 Party Conference. But it was not just that younger Conservatives were not joining; members were leaving.

Part of the problem seems to have been the impression that the same people continued to run the Group; this was bound to be a difficulty, given Fred Tuckman's noted observation that

> [The] B.G. [Bow Group] consists of (1) Politically ambitious (2) Persons wanting to achieve some fulfilment, often of a vaguely compulsive nature. [Therefore] Tend to be touchy on matters involving their status, acknowledgement of contribution made & wish to feel they are consulted, have a share in shaping decisions.[79]

By 1963 – when John MacGregor was Chairman – the Council was aware that the Group appeared to be ageing, partly because little effort had gone into active recruitment, and also presumably because ambitious but frustrated young members were drifting away. Inside the Group the atmosphere was increasingly fractious: presentation meetings, at which draft pamphlets were discussed and cleared for publication, became factional. The case for publishing *No Tame or Minor Role*, by Sir Robin Williams and Len Beaton, who argued the case for remaining outside the Common Market, was fiercely contested. The meeting convened to approve the draft pamphlet split 21–17 in favour of publication, with eight abstentions. The Council's minutes recorded that 'Some members of the research committee felt there was a danger of meetings being "packed", key members not bothering to attend and express their views, and pamphlets being supported through loyalty rather than on their merits.'[80]

A number of members suggested that a solution to the Group's general problems lay in creating a new post of Political Officer. Most prominent among them was a young Australian, Henry Bosch. Bosch had joined the Group unhappy about its support for decolonisation. Immersing himself in the Group's research work, he 'sought to shift the emphasis of the Group more to the right and more towards economic issues'.[81] He believes that membership of the Group had by then acquired a principally social cachet and that 'there was a lack of people prepared to put in the substantial effort needed to produce more of the research pamphlets on which the Group's reputation and influence were based . . . It seemed that there was a danger that the Group would become irrelevant if it did not do more to attract more high quality people and to motivate them to do research.' Corroboration of his view comes from an unlikely source, *The Short List*, a novel written by David Walder MP which centred on the members of the 'Stepney Group'. Asked by an aspiring candidate whether he should join the Group, Walder made his blunt Minister reply: 'Look my dear chap, all ginger groups are useful at first, then they start to die. The first signs of death are when the members start getting into the House of Commons. Then the rest of the Group becomes pompous and opinionated and people start to join who regard the Group as useful as an avenue to the House.'[82]

It may well be that the success of the Group's members encouraged others to relax and more to join for the wrong reasons. Bosch wanted to turn this around. The Council's minutes record that 'As he saw it, the main task was to put across the ideas for which the Bow Group stands to new people and in a new way'; but, as he admits today:

> There was a further strand to the reasoning. The Bow Group had originally been dominated by a small number of people associated with the original founders and advancement through the committees and offices was mainly by invitation. As an Australian and one who had lived overseas I was not part of this inner group and I felt that as the Bow Group became larger it would be better to open up the executive positions to competition.[83]

Bosch saw the new role as a means not only of creating competition for the top offices within the Group, but of reinvigorating the Group at all its levels at the same time.

When the new position, initially described as Political Secretary, was first discussed in September 1963, the Council was split, its members dividing equally on the issue, although the Chairman, John MacGregor, cast his vote in favour. It was clear that to create a new, overtly political post in the Council would be to make an alternative career route to the chairmanship of the Group and break the existing continuum of Chairmen, which was exactly as the ambitious Bosch intended. It may also have been that MacGregor saw the move as a useful way of opening up the Group's political structure; he was a graduate of St Andrew's, at a time when the predominant background of the Group's previous chairmen was Oxford or Cambridge.[84] A further suggestion that the Group was being manoeuvred away from its strong Oxbridge connections came in the same meeting when the Council agreed to rename the Librarian the Research Secretary; the former title reflected a similar position in the Oxford Union's hierarchy.

The creation of a Political Officer responsible for projecting the Group's image was also controversial since it seemed to run counter to having 'no corporate view'. Sir Robin Williams belatedly asked whether the move would make the Group appear to be a pressure group to the outside world. But the attraction of a energetic job presenting the Group's work was undeniable. Given further time to consider the issue, the Council voted narrowly in favour of a Political Officer at the 'second reading' a month later. That three people stood for the post at the Annual General Meeting in March 1964 reflected the immediate recognition of the strategic importance of the job which had been created, both for the Group's future and as a path to running it, a goal which motivated many of its active members.

Perhaps because he had the clearest vision of a job which was still poorly defined, and probably because of his obvious energy, Bosch was elected to be the Group's first Political Officer in spring 1964. He moved rapidly to consolidate his position. In May he proposed that three large colloquia should be set up, each consisting of 30 young and old members. These Standing Committees would discuss social, economic, and defence and foreign policies. Bosch argued for the committees on the grounds that the Group needed to open its research up. But in reality the committees formed a permanent and more dynamic structure which bypassed the traditional research units whose spontaneous work the Research Secretary co-ordinated.

Though the Group's constitution remained unchanged, Bosch's move ended the precedence of the Research Secretary over the Political Officer in practice. In June, one month after proposing the Standing Committees, he secured a budget of £50 for his nascent empire to cover the cost of entertaining contacts and organising discussion meetings. He met considerable ill-will the following year when he stood for the chairmanship, though the political hierarchy of the Group quickly came to reflect the fact that the Political Officer had a more dynamic job which led almost inevitably to the chairmanship the following year. It was not until Norman Lamont's time that a Research Secretary moved to be Political Officer then Chairman. In the six years before 1964, when the post of Political Officer was created, five out of six incoming Chairmen, David Hennessy, Tom Hooson, David Howell, John MacGregor and Leon Brittan, had been the Research Secretary, or Librarian, during the preceding year. This reflected the Group's purpose as a research group; indeed, the only break in this trend for the officer in charge of the Group's research to go on to be Chairman had been John Biffen, who was elected MP for Oswestry during his year as Librarian.

The contrast after 1964 could hardly be clearer. Including Bosch, six out of the first seven Political Officers went straight to the chairmanship. They included Julian Critchley, Reg Watts, Christopher Bland, Michael Howard and Norman Lamont. Every year for the first four years after 1964, the post of Political Officer was contested. Given the nature of the political progression within the Council, at the election of the Political Officer each year Bow Group members were effectively being asked to vote for the Chairman for the year after. Tim Sainsbury recalls the suspense this generated when he stood for the post at the Annual General Meeting at the Royal Commonwealth Society in March 1967. About 110 Bow Groupers attended:

> The candidates were myself and Sir Christopher Bland. As old friends we were sitting next to each other awaiting the result of the count. It seemed to take a very long time in coming and the tellers had come on to the platform and held whispered conversation with the Chairman while we waited. Eventually Christopher said to me maybe it is a dead heat and that did prove to be the situation. The complication was that they could not decide whether the Chairman who had started the meeting should have the casting vote, he [Julian Critchley] having proposed myself, or the Chairman who had just been elected unopposed [Reginald Watts], who had proposed Christopher Bland. Eventually they decided in favour of the former and I became Political Officer. A year or two later the rules were changed.[85]

In fact Sainsbury did not stand for the chairmanship, and so did not make the transition from Political Officer to Chairman.

The intense, if friendly, competition to become Political Officer reflected the job's importance as a stepping stone to the chairmanship. The chairmanship was not contested until Sainsbury's decision not to stand in 1968 suddenly left the succession wide open. That year three out of the five main posts were contested: Christopher Brocklebank-Fowler was elected Chairman, beating the Research Secretary of the previous year, John Nelson-Jones. Looking back, Brocklebank-Fowler attributed his election to his cultivation of the female vote, a process which had begun when, as Secretary, he had encouraged more women to join the Group.[86] Norman Lamont, standing against Peter Lloyd among others, became Political Officer, and Michael Howard was elected Secretary.[87] The uncertainty following Sainsbury's decision marked an end to a period of uncontested elections for the chairmanship which had begun in 1964. This quiescence disguises the mounting significance attached to office-holding in the Group. Perhaps it is enough to say that whereas John Biffen's career in the Bow Group had ended with his election to the House of Commons, Julian Critchley's close involvement with the Bow Group began only when he lost his seat. The Group had become an increasingly serious political activity in itself.

Some members of the Council feared that research Standing Committees of the size which Bosch proposed would make them all too able to resolve policy. So the Council allowed Bosch to set up the groups, with the proviso that they were not allowed to develop policy. Yet it was inevitable that the Standing Committees would develop positions, if not policy, on contemporary events. They were 'a bit more glamorous' than the rather more worthy Research Committees, on which the Group's reputation continued to depend, says Leon Brittan. The Standing Committees' powers further complicated the tenet of 'no corporate view'. As the Council's rule about officers' earnings had indicated, it was difficult to separate the individual from the Group. Invitations for Group members to submit evidence to a number of Royal Commissions increased this blurring, since members invited in this way were invariably seen as representatives of the Group, no matter how much they stressed that the opinions they gave were their own. So, while in theory the Group remained committed to the 'no corporate view' policy – especially when it came under attack – its structure increasingly suggested a co-ordinated organisation which had the capability to make pronouncements and launch publications at short notice. Whether this ability detracted from the Group's intellectual rigour was, however, a moot point. *Crossbow* highlighted Bow Group members' own concerns:

> On the face of it, the Group has passed through the period following the dispersal of the 'Old Guard' and held off the creeping paralysis which so often tends to afflict organisations of this kind and origin.
>
> The impression nevertheless remains that things are not what they used to be. Neither bigness nor busyness provide any real measure of impact. Inevitably, comparisons are made between the sharp, intellectual focus of Bow Group ideas in the mid-fifties . . . and the uncertainties and conflicts of thought within the Group today.[88]

It is difficult to pin down the cause of this sense of unease, though it may have resulted from a recognition that the more overtly political character of the Group might conflict with its fundamental research purpose and ability to remain separate from the views expressed by its members. There are other possible factors. The style of political reporting was changing, due to the birth of independent television and a less deferential interviewing technique pioneered by Robin Day. Other commentators were quick to follow this lead, and the regularly acidic coverage which the Group received in the 1960s marked an important change from the more straightforward reporting of its work which had filled so many column inches in the 1950s. Consequently, perceptions of the Group began to change. In its earliest years the Group had been regarded as a political research society; as the Group's influence and its political role were seen to increase, it became subject to more incisive political reporting.

Another, atmospheric factor was the misfortune of the Conservative Party, which had a powerful effect on the Group's recruitment. The Group's membership had stabilised at about 900 members by the beginning of 1962, as the flow of new members dwindled to one or two per week. It began to dawn on the Bow Group that its role would change significantly were the Tories to lose the General Election. As early as the summer of 1963 the Group's Chairman, John MacGregor, had convened a high-powered 'Future Activities' committee, comprising himself, Tony Newton, Leon Brittan, David Howell and James Ackers, to look into the future of the Group.[89] What would happen to the Group, they asked, when 'minds at present employed in government will be available to the Party again' for thinking through new policies? The doubts whether the Tories would be returned to power for a fourth term must have strengthened when, on top of the Government's political crises, Macmillan suddenly fell ill in October 1963 and then consequently resigned. Against this backdrop, the Group continued to see an opportunity in the Party's general lack of direction.

In confirmation of an expanding role, in November 1963 the Group left its small office at 60 Berners Street for larger rooms at 240 High Holborn. Tying together this move and the work of the Future Activities Committee, *Crossbow* argued that subsequent to a defeat a political shake-up within the Party would 'almost certainly require a large injection of new blood. This means that the job of restoring intellectual respectability to Conservatism will rest heavily on bodies like the Bow Group.' 'It is vital', the editorial concluded, 'that the Group should be properly organised to meet the challenge.'[90]

When the Group's leaders envisaged a creative role in policy renewal if the Conservatives were removed from Government, they presumed that they would be in close contact with the future Conservative leader. Events were to prove this a considerable assumption. Having retired, diagnosed with a benign tumour in 1963, Harold Macmillan recommended Lord Home as his successor. The political engineering which accompanied Lord Home's consequent journey to the House of Commons was regarded with distaste: having renounced his earldom, for three weeks Home was Prime Minister but a member of neither House until he was parachuted into, and won, a coincidental by-election in Kinross and West Perthshire. One of the founder members of the Bow Group, William Rees-Mogg, argued in an article in the Times that the method used to select Home 'produced as a compromise, a man who had decisive support only from his predecessor against three candidates each of whom had stronger claims'. Of the three, Butler, Hailsham and Maudling, the Bow Group was most closely connected to Butler, who had been a frequent guest of honour at the Group's annual dinners, and whose political outlook probably most closely resembled that of many Bow Groupers.

Not only did Butler fail to snatch the opportunity to follow Macmillan, but the choice of Alec Douglas-Home prompted the immediate resignations of both Iain Macleod and Enoch Powell, both politicians with whom the Bow Group enjoyed a close relationship. Home was not known to be receptive to the Group's particular brand of progressive policies and the Group had made no attempt to change the situation by cultivating him while he had been Foreign Secretary. Only after Home had become Prime Minister did John MacGregor belatedly invite him to be guest of honour at the Group's annual dinner in the spring of 1964. Unsurprisingly, Home declined; it was Butler, something of a hardy perennial at the Bow Group's annual dinners, who came to the rescue. So by the beginning of winter 1963 it looked as if the Group had been left out in the political cold.

The Group was, nevertheless, able to influence the future procedure for electing a Party leader by contributing to the debate on how the process might be improved. Writing in *Crossbow*, the MP for Lancaster, Humphry Berkeley, described the existing arrangement – by which influential people were 'sounded out' and a leader thus selected was presented to the Parliamentary Party and the Executive Committee of the National Union – as similar 'to the enstoolment of an African tribal chief'.[91] With some understatement, Berkeley suggested that 'the traditional way of choosing a Conservative Leader could be improved upon', since it had 'the disadvantage of arbitrariness'. The rationale of the existing system had been to avoid a contest if the Party was in power, and Berkeley believed that 'it should be possible . . . to devise rules and procedures which could be equally applicable to a situation of power or one of opposition.' Berkeley believed that the Parliamentary Party should choose, since the Leader was always dependent on the votes of his colleagues; that the power of the National Union Executive Committee should be diluted; and that the procedure should be accomplished by secret ballot. Gamely, given that the article was spurred by the dissatisfaction surrounding his own appointment, Douglas-Home accepted Berkeley's suggestions, which were adopted in February 1965.[92]

Gloom pervaded the atmosphere within the Conservative Party for the twelve months following Home's appointment. Many Tories believed that defeat was likely because the Party had run out of steam, and the Bow Group was no exception. A poll in *Crossbow*, taken just before the Profumo scandal broke in June 1963, revealed almost equal proportions of approval and disapproval of Government policy among readers.[93] Tim Raison, a former *Crossbow* Editor, was commissioned to write *Why Conservative?*, Penguin's contribution to wider public understanding of the issues at stake at the coming General Election. Criticism of Raison's effort was revealing. *Why Conservative?* was described as good in principle; its drawback was that it bore no resemblance to the reality. The October 1964 edition of *Crossbow*, published in time for the General Election, made a half-hearted attempt to play up Douglas-Home's major weakness – his failure to impress on television. 'If then, this election is fought on issues rather than on personalities, it suits the Conservatives,' argued the editorial. But the Editor, by now Michael Wolff, went on to acknowledge – inside a rather unoriginal cover which took off the Beatles' *A Hard Day's Night* album design – that 'This is the age of being "with it".'[94]

'With it' was what many Conservatives, including Alec Douglas-Home, were profoundly not, and one gains an impression of the ambivalence of the Group's leading lights to the Prime Minister from reading the records of their meetings and *Crossbow* at this time. In consequence it was unsurprising that the Group came under suspicion of fomenting resentment against Home. The proceedings of a Group meeting early in 1964, at which Macleod spoke, caused controversy when it appeared that Macleod had suggested that electoral defeat was inevitable with Home at the helm. John MacGregor was forced to write to the *Daily Telegraph* to rebut the claim. He reported that Macleod had said that he was confident that Conservative Governments would forge

the shape of society in the 1970s and 1980s, even if there were brief
periods of opposition. Commentators drew a different conclusion from
the episode. 'It is surely symptomatic of the Tories' present edginess that
a light-hearted remark about the possibility of losing an election some
time in the 1970s or 1980s should be seen as yet another stab in the
back.'[95] From the relative certainty of its activities whilst the
Conservatives were in power, its members' occasional meetings with
ministers, the Bow Group suddenly faced the uncertainties of opposition,
something which it had never collectively experienced before.

NOTES

[1]   *Time and Tide*, January 1961.

[2]   *Sunday Mail*, 12 February 1961.

[3]   Bow Group Council, Minutes, 18 April 1961.

[4]   *Crossbow*, October–December 1963, p. 13.

[5]   CPA, CCO 6/3/38, Hooson to Low, 24 July 1961.

[6]   M. Jean Berger, *Journal du Parlement*, 26 July 1960. Quoted in *Crossbow*, Autumn
      1960.

[7]   Julian Critchley was MP for Rochester and Chatham 1959–64; for Aldershot and N.
      Hants 1970–74; for Aldershot, 1974–97. He died in 2000.

[8]   *Observer*, 11 October 1959.

[9]   *Daily Telegraph*, 7 March 1960.

[10] 'Tories to Use Young Ideas', *Sunday Times*, 6 March 1960.

[11] Conservative Party Archive CRD/ACP (59), quoted in A. Seldon and S. Ball, eds, *The
      Conservative Century*, Oxford 1994, p. 348.

[12] *The Times*, 11 October 1960.

[13] James Lemkin, interview.

[14] Philip Murphy, *Party Politics and Decolonization: The Conservative Party and British
      Colonial Policy in Tropical Africa 1951–1964*, Oxford 1995, p. 213.

[15] Murphy, *Party Politics and Decolonization*, p. 214.

[16] Bow Group Termcard, Summer 1957.

[17] CRD 2/53/28, 24 February 1958, quoted in Murphy, *Party Politics and
      Decolonization*, p. 164.

18   PREM 11/2248 Macleod–Macmillan 3 April 1958, quoted in Murphy, *Party Politics and Decolonization*, p. 164.

19   Robert Shepherd, *Iain Macleod*, London 1994, p. 156.

20   C. Braganza, 'Catharsis for Kenya', *Crossbow*, Summer 1959, p. 33–7.

21   Richard Lamb, *The Macmillan Years, 1957–1963*, London 1995, pp. 231–42.

22   James Lemkin, interview.

23   Bow Group Council, Minutes, 18 April 1959.

24   Murphy, *Party Politics and Decolonization*, p. 178.

25   Shepherd, *Iain Macleod*, p. 156.

26   Ian C. Jarvie, 'One Man, One Vote', *Crossbow*, New Year 1960.

27   PREM 11/2586, PM (60) 3, 5 January 1960, quoted in Murphy, *Party Politics and Decolonization*, p. 217.

28   Lamb, *The Macmillan Years*.

29   Sir Toby Low (later Lord Aldington) was MP for Blackpool North 1945–62. He was Minister of State at the Board of Trade 1954–57, Deputy Chairman of the Conservative Party, 1959–63. In the latter years of his life he was best known for pursuing and winning a libel action against Count Nikolai Tolstoy about his war record. He died in 2000.

30   Bow Group, Minutes of the 9th Annual General Meeting, 1 March 1960, 4.1.

31   Hugo Young, *This Blessed Plot*, London 1998, p. 153.

32   *Frankfurter Allgemeine Zeitung*, 29 April 1960.

33   Patrick Jenkin, 'Integration or Isolation?', *Crossbow*, Spring 1960, p. 14.

34   Nicholas Timmins, *The Five Giants: A Biography of the Welfare State*, London 1995, pp. 254–55.

35   *The Times*, 20 March 1961.

36   *The Times*, 13 June 1961.

37   Peter Lloyd, Memorandum, 'Research 1970/1', 6 July 1970. Lloyd was elected MP for Fareham in 1979. He was a Minister of State, Home Office 1992–94.

38   Julian Critchley, *A Bag of Boiled Sweets*, London 1994, p. 72.

39   *Daily Mail*, 5 January 1961, p. 2.

40   Tom Hooson, Memorandum, 'Mr Harold Watkinson and the Defence Pamphlet', 27 January 1961. Bow Group Confidential File.

41   CPA, CCO 6/3/38, Hooson to Low, 27 January 1961.

42   *Hansard*, 25 November 1957, quoted in Murphy, *Party Politics and Decolonization*, p. 215.

43   *Hansard*, 27 February 1961.

44 'Labour uses Bow Group Ammunition', *Guardian*, 28 February 1961; Denis Healey, *The Time of My Life*, London 1989, pp. 234–48. Healey had written on the nuclear issue for the Fabian Society in 1960.

45 *Hansard*, 27 February 1961.

46 CPA, CCO 3/6/38, Low to Watkinson, 10 January 1961.

47 CPA, CCO 3/6/38, Goldman to Low, 6 February 1961.

48 Kenneth Alsopp, *Harper's Bazaar*, May 1961.

49 *The Times*, 12 April 1960.

50 Quoted by 'Pendennis', *Observer*, 30 October 1960.

51 *Observer*, 16 October 1960.

52 Ronald Chidwick, letter to *The Times*, 14 January 1962.

53 CPA, CCO 6/3/38 COO, to Slinn, 25 April 1962.

54 David Walder, 'What Young Conservatives Are Really Like', *Crossbow*, October–December 1967.

55 Julian Critchley, 'How the Bow Group Lost its Tinge of Pink and Became True Blue', *The Times*, 17 March 1976.

56 *Punch*, 16 November 1960.

57 'Bow Notebook', *Crossbow*, Spring 1961, p. 49.

58 *Reform of the Licensing Laws*, Bow Group, September 1960.

59 *Glasgow Herald*, 13 September 1961. The Labour Youth Campaign's members included Donald Dewar and John Smith. Tom Hooson, contesting Caernarvon in 1961, was forced to deny that the Bow Group was either angry, or splitting the Conservative Party. *Daily Telegraph*, 7 March 1960.

60 *Guardian*, 7 February 1961.

61 *Evening Standard*, 9 January 1960.

62 *Daily Telegraph*, 18 February 1960.

63 Charles Longbottom was MP for York, 1959–66.

64 *Daily Telegraph*, 29 January 1962.

65 John Biffen was elected MP for Oswestry, November 1961–83; Shropshire North 1983–97. Chief Secretary to the Treasury 1979–81, Secretary of State for Trade 1981–82, Leader of the House of Commons 1982–87.

66 *Crossbow*, New Year 1962, p. 53.

67 *Yorkshire Post*, 26 January 1962.

68 CPA, CCO 3/6/16, Monday Club. Quoted in John Ramsden, *The Winds of Change: Macmillan to Heath 1957–1975*, London 1996 p. 148.

69 Bow Group Council, Minutes, 6 April 1963.

70 Bow Group Council, Minutes, 28 February 1962.

71 George Gardiner, 'The Challenges of the Time', *Crossbow*, Autumn 1986, p. 24. Gardiner was MP for Reigate, February 1974–97.

72 Colin Baillieu unsuccessfully contested Rossendale in 1964 and 1966.

73 Anthony Howard, 'Bow Group – A Tory Fig Leaf?', *New Statesman*, 2 March 1962.

74 Londoner's Diary, *Evening Standard*, 6 March 1962.

75 Howell, interview.

76 Hobbs to Hooson, 1 February 1961.

77 The Rt Hon. Sir Leon Brittan, interview, 14 January 2000.

78 Bow Group Council, Minutes, 12 May 1964. Tony Newton spent almost ten years in the Conservative Research Department 1965–74. MP for Braintree, February 1974–1997. Secretary of State for Social Security 1989–92; Leader of the House of Commons 1992–97.

79 Fred Tuckman, note in the Bow Group Confidential File, not dated, but c.1961.

80 Bow Group Council, Minutes, 23rd July 1963.

81 Henry Bosch, email to the author, 18 November 2000. Henry Bosch was educated at Sydney and Oxford Universities and at the Centre d'Etudes Industrielles in Geneva. After serving as Bow Group Chairman, he returned to Australia. He was Chairman of the National Companies and Securities Commission and was made an Officer of the Order of Australia in 1991.

82 David Walder, *The Short List*, London 1964, p. 10. Walder was MP for High Peak, 1961–66; for Clitheroe from 1970 until his death in 1978.

83 Bosch, email.

84 John MacGregor was elected MP for South Norfolk in February 1974. Chief Secretary to the Treasury 1985–87; Minister of Agriculture, Fisheries and Food, 1987–89; Secretary of State for Education and Science 1989–90, Leader of the House of Commons 1992–94; Secretary of State for Transport 1992–94.

85 The Rt Hon. Sir Timothy Sainsbury, letter to the author, 23rd April 1999. Tim Sainsbury was MP for Hove, November 1973–97. Minister of State at the DTI, 1990–94. Christopher Bland was Chairman of LWT 1984–94. Since 1996 he has been Chairman of the Board of Governors of the BBC.

86 'Crosstalk', *Crossbow*, Summer 1980. Christopher Brocklebank–Fowler was MP for King's Lynn, 1970–74; for Norfolk North West, 1974–83. He crossed the floor to join the SDP in 1981, and joined the Labour Party in 1996.

87 Norman Lamont was President of the Cambridge Union. He was MP for Kingston-upon-Thames May 1972–97. After a period as Minister for Defence Procurement 1985–86, then at the Treasury, he was Financial Secretary, 1986–89; Chief Secretary 1989–90, Chancellor of the Exchequer 1990–93. Michael Howard

has been MP for Folkestone and Hythe since 1983. He was Secretary of State for Employment, 1990–92; for the Environment 1992–93, for the Home Department 1993–97.

88 *Crossbow*, October–December 1963, p. 10.

89 Leon Brittan was a President of the Cambridge Union. He was MP for Cleveland and Whitby, February 1974–1983; for Richmond, Yorkshire, 1983–88. He was a member of the European Commission, 1989–99 and its Vice-President 1989–93, and 1995–99. James Ackers was chairman of FUCUA in 1958. A businessman who also served on the Monopolies and Mergers Commission and the NEDC, he was knighted in 1987.

90 Bow Notebook, *Crossbow*, October–December 1963, p. 10.

91 Humphry Berkeley, 'Choosing a Leader', *Crossbow*, October–December 1963, pp. 29–31.

92 Robert Blake, *The Conservative Party from Peel to Major*, p. 297.

93 Michael White, '*Crossbow* Readers', *Crossbow*, July–September 1963, p. 18.

94 'A Hard Day's Vote', *Crossbow*, October–December 1964, p. 5. Michael Wolff was concurrently leading research for the official biography of Winston Churchill. He was Director General, Conservative Party Organisation 1974–75. He died in 1976.

95 'London Letter', *Guardian*, 6 February 1964.

Four

'ON THE MAKE': 1964–70

On 15 October 1964, Harold Wilson won the General Election by a slim majority of four seats. This narrow margin meant that there was no let-up in the political pressure, since another election seemed likely soon. As the Tories moved from Government to Opposition for the first time in the Bow Group's collective memory, the Group's Chairman was Leon Brittan. Though only 24 years old, he had already been a member for several years, travelling down from Cambridge to attend Group meetings. One anonymous contemporary vividly recalled this precocious undergraduate 'amazing graduate members with his self-confidence from the floor as he held forth, thumbs tucked under his jacket lapels'.[1] Another member of the Group, Graham Norton, told Peter Lloyd that he 'never knew what a muscular intellect was until he got into an argument with Leon Brittan one day'.[2] Among those who were impressed by Brittan's drive was John MacGregor, who suggested that Brittan should stand as the Group's Librarian in spring 1963. He was elected unopposed, then became Chairman a year later, again to no ostensible opposition. His own opinion of what the Group should do at this juncture mirrored Iain Macleod's. At the Bow Group's first post-election Council meeting, four days after the Tories' defeat, Brittan announced his strategy. He thought that the Group should concentrate more fully on being a research society; it should set up 'fundamental study groups' that should report inside one year. Further, putting into practice the beliefs of the Future Activities Committee of which he had been a member, Brittan proposed that *Crossbow* should become 'a vehicle for top politicians to put forward ideas'.[3] The theme of the following issue was 'Election 64'. The prospect that Wilson would

call a second general election to try to reinforce his majority was the catalyst for activity at this pitch.

There were signs that the Bow Group expected a longer spell in Opposition. In the same issue of *Crossbow* Iain Macleod wrote an article, 'In Opposition', in which he joined the debate on tactics:

> There is first the 'give them enough rope school'. I am not a member of this company. The fallacy lies in the assumption that you can whenever you wish tighten the rope. This is not so. If in politics you concede the initiative as for example Attlee did in 1951 it may well take you many long weary years to regain it. Nor do I believe in the theory of all out attack on all fronts. Harrying the Government would strengthen it. I believe in guerrilla raids, in concentrated assaults on weak ministers, in occasional carefully planned set piece attacks on the Labour Party in general and the Prime Minister in particular . . . together with this I believe in calling on all the cells of our Party, inside and outside Westminster, to hard, concentrated work on policy. So much to do. So little time. 4

Here was a hint of the unhappiness with Douglas-Home. The request to Macleod to contribute was significant since he had refused to take a job in Douglas-Home's Cabinet in October 1963. *Crossbow*'s editorial team hoped that Douglas-Home would step down after a second election later in the year, if the Tories lost again. In the same issue *Crossbow*'s Editor, Michael Wolff, suggested that 'It will indeed be Sir Alec's duty to lead the Party for a long time if no alternative emerges.' The implication of his editorial was that the longer the duration of Douglas-Home's leadership, the greater the length of time the Party would spend in Opposition.5 But with another election likely, such criticism remained veiled.

This changed in June 1965 when Wilson made it clear that he had no plans to call a second election immediately to fortify his majority. *Crossbow*'s opposition to the Conservatives' leader became overt. 'Are we Losing our Way?', a leader in the July 1965 *Crossbow*, edited by Wolff, complained that 'the entire Party still remains burdened, however unfairly, with the grouse moor image . . . There must be sympathy for those who are reluctant to entrust new policies to a spokesman who can neither inspire nor carry conviction.' The image of the grouse moor caught the eye of several cartoonists and the phrase seemed to summarise the concern that a 14th earl would not be the man who would lead the Conservatives back to office. On 23 July, Douglas-Home resigned.

Edward Heath's election as Conservative Party leader was, in contrast to his predecessor's, initially very encouraging for the Group. As his chief of staff, Heath employed the 28-year-old John MacGregor, who had completed his term as Chairman of the Bow Group a year earlier. At the same time, Heath drafted in David Howell, another former Chairman, to help with rethinking policy. Howell was appointed director of the Conservative Political Centre. Only two years earlier both MacGregor and Howell had been busy considering the Bow Group's future together; by late 1965 they were discussing the future policy of the Conservative Party as a whole. Here – finally – was the meteoric rise to personal influence of which the early Bow Groupers had dreamed. Howell remembers a well-publicised trip to Scotland which he made with Heath to discuss the future with Alec Douglas-Home. The front page of the *Sunday Times* carried a photograph of Heath and Home, with Howell – in his own words – 'like some ghastly youth, popping up in between'.[6] Just as Macmillan had successfully done before him, Heath was trying to promote the image that he was involving energetic young thinkers in the process which led up to the writing of the 1966 Manifesto. *Putting Britain Right Ahead*, the first instalment of this process, was published in time for the 1965 Party Conference. *Putting Britain Right Ahead*'s stress on the importance of incentive, competition and the consumer, through joining 'Europe', was widely supported. But Susanne Puddefoot, a fashion journalist and Bow Group member, attacked its title in *Crossbow* as 'no more than an artless assembly of the necessary nuts and bolts'.[7] She was partly right. 'Ahead' had been added to the title of the document only at the last minute, when it was realised that 'Putting Britain Right' might beg the question: who had put Britain wrong?

Anthony King believed that *Putting Britain Right Ahead* was covered in the Bow Group's fingerprints. The almost total correlation between those who had contributed to the Bow Group's latest book of essays, *The Conservative Opportunity* and those involved in *Putting Britain Right*

Ahead led King to believe that the Bow Group's alumni had found a place at the heart of Opposition policy-making. He argued that 'This role [of a Tory intelligentsia] was played during the 1950s by the Bow Group, but of course Conservatives outside government could achieve little as long as their party remained in power, and while it retained its sense of direction. Their opportunity has come during the last two years.'[8] Anthony Howard made a similar connection in a critical article entitled 'Tough Bowmen', in which he asserted that the tone of the policies being proposed was 'tough to the point of being ruthless'.[9] The influence which the Group once again seemed to be wielding reactivated opposition among other Tories. One article in the *Spectator* in early 1966 suggested that Edward Heath was being led astray by the Bow Group's concentration on reducing the burden of the welfare state.[10] The secrecy surrounding Howell's policy shake-up encouraged the rumours, but the strong emphasis on economics in both *Putting Britain Right Ahead* and *The Conservative Opportunity* reinforced the impression that members of the Group carried much influence with Edward Heath and stimulated greater press interest in *The Conservative Opportunity*. Critical acclaim was not matched by commercial success however, a fact brought home to Peter Lloyd when he discovered copies of the book remaindered on the Charing Cross Road.[11]

Like Anthony King, Leon Brittan believed that the Bow Group and its calendar could benefit from the extra time top politicians would have on their hands, out of Government. This was not a universal interpretation. Though his judgement may be influenced by the fact that he became Chairman as the Conservatives regained power in 1970, Michael Howard – who joined the Bow Group Council in 1965 fresh from Cambridge – believes with hindsight that the Group was less influential when the Conservatives were in Opposition.[12] Certainly the Conservative Research Department had more time to consider possible new policies in Opposition. That left the part-time Bow Group jockeying with the permanent CRD for an influence on the Shadow Cabinet's policy-making during the years out of office. The potential for tension between these two organisations had increased before the General Election, when the Group's great friend R. A. Butler was encouraged to relinquish the chairmanship of the CRD. Butler had always valued the Group for its integral but independent work on a range of topical issues and brought Bow Group experts onto Party policy committees. No one replaced Butler in this post, and the lack of co-ordination between the Group and the CRD manifested itself in several moments of friction over industrial policy during the later 1960s. Opposition also meant a subtle shift in the type of ideas which were needed. With the Tories in Government, Ministers required ways and means to achieve objectives; in Opposition, Shadow Ministers sought broader ideas about the future direction that the Party should take. Leon Brittan recalls the difficult period between 1964 and 1966 when, due to the impending second General Election, thinking was divided between concrete policies for use in an election campaign, and more abstract thinking should the election be lost.[13] By this time the CRD was freer to perform the role of think-tank, and this competition, plus the success of the Group's former members, seems to have changed the Bow Group's priorities.

'I cannot claim that my year in office was especially distinguished,' admitted Julian Critchley about his chairmanship of the Group, which began in 1966. At the 1964 election he found himself, like many other unexpected new Conservative MPs of 1959, unceremoniously ejected from Parliament. His involvement with the Group seems to have catalysed a change of emphasis away from intellectual influence on policy and towards involvement in politics. At 35, just young enough to stand for office in the Bow Group, and seeing it as a springboard to his return to Parliament, Critchley immersed himself in the Group, becoming its Political Officer at the first opportunity after he had lost his seat. Like his predecessor Henry Bosch, he used the job of Political Officer as the staging post to the chairmanship the following year. Also with his eyes on the chairmanship was Hugh Dykes.[14] The decisive factor in the leadership contest which followed, believed Critchley, was his former job: 'The reputation I had gained as a maverick backbencher enabled me to stand for and win the chairmanship of the Bow Group in the spring of 1966'; Peter Lloyd adds that he was also good at jokes.[15] Back in the Group, Critchley resembled a carp in a goldfish bowl and Dykes, especially, was put out by his decision to return. Critchley's influence was an important stimulus for the parliamentary aspirations of others and his own political views set the tone for the Group until the beginning of the 1970s. In a typically light-hearted retrospective written in 1980, Critchley recalled the era for *Crossbow*. It is worth quoting at length for its portrayal of the Group:

> When I joined the Bow Group in the late 50 the pattern was already set. The group was for blue-stockings of both sexes. We met frequently in tiny rooms where we were hectored by Peter Goldman, travelled yearly to either Oxford or Cambridge where we listened to Cuth Alport, and in the summer took taxis to Hurlingham where to the contempt of the resident hearties, we danced decorously with other people's wives to the accompaniment of chicken. In the interval between fowl and flesh we were exhorted by R. A Butler at his most 'Rabish'.
>
> We were all on the make. We wanted desperately to get on in politics, and, in consequence, the chief topic of conversation was candidate selection. We would bump into each other in the dingy offices of North and East London Conservative Associations perched on the hardest of chairs waiting nervously for the summons to sing and dance.
>
> . . . My period of office passed uneventfully (we did not hold a dance as I decided that it was not our scene) and I was succeeded by Christopher Brocklebank-Fowler whom the years have turned into a pillar of the 1922 committee. It seems that the Bow Group has always preferred 'low' to 'high' politics, defence and foreign affairs being neglected for the dismal science . . . The Bow Group has been a ladder up which the cleverer Tories can climb, and it takes its intellectual tone from the prevailing orthodoxy.[16]

Credible though this sounds, it does not accurately reflect the dynamics of the Group before Critchley immersed himself in it from late 1964. True, early Bow Group members were ambitious; but it would be anachronistic to suggest that they saw the Bow Group in its early days as their *ladder* rather than as a simple vehicle for publicity: it was far too precarious and had no political hierarchy up which to climb. The rungs of a 'ladder' developed only as the Group established itself as a permanent fixture in the eyes of Conservative MPs and commentators alike, and as an internal political hierarchy developed. Nor had the Group's tone always been consonant with the Party line, as the furore surrounding Critchley's own involvement in the decidedly heterodox *Stability and Survival* and *The New Africa* had showed. Neither suggests that Critchley was right to say that the Group had neglected 'high' politics in favour of the dismal science of economics. Rather, it was the range, and heretical yet influential quality, of the Group's work which had caused aggravation and recognition in equal measure. Both led to the Group's image of influence. That is not to say that Critchley's view was not valid, but it did not predate his involvement in the Group. Rather, his opinion seems to be an insight into why he rejoined the Group in 1964. He was making the best use of an organisation which he and others had built from research. Its consequent gradual increase in influence meant that by 1966 it was a credible means of returning to full-time politics. Simon Jenkins, who became a member of the Group in the later 1960s, concurs: by the mid-1960s, in his opinion, the Group had acquired 'a centrality in the career structure of the Party'.[17] Critchley's recollections were an admission that it was his own political advancement rather than the nurturing of new ideas which attracted him to the Bow Group.

Crossbow is the most sensitive weathervane of this change of priorities from political research to political careerism, since its content reflected the interests of both its editorial board and its readership. Although selection was a constant topic of conversation for Bow Groupers drinking in the Sherlock Holmes pub off Northumberland Avenue after meetings across the road at the Constitutional Club, and the Party Vice-Chairman in charge of candidates was a perennial and favourite speaker, the interest never crossed into print. Peter Riddell observed how this changed around 1968. He has recently written, with some exaggeration, that 'Copies of *Crossbow* . . . read during the late 1960s like a manual on how to become a parliamentary candidate.'[18] Before, the subject of members' success in constituency selection contests had merited coverage only in *Crossbow*'s diary column. This column had seen several identities and was called 'Ladbroke' by the late 1960s. This in itself was a reference to the political aspirations of the then Editor, Leon Brittan, which were focused on Ladbroke Grove in West London.

Until 1968 there was not a mention in *Crossbow* of which seat to try to fight, nor how best to be selected to fight it. Both these subjects have been dealt with repetitively in *Crossbow*s since. It all began with one rather macabre article, written as the constituency selection process rolled into action once again in 1968, by the anonymous 'Psephologue'. The author was more than likely one of the members of *Crossbow*'s Editorial Board, which that year comprised a star-studded cast of seat-hunters: Leon Brittan, Jonathan Aitken, Christopher Bland, Julian Critchley, Norman Fowler and Norman Lamont.[19] Psephologue listed the 49 Tory MPs aged over 60 in January 1968 and noted that 'Already five of those listed . . . have indicated that they will not seek re-election. Undoubtedly, more will follow. Sadly, illness and death will claim their victims.' In 1970 Julian Critchley was to benefit from the retirement of Sir Eric Errington, the septuagenarian MP for Aldershot, who was seventh on Psephologue's list.

Psephologue returned in the following Parliament with an update. '23 of the original 49 have now either been promoted to the House of Lords, retired or died.' Top of the list in 1971 was Dame Irene Ward, the MP for Tynemouth first elected in 1931. 'Out of respect we have refrained from printing this redoubtable parliamentarian's age; it will be a bold man who mentions retirement in her presence.' The following year Norman Lamont, the Group's Chairman at the time, was to benefit from the selection following the death of John Boyd Carpenter, MP for Kingston-upon-Thames, who had been 29th on Psephologue's list.[20] Coincidentally, his opponent in the subsequent by-election was Tony Judge, the Editor of the *Police Federation Journal*, who had spoken at the Bow Group's Conference on crime and punishment earlier in the year. And, in addition to seats vacated by retiring Conservative MPs, there was a host of marginal constituencies which might turn Conservative given an overall swing in the Tories' favour.

Describing the ongoing selection process added further dramatic scope to the genre. *Crossbow* readers in January 1969 were treated to an eye witness account by Elspeth Howe of her role as the candidate's wife in the extraordinary Reigate selection meeting, in which she and other wives were obliged to make a four-minute speech. David Walder followed up *The Short List*, his novel on a fictional selection contest which had featured the 'Stepney Group', with a satirical article in *Crossbow* developing an imaginary political assault course for budding parliamentary candidates. In another anonymous article, 'You Too Can Enter Parliament', printed in late 1969, readers were provided with a parody of a selection speech, 'guaranteed to secure adoption' because it successfully appeared to be all things to all men. On the following page, Michael Pinto-Duschinsky surveyed the Bow Group's candidates for the General Election, estimating who would be elected depending on the extent of the swing to the Conservatives. With the Tories up to 20 points ahead of Labour in the opinion polls, this was a highly appetising look ahead to the political comeback of the following year. Most revealing about the list of candidates were their backgrounds and education: almost all had been to Oxford or Cambridge; but whereas Oxford graduates dominated the Parliamentary Party, true to the Group's origins, Cambridge-educated Bow Group candidates significantly exceeded those from Oxford, by 28 to 16.

Twenty years later, the genre remained as compelling: in summer 1988 Stuart Jackson, a market researcher, methodically assessed the best strategy for each stage of the selection procedure in 'That Safe Seat'. The article was subtitled 'For at least a quarter of Bow Groupers, this will be the only article they ever remember'.[21] While it would be wrong to over-emphasise the importance of articles on the selection process, they do stand out from *Crossbow*'s other content. As an example, Psephologue's 'What Vacancies at Westminster?' came in an issue – that of January–March 1968 – when the alternative reading included an assessment of Charles Morrison MP and a perceptive, but less than gripping, article on 'The New Quasi-governmental Institutions' by Christopher Tugendhat.[22] The question is, whether this new interest in practical politics came at the expense of the more profound research, from which the Group had gained its reputation. It seems that it may have.

Concerns about the direction in which the Group was heading had emerged before Critchley succeeded Henry Bosch as Chairman. But

Critchley did not intervene, as Brittan had in 1964, to re-emphasise the Group's reliance on quality research. Some years earlier James Lemkin had described 'political influence' as 'the be-all and end-all' of the Group. By the second half of the 1960s, judging by *Crossbow* and the activities of the Group's members, the driving force behind the Group was a more disparate search for political self-advancement. In *Crossbow* one member, Garth Nicholas, concluded a critique of the Bow Group's research groups, which he branded as either 'vague', 'trivial' or 'politically irrelevant', with a pithy reminder: 'There is no reason why the Bow Group should not develop into a pleasant social club with political overtones or into a convenient rung on the political ladder – if that is what members want. Personally, I would hope that the Bow Group will once again devote itself to serious political research, which, after all, is how it gained its reputation.'[23] The implication is that networking had distracted the Group.

It also seems as if the Group may have lost some of its political breadth, for which there were two possible reasons: the 'Left of Right' outlook of key members of several consecutive Bow Group Councils, and the continued advance of the right-wing Monday Club. Julian Critchley made a dry allusion to the former factor when, on retiring from the chairmanship, he gave each member of his Council a copy of *Quotations from Mao Tse Tung*.[24] Earlier in the year he had attracted the anger of Lord Grimston, the Carlton Club's Chairman, by inviting the Liberal leader Jo Grimond to dine at the Club before he spoke to the Group, an act to which other members of the Carlton had predictably objected.[25] 'The Bow Group wants to demolish our defences East of Suez. As do the Liberals. And now the Bow Group entertains the Liberal leader Mr Jo Grimond to dinner. Isn't it time the Bow Group went all the way and joined the Liberals?' fulminated the *Daily Express*' leader-writer.[26] Critchley was summoned to a meeting with Grimston, which he missed because his bus was late.[27] Critchley's successors were similar. Christopher Brocklebank-Fowler, who had been the Group's Secretary when Critchley was its Chairman, and was himself Chairman of the Group two years later, is well known for having dramatically crossed the floor of the House to join the SDP after Howe's 1981 Budget. And

Christopher Bland, the Political Officer in Brocklebank-Fowler's year, who was elected Chairman in 1969, had represented Oxford University at fencing as an undergraduate, a fact which became the hook for a witty diary piece on his views in *Crossbow* the following year: 'And his [Bland's] politics? "At Oxford, he was a half-blue," one of his friends reports, "and I think he probably still is."'

The impression that the Group stood at the left-hand end of the Conservative spectrum was willingly reinforced by critics, whom *Crossbow* continued to antagonise. In October 1967 *Crossbow*'s designers George Perry and David Hillman decided to enliven the Party Conference issue with a cover photograph of an anonymous girl in her bra and knickers under an unbuttoned man's shirt, sitting beside an empty wine glass, to illustrate the headline question 'What are Young Conservatives really like?' 'I don't think any of us were prepared for the amount of publicity generated by that *Crossbow* cover,' says the model, who was Gilvrie Misstear, assistant art editor on the *Sunday Times Magazine*, where Hillman and Perry both worked. When *Crossbow* came out, speculation over her identity erupted as the press yearned for her to have some scandalous connection with a politician. The photographer, Rayment Kirby, remembers journalists gathering outside his studio. They discovered that he did freelance work for the *Sunday Times* and guessed a connection. 'I could not go into the *Sunday Times* office for about a week' as the press had 'staked out the building', remembers Gilvrie Lock today. *Crossbow*'s editor, Leon Brittan 'was somewhat bemused but behaved magnificently, standing firm in spite of all the outrage. Even he didn't know it was Gilvrie, so he could not in any case reveal her identity', remembers Perry.[28] *Crossbow*'s cover was reprinted in just about every national newspaper, as well as many local ones, taken off or alluded to in a host of cartoons and earned a mention on the weekly television round-up of the press, *What the Papers Say*.

But the implication that a female Young Conservative was anyone's after a drink rankled with some. 'I deplore the picture of a scantily-clad girl on the cover of *Crossbow*', wrote IC Bellamy from Southampton to the *Daily Sketch*, 'I have been a Conservative for some years, but not any more if this picture represents the young Conservatives of today'.[29] Sir

Cyril Osborne MP called the photograph 'a libel on the Young Conservatives'. The *Daily Mail*'s cartoonist juxtaposed the picture asking 'What are the Young Conservatives really like?' beside a poster of Osborne, with the caption 'A lot more attractive than some of the old ones'. Central Office said it had no complaint and, at Perry's suggestion, Edward Heath sent a box of chocolates to Gilvrie Misstear for her to pose with in a recreation of the shot for the *Sunday Times Magazine*'s round-up of the year.

The long-term damage was done not by the picture, but the accompanying article which described the Young Conservatives, in much less glamorous terms, as 'the political infantry', rather than future stars in the political firmament.[30]

The publicity the Group gained at the Young Conservatives' expense may explain why one internal examination of the Bow Group's image which was completed in April 1971 noted that relations with the Conservative Party as a whole had deteriorated since the Group was often 'thought of simply as a left-wing pressure group'. To some extent the personalised nature of recruitment campaigns may have helped to strengthen this image, since it was usual for the Bow Group to begin a drive for members with each Council Member being asked to find a handful of new members from among their friends and acquaintances. Richard Crossman, the Secretary of State for the Social Services and the first Labour Minister to address the Group, suggested that the line between the Labour Government and the Bow Group was indeed a fine one. His account is a unique speaker's-eye view of a Bow Group meeting:

> This evening I found myself at the Bow Group, the Fabian Society of the Conservatives, to talk to them about the NHS . . . They asked me to dine at the Cavalry Club, magnificent place in Piccadilly, where I found standing at the bar elegant young men who then took me upstairs for an excellent dinner. Out after that to the Royal Commonwealth Association, where I found they had gathered about 160 intelligent, prosperous, upper-class men and women. I gave them a racy account of what we are doing and enormously enjoyed myself. I explained why we couldn't put the Health Service under local government . . . I was fairly confident

because no journalists were there, and as Bow Group meetings are
off the record nothing can be printed. But in a way I felt uneasy at
the fact that I didn't feel wholly out of place in that company,
having that kind of discussion.[31]

Crossman's slight discomfort is corroborated by someone who has a
chance political symmetry: Peter Lilley, a future Secretary of State for
Social Security. He recalls that when he became Chairman of the Bow
Group in 1973, the atmosphere inside the Group was such that he had no
idea that his immediate predecessors, Michael Howard, Norman Lamont
and Peter Lloyd, shared similar views on the economy to himself.[32] The
reason for this was that economics was not a key interest of many Bow
Group members at the time. Peter Lloyd had little interest in the subject
until the failure of Heath's prices and incomes policy began to erode the
preceding economic policy consensus.

The other factor, the growth of the Monday Club, encouraged
commentators to view the Bow Group in factional terms. Whether the
Group liked it or not, the existence of the Monday Club increasingly
turned the Bow Group into a gravitational point for those who disliked
the Club's views. Once, the Bow Group's outstanding characteristic had
been its fusion of youth and intellect. As one commentator pithily asked:
'How did one describe a bright young Tory before you could call him a
Bow Grouper?'[33] Youth was no longer the distinguishing factor it had
been for the Group in the 1950s. The average age of members had slowly
crept up over the years, and many of the active participants from the
1950s remained closely involved in the Group's work late into the 1960s.
This had its associated kudos. In 1966, for example, the Bow Group's
three Standing Committees for research into economic, foreign and social
affairs were chaired respectively by John Biffen, MP for Oswestry, David
Howell, the new MP for Guildford, and Geoffrey Howe, whose brief
career as MP for Bebington which began in 1964 had been rudely termi-
nated at the March 1966 General Election.[34] Like Critchley, Howe saw the
Group as a way of maintaining his political profile while out of
Parliament. Although the purpose of appointing the three MPs to run the
Standing Committees had been to raise the Group's profile, it perhaps

also reflected a paucity of talent within the Group's younger ranks or simply discouraged new members. And the Monday Club had become a viable alternative for those who did not approve of progressive political thinking.

Following the divide on decolonisation, immigration formed the basis for contention in the later 1960s. Unlike the Monday Club, which believed that race relations laws simply embedded positive discrimination in society, the Bow Group supported the principle of the laws. Following the Race Relations Act of 1965, in *Commonwealth Immigration* Christopher Bland, Christopher Brocklebank-Fowler and Tim Farmer attacked both the Labour Government and Conservative Opposition for an overly inflexible attitude to race relations which failed to achieve closer integration. Rather than setting annual quotas of immigrants, the three authors argued, the Government should actively manage the placement of immigrants in the community by buying up houses to engineer an acceptable balance of immigrants. This suggestion was controversial and it was attacked in an article syndicated to several newspapers, which accused the Group of 'leaning too far in the other direction, of creating – paradoxical though it may sound – an impression of pro-immigrant bias and preferential treatment which may cause resentment among local people'.[35]

As Critchley ended his term as Chairman, there is some indication of disquiet at the direction in which the Group had gone during the previous year. His successor, Reginald Watts, announced that he feared there was 'a danger that the Bow Group was talking itself into insignificance'. The answer, he believed, was not necessarily less talk, since he felt that the quality of the research was high, but greater relevance and better timing. It was not, in Watts' opinion, that the Group was becoming too political; it was that it was not political enough. It seems his immediate criticism about the Group's poor timing may have been a way of reasserting greater control over the power to issue statements to the press, which had been gradually dispersed among the Standing Committees.[36] The previous informal circle which had caused so much controversy over the Africa Memorandum was formally re-instituted as the 'Political Committee' from June 1967. The Chairman, Research Secretary, Political

Officer and *Crossbow*'s Editor were permanent members; the author of
the statement – often the Chairman of the Standing Committee involved
– joined them to decide what the Group would say. Dealings with the
media were passed exclusively to the Political Officer, then Tim
Sainsbury, on the grounds that a faster reaction to events necessitated a
slimmer structure.

But it was far from clear that a better strategy for engaging the
media's interest was all that was needed. Contrary to Watts' personal
opinion, there were doubts over the quality of the Group's research, and
not just from inside the Group. One influential critic was the director of
the Conservative Political Centre, Russell Lewis, who was also an ex-
Chairman of the Group. His view, which was important because the CPC
had taken on the role of the Bow Group's publisher from 1956 with first
option on any pamphlet, was that many of the drafts were unfocused,
intellectual observations of modern problems, not sharply political
contributions to contemporary debate.[37] Archie Hamilton, then a 28-
year-old Borough Councillor in Kensington and Chelsea, agreed with
him. In an article for *Crossbow* entitled 'Whither the Bow Group?', he
attacked the Group's research for lacking pertinence and its structure for
failing to use 'the views of a thousand intelligent younger Conservatives'.
'Can we really pretend', he asked, 'that a 60 page pamphlet on developing
the ocean bed is highlighting a vital political issue today?'[38] This was
debatable. Russell Lewis was piqued that the Group had published
Laurance Reed's *Ocean-Space: Europe's New Frontier* without offering
him first refusal since he thought it was so good; but Hamilton's point
was that material like this, though undoubtedly visionary, was not useful
to a party in Opposition.[39]

One author wrote pamphlets which were universally acclaimed
within the Group and the CPC. He was Simon Jenkins, a young Oxford
graduate whom Reg Watts had headhunted to write a pamphlet which
would put the Bow Group's seal of approval on the comprehensive
system. Jenkins was flattered to have been asked, although he wondered
whether he would fit in with the Bow Group. 'You would have had to
have been in an isolated cocoon to have got through the 60s as a
Conservative at university,' he believes today, having himself held broadly

left-wing views whilst an undergraduate at Oxford.[40] His first pamphlet for the Group, *Conservatives and Comprehensives*, was published in December 1967, its purpose being to exorcise the ghost of the eleven-plus exam, to which some imputed part of the blame for the 1964 election defeat. Jenkins went on to produce a series of pamphlets defending the comprehensive system and attacking Labour's education policy. In Russell Lewis' judgement they outshone most of the Group's other publications, and by 1967 Lewis' opinion mattered greatly.

Lewis realised he was in a good position to improve the quality of the Group's output, given that the CPC had first option on publishing work from the Bow Group. By the mid-1960s the Bow Group was short of money. Advertising in *Crossbow* was dwindling, despite the efforts of the Bow Group Council and the Group's friendly MPs to secure commitments. The Group had lost Michael Heseltine's expertise when he resigned late in 1965, under pressure from his own financial problems. When the Tories lost the election in 1966, the situation worsened. The Group's own analysis suggested that between 1965 and 1966 advertising revenue had dropped by one third. *Crossbow* entered a vicious cycle of reduced coverage in the press and dwindling advertising. Suddenly the Group, which had become more financially independent, was once again reliant on donations for a substantial proportion of its income.

In such straitened circumstances the publishing arrangement which the Group had reached with the CPC was beneficial. The CPC guaranteed a wide circulation among its subscribers and removed much of the burden of distribution and marketing from the Bow Group's shoulders. Only occasionally would the Group publish work itself, usually pamphlets in which the CPC was not interested. Realising that the Group's finances did not leave it in a position to refuse, Lewis was able to dictate terms. He stipulated a limit of 7,500 words, at a time when the average length of manuscripts submitted was 17,500–20,000 words. But it was not simply a question of the style and quality of the drafts; CPC's own lack of money seems to have been just as important a reason for Lewis' stubborn editorial policy. In September 1967, soon after he had set this limit, Lewis returned draft pamphlets on the monarchy and censorship to the Bow Group with the advice that if they were cut by a third each, he would consider publishing them. Both *An Evolving Monarchy* and *Not for Publication*, by Peter Lloyd, were eventually published during 1968. A pamphlet on drugs, drafted in 1969, was cut to 8,000 words at Lewis's demand, and was not published until April 1970. The Research Secretary in 1968, Norman Lamont, attempted to make Lewis commit himself to a programme of future publications, but Lewis proved impossible to tie down. Instead, in an incentive to induce the Group to focus its work on popular political issues, Lewis promised the Bow Group a discount of 40% on the cost price if more than 700 copies were ordered. Rather sourly, Roger Freeman reported during one meeting of Bow Publications that 'although Russell Lewis had said he would take a proportion of our pamphlets, he had turned down every one he had been offered.'

Following advice from Edward Du Cann, the Bow Group Council considered trying to put pressure on Lewis by seeking the support of more senior Party officials, but Lewis proved to be immune to such tactics, if they were indeed employed. The Group tried another tactic: in November 1968, independently of the CPC, it published a critique of *A Fair Deal at Work*, Heath's new trades union policy. *A Fair Deal at Work* advocated placing industrial relations on a formal, contractual footing and was generally welcomed in the press. The Bow Group's response seems deliberately perverse, given that previously it had published arguments supporting measures to limit trade union powers, and it earned the irritation of *A Fair Deal*'s author, the MP Robert Carr. Eventually the Group had no choice but to accept the wisdom of Lewis's strictures.[41] In March 1971 a committee convened to examine the Group's research came to the same conclusions that Lewis had arrived at four years earlier. The Research Secretary, Peter Lloyd, recommended that future pamphlets should 'pin-point political and social problems and provide solutions to them rather than survey political fields', and thus be 'more politically relevant when published'.[42]

Immigration, the hot domestic issue of 1968, provided the Group with further opportunities to demonstrate its political weight. Interest in the issue was reinvigorated when it appeared that the Shadow Cabinet would oppose the new Race Relations Bill in April 1968. Brocklebank-Fowler and his predecessor as Chairman, Reg Watts, signed an open

Bruce Griffiths, first Chairman of the Bow Group.

CONSERVATIVE CLUB,
ST. JAMES'S STREET,
S.W.1.

TELEGRAMS & TRADITIONS, PICCY, LONDON.
TELEPHONE Nº 9341 WHITEHALL.

AGENDA.

1. **Membership**
   a) Numbers. — 50, minimum
   B) Qualification. — Members of Universities & Professions.
   c). Age — 35 (altered easily)
   D) Subscription. — £1-1-0. (Minimum)
   E) Senior Members. — Yes. Drawing up a list.

2. Objects. *Publishing Cttee.*
   a) Publishing. — To be left fairly loose at first. But that an initial effort should be made — in conjunction with F.U.C.U.A.? & Grads
   B). Discussion Groups. above.? — + Academic staff?
   c. Social Activities. — Cttee-Dinner.
   D). Undergrad / Grad link up.
   E). Relations with F.U.C.U.A.
   F). Speaking Groups. — Yes.

3). Accomodation.
   a) Bow
   B) Other.

4) Agenda for Bow

5). (Recommendation of officers of)
   Steering Cttee.

6) Proposed Members

Bruce Griffiths's draft agenda, 1950.

Geoffrey Howe at work as editor of *Crossbow*, 1960.

David Howell addressing a Bow Group meeting at the
Constitutional Club in 1960.

Four aspiring young men from the pages of *Crossbow* in the 1960s: *clockwise from top left*, Norman Lamont, Norman Fowler, Michael Howard, Christopher Bland.

Leon Brittan networking on the terrace of the Houses of Parliament.

Four prominent Conservatives before the Bow Group's twenty-fifth anniversary dinner on 16 March 1976 – the day Harold Wilson announced his resignation.

CROSSBOW

The Bow Group Quarterly
October-December 1967
2/-

WHAT ARE
YOUNG
CONSERVATIVES
REALLY LIKE?
A report by
David Walder

The notorious cover girl of *Crossbow*, October 1967 . . .

High tide next week

. . . transformed to Edward Heath by Illingworth in the *Daily Mail*.

'Recession is when your neighbour loses his job. Depression is when
you lose your job. Recovery is when the Chancellor loses his job.'
Norman Lamont addressing the Bow Group meeting at the
Conservative Party Conference, 1993.

letter to Heath which was published in *The Times*. They were joined by
the National Chairman of the YCs, and the Chairman of the Federation
of Conservative Students, but not the Monday Club. In Parliament the
Tories were pressured to adopt a reasoned amendment, which acknowledged the need for a new law but opposed the Bill's second reading.[43]
Late in the year, the Group invited Enoch Powell – by now exiled from the
Shadow Cabinet after his remarks on race – to be the target in one of its
new 'Under Fire' meetings, in which leading members of the Group inter-
rogated a senior political figure. Critchley, who was to have been one of
the inquisitors, refused to take part; Michael Howard took his place.
Given the importance of the issue in the West Midlands, it was not
surprising that three members of the Birmingham Group decided to
write 'A Birmingham View' on the subject. Two out of the three authors
were to become MPs: Ken Clarke and Nicholas Budgen made an unlikely
pairing; the other was John Lenton, the Birmingham Group's Vice-
Chairman. The London Bow Group was alarmed at the line the
Birmingham Group might take, and the Council was anxious to discover
what it was in advance of publication. Birmingham's was a more
trenchant approach, which advocated a 'temporary pause in the flow of
immigrants for a period of say five years'. They supported greater
requirements for potential immigrants, including English language tests
and health checks. But, like the previous pamphlet, Clarke's and Budgen's
accent was on ensuring that the immigrants were effectively absorbed
into the white community through careful dispersal.

Throughout this period, however, a latent problem persisted. By the
late 1960s, the Bow Group was living beyond even the means provided by
an expanding income. Roger Freeman, who at the time was Managing
Director of the publishing arm of the Bow Group, Bow Publications,
frankly described the problem:

> Bow Groupers have always seemed either unable or unwilling to
> grasp the elements of financial control. Council members tend to
> debate endlessly the principle of paying for the chairman's cigars,
> but can never concentrate their minds on major financial issues,
> like the profitability of *Crossbow* . . . Many members seem to talk

as if all our work is limitlessly subsidised by unnamed, yet
obviously rich financial backers. Needless to say, this is a myth.44

It is possible that Freeman sounded overly apocalyptic by 1969. On the
face of it – and that was perhaps part of the problem – the Group
appeared to be in rude financial health, and the Conservatives' political
prospects looked excellent. A decline in the Group's membership, from a
peak of 927 at the beginning of 1963 to a low of 708 in the second half
of 1966, had quickly reversed as the country became disillusioned with
Wilson's Government. This was the main catalyst for an increase in
membership of almost 50% in just under two years. For the first three
quarters of 1968, the total membership had reached an all-time high, just
under the magical 1,000 mark.

The upturn in the membership had happened irrespective of the
Group's direct attempts to stimulate interest. Advertising was never
successful: one advert in the *Spectator* in late 1968, for example,
generated just seven replies. Similarly, a sherry party organised by the
Group to raise its profile among final year students in Cambridge, which
was attended by 70 undergraduates, resulted in the recruitment of only
four new members. To acquire these, as someone in Council ruefully
noted, had cost £10 of sherry each. Peter Lilley, who as a junior officer on
the Council was responsible for the Bow Group's University and Branch
liaison in 1970, conducted a detailed survey of the economics of the Bow
Group's recruitment policy. He starkly concluded that the cost of recruitment at the universities was such that 'it is only if a university member
maintains his membership for at least four years . . . that he begins to
contribute to the Group's finances.'45 This was an important observation. It meant that the effects of the loss of members following the
Conservative defeat in 1964 would continue to have an impact on the
Group's balance sheet almost until 1970. 'An important subsidiary aim
[of recruitment]', Lilley added, 'is to increase our subscription revenue.'
It seems that this was far from the minds of many Council members.
Christopher Bland, the Group's acerbic Chairman at this time, preferred
to use his contacts in the City and the British United Industrialists to
make up any shortfall between revenue and expenditure.

The continuing financial pressures of these years superimposed themselves on the rigour of the Group's interviewing procedure. By 1969, two alternatives seemed to crystallise: that espoused by the then Secretary, Michael Howard, that the Group should admit anyone who would make some contribution; and that of Peter Watherston, that the Group should not admit anyone likely to be a 'positive nuisance'.[46] Although some members of the Group still took pride in its intellectual exclusivity, there was growing support for a relaxed membership policy, and Watherston's view prevailed. 'I didn't like the pomposity of refusing people,' says former Council member Peter Lloyd today.[47] The membership of the Group grew, mainly because Conservative fortunes were improving, but partly because the Group was less discriminating. Whereas Richard Bing had reported in 1965 that of 123 people who had applied for membership, 25.2% had been rejected, by 1970, of the 116 applications since April the previous year, just five were rejected. Of the applicants, 43 were current university members, of whom two were female. There were 73 'others', 56 men and 17 women.

The Group was still short of money and approached the Sainsbury Trust, which does not appear to have been able to help, and Conservative Central Office. Lord Chelmer, one of the Party's two Treasurers, accepted the Group's contention that it was not sufficiently well off to support itself on an indefinite basis and agreed to speak to Colonel Hobbs of the British United Industrialists. Having been the regular contributor of £4,500 annually to the Group since 1958, the BUI had been forced to reassess its support in 1967. That year it paid out only £1,000, owing to the new Companies Act which made it mandatory for listed companies to declare their political donations. The BUI feared its subscribers would take fright and that it would itself have to focus its support on the Conservative Party alone. Fortunately, it was able to wriggle out of the problem by making itself an unincorporated association, thus protecting its secrecy.[48] In January 1969, as a result, Hobbs was able to agree in principle to give £3,000 to the Group. This amount represented almost half of the Group's income for that year, but the final donation seems to have been somewhat less, at £2,200.[49] The Group's appetite continued to grow, however, and even the substantial support of two new donors, John Baring and Sir Siegmund Warburg, failed to reduce its dependency.[50] Whereas the Group had recorded a surplus of £3,437 in 1968, it was £1,800 in deficit at the end of 1969, and this debt was expected to double during 1970. For several years the Council had postponed putting up the cost of membership, but now it had to accept that an increase was inevitable. A rise of almost 100% over two years was finally agreed to in March 1971.

Even though the Bow Group's membership was once again expanding in the late 1960s, topping 1,150 at the end of 1971, relative to the development of other Tory organisations the increase in members was insignificant. When the Group's membership reached 1,000, with the enrolment of a Mr Bruce Kyle in November 1968, it was a reflection not only of the declining profile of the Group itself, but of the relative insignificance of the number, that the Group earned no coverage for this event, which was an important landmark by its own standards. A glance at the Bow Group's competition quickly explains why this was the case. The Monday Club was, as one Bow Group Council member noticed, 'getting the type of "shocked publicity" that perhaps the [Bow] Group got in the 1950s'.[51] The Bow Group tended to dismiss the intellectual abilities of the Club's members: at a well-attended press conference to trail the Group's forthcoming events in the summer of 1969, Christopher Bland dismissed the Monday Club's policies as 'graffiti'. Several years earlier, John MacGregor observed that 'the standard of research as shown by their published work was not particularly good.' This was to miss the point. The Club was a campaigning organisation. As early as the Party Conference in 1966, the *Guardian* noted that 'the Monday Club stand was yesterday pulsating with dynamic purposive action while the Bow Group's was deserted.'

By the start of the 1970s the Monday Club was believed to have a membership at least twice the size of the Bow Group's, at 2,000, of which it claimed 10% held office in constituency associations. From being an organisation initially regarded with great suspicion, the Club had gained acceptability, and probably enjoyed the support, like the Bow Group, of the British United Industrialists.[52] Whereas the Bow Group remained a largely metropolitan operation, the Monday Club had a much wider regional influence. About 70% of its members were provincially based. The Club's nationwide spread and its influence in constituency associations had clear implications for Bow Group members' chances of selection relative to Monday Club members. Harold Soref, chairman of the Monday Club's Africa Group, was selected for Ormskirk. His selection speech had demanded an end to what he saw as the 'post-imperial retreat', a direct attack on the position closely identified with the Bow Group.[53] *The Times* noted that an attack in *Crossbow* on Heath's 'gratuitous concessions . . . to the Party's reactionary wing' early in 1969 came just as the Shadow Defence Secretary, Geoffrey Rippon, published a pamphlet through the Monday Club.[54] Edward Heath also spoke to the Monday Club in 1969; he did not speak to the Bow Group that year. The Tory leadership used the Monday Club to publish its thoughts, just as ten years before the previous leadership had used the Bow Group to fly kites to test party opinion on Africa.

Anthony Howard provided an epitaph for the Group in the 1960s: 'In the late 1950s it was Butler and the Bow Group who set the whole tone of Tory attitudes: today it is the Monday Club.'[55] Simon Jenkins recalls the 'distaste' within the Group at the time for the Monday Club's and Selsdon Group's agendas.[56] For the Bow Group, the problem was that both of these competitors were working along the right lines: reinforcing a set of basic principles which formed not only the platform for the 1970 manifesto, but made the public aware of what Edward Heath stood for. With its constitutional requirement to remain a broad church, it was harder for the Bow Group to perform a similar role. The Group was also smaller, and the mood of the party as a whole was moving rightwards and away from the progressive approach which had epitomised Bow Group thinking. The *Guardian* caught up with Bill Cash at the Party Conference in 1969: 'We are not particularly sympathetic to the permissive society,' the newspaper quoted him saying.[57] Cash had been lobbying conference delegates with plans to set up research groups which would return to Tory first principles. T. E. Utley broadly agreed. He argued that although there were plenty of energetic young Conservatives, Tory principles were being eroded, and the reasons for support were losing their resonance. It was the Monday Club and the Selsdon Group, and not the Bow Group, which benefited from the gathering momentum of these views.

Although the Group continued its political programme regardless, the impression was that it was not as influential at the end of the 1960s as it had been at the beginning. The Group failed to persuade Michael Ancram and Malcolm Rifkind, both members of the Scottish Thistle Group, that they wanted to become 'the Bow Group in Scotland'.[58] At the Federation of Conservative Students' Conference, Peter Lilley reported that he had 'encountered some 'light-hearted ribaldry from the audience who seemed to suffer from considerable misapprehension as to what the Group stood for'.[59] Nevertheless, politicians from both sides in Northern Ireland addressed the Group as part of their lobbying activities, just as the main protagonists in African politics had met the Group early in the 1960s. The Group's leadership appeared to support Terence O'Neill, the Northern Irish Prime Minister, in his call for devolution when they framed a motion for a meeting on Ulster at the 1969 Party Conference. The Group had habitually debated a controversial 'missing motion' at party conferences during the 1960s; in 1969, the Group posed that the Ulster Unionist Party should accelerate its programme of reform and cut its links with the Orange Order. The issue was sufficiently inflammatory to be cancelled after one speaker withdrew and the other, Peter Kirk MP, mysteriously found that he had double-booked himself.

Whereas the Bow Group had appeared well placed to gain from Heath's election as Conservative Leader in 1965, the hope had failed to translate into reality by 1970. 'It had been an average year for the Group,' concluded Christopher Bland at the Group's AGM in 1970. 'In terms of its impact on the country as a whole it was always less significant in the immediate short-term when the Party was in Opposition than when it was in power.'[60] Politically, the Monday Club was larger and a more visible lobbying force than the Bow Group, which remained, true to its constitution, without a corporate view. Perhaps, because of this fundamental difference of aims, it is unfair to compare the two organisations; yet that was what contemporaries did.

Perhaps experience had proved wrong those who believed that the Group stood to benefit from a spell out of power. But other factors seem a more likely cause for the Group's disappointment. The Tories were at least initially unpopular, and the Group was marginalised within a Party which was out of power and in which a number of factional groups were competing for influence and limited financial resources. Unpopularity hit the Group's subscription revenue, as did careless financial management. Both the Group's annual dinner and its weekend conference made substantial losses.[61] The priorities of those who ran the Group were also a factor. Despite the ambitions of these men, the Group's particular blend of careerism and intellectualism failed to propel it as perhaps its members expected. Whereas the Group had been suspected of influencing Heath in Conservative circles in 1965, by 1970 it was widely believed to have little clout. There was a variety of alternative ports of call for politicians looking for new ideas by the end of the 1960s. Geoffrey Howe went to the Institute of Economic Affairs when researching pension arrangements in 1969 for a pamphlet he was writing with the Bow Group's Research Secretary at the time, Norman Lamont. The Bow Group could not provide the level of expertise on the semi-professional basis which the IEA's founders, Arthur Seldon and Ralph Harris, could.[62]

The Group hit financial problems just as the domestic issues of the decade and the Conservatives' policy requirements favoured a more trenchant political position which the Monday Club was more easily able to adopt. 'Not only has the Group had to bump up its annual subscription from £5.25 to £8 to avoid bankruptcy, its political influence is undoubtedly waning. The Group's philosophy has little in common with Mr Heath's brand of Conservatism,' believed one commentator in the *Sunday Telegraph*.[63] By contrast, a year's subscription to the Monday Club cost £3. At the 1970 election, the Bow Group tried hard to present the eighty-two candidates who were its members as a rebuttal of the allegation that the Conservatives had moved to the right. Mr Heath, the Group argued, 'has brought to the Conservative Party moderate and careful thinking of the type the Bow Group has always tried to promote'.[64]

At the same time a pamphlet was published, *We Not Only Cope, We Care* – the title encapsulating the point the Group was trying to make.

The truth was that many in the Bow Group despised the politics of
Selsdon Man and the views reproduced in Monday Club pamphlets. In
fact, many more MPs were members of the Bow Group than of the
Monday Club, but in the climate of the late 1960s, the Bow Group was a
fish out of water. In that era Robert Rhodes James observed, if a little
pessimistically:

> [a] disturbing trend . . . towards what must be described as the
> revival of anti-intellectualism in the Conservative Party. The Party,
> no less than the country, requires men and women of first-class
> brains . . . It is a striking feature of British politics in the 1960s
> that, with a few exceptions, the Conservative Party failed to attract
> many people of this calibre; even more alarming, from the
> Conservative point of view, is the fact that many have been
> positively alienated.[65]

At the Group's tenth anniversary dinner in 1961, Butler had expressed the
wish that what he saw as a rather poor group of backbenchers should be
supplemented by some new talent from the Bow Group. The Bow Group
remained closely associated both with the man and with 'Butskellite'
politics to the end of the decade. In the wake of riots at the London
School of Economics, Butler, now a peer and Master of Trinity College,
Cambridge, spoke out at the Group's annual dinner in 1969 against
sending students down for making a political point. Enlightened though
this view may have been, whether it resonated was another matter.
Tellingly, the *Evening Standard*'s comment on the speech was entitled
'Butler's vintage'. It was the Group's association with a group of people
who were no longer in charge of the Party which limited its influence by
1970.

NOTES

1   Peter Riddell, *Honest Opportunism*, 2nd edn London 1996, p. 97.

2   The Rt Hon. Sir Peter Lloyd MP, interview, 17 October 2000.

3 Bow Group Council, Minutes, 19 October 1964.

4 Iain Macleod, 'In Opposition', *Crossbow*, January–March 1965, p. 33.

5 Editorial, *Crossbow*, January–March 1965, p. 5.

6 Howell, interview.

7 Susanne Puddefoot, 'Vague and Incompetent', *Crossbow*, January–March 1966, pp. 8–10.

8 Anthony King, 'New Stirrings on the Right', *New Society*, 14 October 1965, pp. 7–11.

9 Anthony Howard, 'Tough Bowmen', *The Sunday Times*, 27 June 1965.

10 Alan Watkins, 'How the Election will be Fought', *The Spectator*, 25 February 1966.

11 Lloyd, interview.

12 The Rt Hon. Michael Howard MP, interview, 13 April 1999.

13 Brittan, interview.

14 Hugh Dykes was MP for Harrow West, 1974–97. Concurrently, before the change to direct elections, he was an MEP, 1974–77. In the latter part of his Parliamentary career he devoted his energies to the European Movement, of which he was Chairman, 1990–97.

15 Critchley, *A Bag of Boiled Sweets*, p. 97.

16 Julian Critchley, 'Bluestockings Inc.' *Crossbow*, Summer 1980, pp. 21–2.

17 Simon Jenkins, interview, 19 October 1999. He was Editor of the London *Evening Standard*, 1976–78; Political Editor of the *Economist*, 1979–86. After a period as a columnist on *The Sunday Times*, he became Editor of *The Times*, 1990–2. Since 1992 he has written, with a special interest in the railways and church architecture, for *The Times*.

18 Riddell, *Honest Opportunism*, p. 97.

19 Jonathan Aitken graduated from Oxford to take up a job as Selwyn Lloyd's Private Secretary, 1964–66. He was a foreign correspondent on the *Evening Standard*, 1966–71. While MP for Thanet East, February 1974–87: and for Thanet South 1987–97, he was Minister of State for Defence Procurement 1992–94 then Chief Secretary to the Treasury 1994–95 before resigning to fight an unsuccessful libel action. Convicted of perjury, he spent a short time in prison and returned to Oxford to read theology. Norman Fowler was Chairman of CUCA. After a period as a *Times* reporter, when he specialised in Home Affairs, he was elected MP for Sutton Coldfield in February 1974. He was Secretary of State for Transport 1981; for Social Services 1981–87; for Employment 1987–90.

20 'Psephologue', *Crossbow* October–December 1971, pp. 28–9.

21 Stuart Jackson, 'That Safe Seat', *Crossbow*, Summer 1988, pp. 16–17; interview, May 1999.

22   Tugendhat was President of the Cambridge Union. After ten years as a leader writer for the *Financial Times*, he was elected MP for the Cities of London and Westminster 1970–74; City of London and Westminster South 1974–76; he was a European Commissioner, 1977–85 and a Commission Vice-President 1981–85. Since 1991 he has been the Chairman of Abbey National.

23   'Is Bow Group Research on the Wrong Lines?', *Crossbow*, January–March 1966, p. 41.

24   Bow Group Council, Minutes, 16 March 1967.

25   Critchley, *A Bag of Boiled Sweets*, p. 97.

26   *Daily Express*, 11 October 1966.

27   Critchley, *A Bag of Boiled Sweets*, p. 97.

28   Gilvrie Lock (neé Misstear) email to the author, 7 January 2001; George Perry, email to the author, 10 January 2001. David Hillman later restyled the *Guardian*.

29   *Daily Sketch*, 16 October 1967.

30   David Walder, 'What Young Conservatives Are Really Like', *Crossbow*, October–December 1967.

31   Richard Crossman, *The Diaries of a Cabinet Minister*, London 1977, Vol. III, pp. 816–17. Entry for 12 February 1970.

32   The Rt Hon. Peter Lilley MP, interview, 13 April 1999.

33   Katharine Whitehorn, *Observer*, 10 September 1967.

34   'Experience Gap Bridged by Bow Group', *Daily Telegraph*, 20 October 1966. Howe had been elected to represent Bebington in 1964.

35   'The Problem of Immigration', *Yorkshire Evening Post*, 9 October 1965.

36   Bow Group Council, Minutes, 4 April 1967. An independent management consultant, Watts went on to become the Chief Executive of Burson Marsteller. He is a member of the Metropolitan Police Committee.

37   Lewis, interview.

38   Archie Hamilton, 'Whither the Bow Group?', *Crossbow*, July–September 1969, p. 46. Hamilton was elected MP for Epsom and Ewell in April 1978. He was Parliamentary Under-Secretary of State for Defence Procurement, MoD 1986–87; PPS to the Prime Minister 1987–88; Minister of State, MoD, 1988–93.

39   Laurance Reed was MP for Bolton East, 1970–February 74.

40   Jenkins, interview.

41   Bow Publications, Minutes, 15 January 1969.

42   Peter Lloyd, *Report of the Sub–Committee on Research to the Council*, 1 March 1971, objectives 8 and 5 respectively.

43   Edward Heath, *The Course of My Life*, London 1998, p. 292.

44 Roger Freeman, 'Ladies and Gentlemen', *Crossbow*, January–March 1969, p. 38. MP for Kettering 1983–97. Chancellor of the Duchy of Lancaster, 1995–97.

45 Report by University and Branch Liaison Officer, 6 July 1970.

46 Bow Group Council, Minutes, 31 March 1969.

47 Lloyd, interview.

48 CPA, CCO 20/29/1, Drewe to Chairman, 13 December 1967.

49 Bow Group Council, Minutes, 31 March 1969 and Amended Budget for 1969; Minutes, 30 June 1969.

50 John Baring succeeded to his father's title in 1991 as Lord Ashburton. He was Chairman of Barings 1985–89; of BP, 1992–95. He first married Sir Robin Renwick's elder daughter. Sir Siegmund Warburg was Chairman of SG Warburg from 1978 until he died in 1982.

51 Bow Group Council, Minutes, 21 April 1971.

52 *Birmingham Post*, 18 December 1968.

53 Diary, *Times*, 29 August 1969.

54 *Times*, 22 April 1969.

55 Anthony Howard, *New Statesman*, 4 April 1969.

56 Jenkins, interview.

57 'Path of Glory', *Guardian*, 11 October 1969. Bill Cash was MP for Stafford 1984–97; for Stone 1997–.

58 Bow Group Council, Minutes, 3rd December 1969.

59 Bow Group Council, Minutes, 10 November 1970.

60 Bow Group Annual General Meeting, 16 April 1970.

61 Bow Group Council, Minutes, 6 July 1970.

62 Richard Cockett, *Thinking the Unthinkable*, London 1994, p. 171.

63 Ian Waller, 'How Ginger Groups Fare', *Sunday Telegraph,* 9 May 1971.

64 'Morale Booster for Tories', *Daily Telegraph*, 1 June 1970.

65 Robert Rhodes James, *Ambitions and Realities*, London 1972, pp. 290–1.

Five

'SO WE WON AFTER ALL': 1970–5

Given that *Crossbow* had spent much of the previous two years whetting its readers' appetites for Government, the Conservatives' victory in the 1970 General Election seemed to catch the Bow Group by surprise. Several local election defeats earlier in the year had suggested that Labour might cling on to power. Although Heath was confident that the polls were underestimating Conservative support, others did not have access to the results of Conservative Central Office's private polling.[1] A planned summer edition of *Crossbow* was shelved when Wilson requested a dissolution of Parliament, so it was not until the autumn of 1970 that the new Editor of *Crossbow*, Simon Jenkins, had an opportunity to comment on the Conservative election victory. His opening words were 'So we won after all. And we won not by the skins of our teeth but decisively.' Michael Howard, who took over as Chairman of the Group early in 1970, remembers the shock of the transition into Government. Having volunteered to drive Robert Carr, the new Secretary of State for Employment, to a Bow Group meeting at the Royal Commonwealth Society on Northumberland Avenue shortly after the election, he had difficulty finding a space to park. With not long to go before the meeting was due to start, Howard decided that it was best to leave the car in the middle of the wide street, which, as he puts it today, was 'not entirely illegal'. 'Are you sure this is a good idea?' asked Carr. 'Oh, don't worry,' Howard reassured the nervous new Minister, 'no one will recognise you.' Realising his gaffe, he quickly added: 'not this early in the term'.[2]

Thirty-nine members of the Bow Group were elected in June 1970, compared to 17 in 1966. Heath's choice of Government appointees temporarily allayed the Group's concerns that it had strictly limited ability to influence him: of the 39, he gave eight ministerial positions.[3] A ninth, the former Chairman of the Group and hereditary peer, Lord Windlesham (David Hennessy), was also appointed as a minister. 'Whoops of joy', hyperbolised the *Evening Standard*'s Londoner's Diary, could be heard 'in Bow Group circles at the final complexion of Mr Heath's administration.'[4] In keeping with Howard's belief that more influence could be exerted with the Conservatives in Government than out, the Council invited the Bow Group's MPs to a drinks party early in July. That month the Council moved to strengthen the Group's Standing Committees. 'It was felt that the Election results giving a greater Bow Group representation in the House had increased the potential of these Committees' to produce 'short term research', and 'to maintain contact with older, distinguished members of the Group' – in other words, MPs.[5] In the same meeting the Research Secretary, Peter Lloyd, presented a paper on the Group's future research. Lloyd advocated 'The setting up of groups which will cover the main areas where Government is still formu-lating, or has yet to formulate, policy and where the Bow Group can make a well-considered contribution'.[6] Lloyd believed that the Bow Group should investigate the National Health Service, the constitution and housing. Gaps in Government policy provided an opportunity for the Group. Later that year, in its October issue, *Crossbow* gave four new MPs space to write about a key issue. Christopher Brocklebank-Fowler chose South Africa, Barney Hayhoe the political levy raised by trades unions; Laurance Reed returned to his pet subject the sea, and Tim Raison picked playgroups.

But before *Crossbow* had gone to press, tragedy struck. The October issue also carried the obituary of Iain Macleod, written by his Parliamentary Private Secretary, Nicholas Scott MP. 'There can be few groups who will miss him more than that generation of young men and women in politics to whom his inspiration meant so much. In the Bow Group, the Young Conservatives, the Research Department and the House of Commons they looked to him to represent their views and to articulate their idealism.'[7] It was a two-way relationship: one of the first new MPs whom Macleod had rung to congratulate was Barney Hayhoe, whose thoughts on the future *Crossbow* were printed in the same issue as Macleod's obituary.[8] The Bow Group had prematurely lost an important ally: it is worth speculating whether the Group would have once again flown kites for Macleod as Chancellor of the Exchequer, had he lived, as it had for him as Colonial Secretary.

The autumn issue of *Crossbow* also revealed a marked difference of opinion over what the future held between the Chairman of the Group and the journal's Editor, which partly reflected their differing ambitions. Although Michael Howard retrospectively expresses his own reservations about the Heath Government, there was little sign of this in an open letter he wrote to the Prime Minister published at the 1970 Party Conference and every indication he was hunting a seat at the next General Election. 'It is surprising how some people have yet to grasp that the lack of hasty deeds from your Government is indicative of the fact that it is a Government which to an almost unprecedented extent is eschewing the shadow of gesture for the substance of premeditated action.'

Free from the self-censorship of the aspiring parliamentary candidate, Simon Jenkins struck a caustic note. 'If it can be said that we did not win the last election on a false economic prospectus, we at least did so on an extremely naïve one.' Acutely, Jenkins observed that the 'ringing phrases about massive cuts in public spending . . . are beginning to look a little thin in the eyes of the electorate.'[9] His dislike of the Selsdon rhetoric was barely concealed:

> Before the election, the Conservative leadership, for reasons best known to itself and its private pollsters, acquired the image of being the party first and foremost which would put spending power back into the pockets of the people. This was overlaid with a veneer of right-wing tough-mindedness on non-economic issues, which in the case of most of the Shadow Cabinet was fortunately only skin deep.[10]

The Bow Group could not resist testing just how thick this right-wing gloss was. Its first short memorandum focused on the plight of African Asians. Taking as their title *The Greatest Claim* – a phrase used by

Reginald Maudling to describe the right of Asian British passport holders to enter the United Kingdom – the authors, Michael Howard and four MPs, Julian Critchley, Sir Anthony Meyer, Tim Raison and David Walder, addressed the shortcomings of the 1968 Immigration Act.[11] This law limited entry to 1,500 Kenyan Asians each year. By May 1970, 7,180 were waiting to enter the UK. There was pressure to amend the immigration rules.

The Bow Group set out to open the debate and put pressure on the Government to relax the requirements. The timing was crucial. The Home Office had just begun to draft a new Bill, which, it was rumoured, would put Commonwealth citizens on the same footing as other foreigners and enable them to apply for work permits. Perhaps the authors thought they were in a strong position to influence the minister responsible for immigration, Lord Windlesham, whose appointment Jenkins saw as 'the surest sign of the Government's determination not to yield an inch to the backwoodsmen in this field'.[12] Michael Howard suggested reallocating the under-utilised Commonwealth work vouchers to Kenyan Asians. Coming in August when other political news was scarce, the Bow Group's contribution was widely reported. Simon Jenkins believed that it supported the private views of a substantial proportion of the Government and the Cabinet as well as the Foreign Office. Furthermore, the Group's idea attracted generally favourable editorial comment, although not everyone agreed. Nigel Lawson felt the plan was a non-starter, since 'It would amount to a significant net increase in the rate of coloured immigration into Britain, which would be bad for race relations and contrary to what the Conservatives led people to believe before the election.'[13] In fact the Bill the Government published in February the following year replaced employment vouchers with work permits which did not carry permanent residence rights. It was only during the summer of 1972, when Idi Amin began his expulsion of Asians from Uganda, that Heath was obliged to take almost half of all those expelled. The Bow Group was once again enjoying greater recognition from the Party's leadership. But it was more the wayward 'Halt Immigration Now' campaign of its main competitor which pushed the Monday Club to the outer margins of the Party, leaving the way clear for the Group.[14]

But, as Heath intended, it was not immigration but Europe which dominated his political agenda. The programme which Michael Howard proposed to the Group reflected this focus. Franz Josef Strauss, the leader of the Bavarian Christian Social Union, and Valéry Giscard d'Estaing were both invited to speak, although neither in the event accepted Howard's offer. Behind the scenes the Group understood that 'the Party was particularly anxious for the Group to do everything to help with the promotion of Britain's entry into the Common Market.'[15] In his comprehensive study of Conservative views towards Europe up to the 1975 Referendum, Nigel Ashford believes that the Bow Group's involvement was welcomed, since 'it helped to identify Europe with the younger, intellectually able and more forward-looking members of the party, and therefore helped to make Europe an attractive political proposal for the Conservatives.'[16] At the UK's previous application for Common Market membership in 1962, the Group's then Chairman, David Howell, had been among the public figures who soberly endorsed the unsuccessful British attempt to join, in *The Times*. The manner in which the message was delivered changed a little in the intervening nine years. In the summer of 1971 the Bow Group Chairman, Norman Lamont, surrounded by girls in hot pants, put the case for membership over a megaphone to a rally in Trafalgar Square.[17] At his side were the new MPs Kenneth Clarke and John Gummer.[18]

The Group devoted its July 1971 *Crossbow* to the theme of Europe, just as the Government published its White Paper, *The United Kingdom and the European Communities*, which opened the campaign in favour of membership. Although the 'no corporate view' policy still held, *Crossbow* noted that 'The Group has always contained many passionate Europeans, including the last five or six Chairmen, and is probably broadly in favour of entry'. The only significant opposition to Common Market membership came from Simon Jenkins, and he had just resigned the editorship of *Crossbow*, to be replaced by the strongly pro-European Christopher Bland. By 1970 Jenkins had decided to pursue a career in journalism; his views on Europe were one reason why he doubted his political career would go far with Heath as the Conservative Leader. Looking back, he thinks that 'the ferocity of the pro-Europeanism which came down from Heath's operation affected the Bow Group and its working.'[19] The Group developed close relations with both the European Forum (the forerunner of the Conservative Group for Europe) and the European Movement. In February 1970 the Council invited the new Chairman of the European Movement, Lord Harlech, to become a patron of the Bow Group, an offer which he accepted.[20] Harlech's involvement marked the beginning of a strong relationship between the Group and the European Movement, which volunteered to foot the bill for the Bow Group's Spring Conference at Keele in 1971. However, this Conference was not a success: the location – which was inconvenient for many of the London members – a postal strike and the difficulty of obtaining speakers who were involved in the EEC membership negotiations were all factors. In 1973 the European Movement subsidised a Bow Group trip to Brussels as well as making an agreement in principle to sponsor up to three Bow Group publications on Europe each year, for £150 each. In return, the Group was to ensure that European Movement publications and the new quarterly *Federalist* were circulated among its members.[21]

Christine Stewart-Munro was co-opted onto the Council to act as European Liaison Officer and the Group set up branches in Paris, Bonn and Brussels. Of these, the most successful was the Paris Bow Group – 'les Bowistes'. At its launch party on 4 December 1972, Sir Christopher Soames, Britain's first European Commissioner, was guest of honour. In London the Council was later informed that, of the officers on the Paris Branch's Council, half were English, half French. Bonn's branch was started by a Professor Kaltefleiter in the summer of 1973 after the Bow Group had met representatives of the German Christian Democratic Union several times in the previous two years. A Brussels Bow Group drew its impetus from the handful of Bow Group members who went there to work in the European Commission after Britain's membership had been agreed. The Paris Branch seems, however, to have fallen foul of the legal requirement in France for it to register as a political grouping, and there are few signs that either the Bonn or the Brussels groupings ever gathered momentum. By 1974, all three continental Bow Groups were quiescent; but they had demonstrated the Bow Group's enthusiasm for 'Europe'.

With sceptics in a minority in London – and silent if they had political aspirations – the Bow Group's publications on Europe assumed an increasingly favourable tone, though this may also be attributed to the influence of the European Movement's sponsorship. In the run-up to the abortive campaign of 1962 the Group had published, amidst much controversy, both sides of the argument. By contrast, in 1971 *Crossbow* observed that when the Group published *Our Future in Europe*, which put the long-term case for entry, 'it was not greeted by a counter pamphlet and is one of the best-selling pamphlets of recent years'. The pamphlet had no named authors, and marked a return to the anonymous memorandums with which the Group's leadership had put the case for decolonisation over ten years earlier, and similarly infringed the position of 'no corporate view'.

As Editor of *Crossbow*, Christopher Bland was in a position to be as partisan as he liked without any constitutional implications for the Bow Group. He strongly supported more open advocacy of the case for Europe: 'it has generally been accepted that a favourable attitude to Europe should be prudently played down on the hustings. It is up to Mr Heath to ensure that the European case is put well and realistically, so that the success of Britain's application not only ceases to be thought a liability in by-elections, but becomes a major plank in the Conservative Party's eventual election platform.'[22] In July 1971 he opened *Crossbow* with an editorial which depicted the European issue in geographical yet also metaphorical terms. In 'Mainland or Open Sea', he attacked Jim Callaghan's own invocation of Churchill, 'I choose the open sea', as 'inappropriate and out of context'. 'Britain is no longer a maritime power,' Bland went on to observe, interpreting one of *Crossbow*'s guiding editorial mantras, 'a realistic appraisal of Britain's place in the world', to mean a pro-European stance. And so a degree of fatalism imbued the piece: 'The risk in going in is only outweighed by the certainty of failure if we stay out.' In this vein, active support for involvement in Europe followed logically from the Group's much earlier work on a post-colonial policy for Africa.

The remainder of that issue of *Crossbow* concentrated on the advantages and challenges of membership. Leon Brittan looked forward to a time when Europe could be more self-sufficient in its defence. James Scott-Hopkins, the MP for West Derbyshire, argued that agriculture was no longer a stumbling block to EEC entry, so long as British farmers adapted rapidly. In fact *Crossbow* had already published an article which came to the same conclusion, in Spring 1961, when Graham Hallett argued that farmers' fears of the consequences of joining a common agricultural policy were overblown. Criticisms that the CAP would either ruin British agriculture or produce 'an over-protected, high-cost' system were, he believed, 'exaggerated'.[23] Ultimately, however, Hallett accepted that the farming issue was subordinate to the fundamental question: 'Is it in our interest to give up some of our independence in economic affairs and take part in a collective process of decision-making, with some form of political union as the ultimate goal?'

This was the real question, but it was almost as if there was a tacit recognition that although *Crossbow* readers deserved to know the full implications of the European project, this was not something to which the wider public should be privy. A spoof selection address, published in *Crossbow* just as safe seat fever gripped the Bow Group in the run-up to the 1970 election, was the funnier for being close to the truth:

> I am a supporter of Britain's entry into the Common Market. Mr Heath, of course, did great work at Brussels. Entry into this wider grouping will give this country a new role, and new opportunities. This is an age of big groupings. Britain must become a member of one. And let me assure you that she can do without any loss of sovereignty whatsoever. Let no one tell you otherwise. We have much to offer, not least our political skills and leadership. Sir Alec Douglas-Home has unrivalled experience as a statesman of world calibre. We will lead the new Europe.[24]

It is hard to believe that with as opinionated a membership as the Bow Group's there was unanimous support for the Bow Group Council's apparently ardent support for Common Market membership. Just as the Council had enraged certain members of the Group in 1961 with its pronouncements on Africa, so the Council's handling of the European issue seems to have aroused discontent.

Some time in advance of the Annual General Meeting in 1971 an anonymous letter entitled 'Crisis at the Bow Group?' began to circulate among members. Before calling for the adoption of his report at the AGM, Michael Howard, the outgoing Chairman, said that he deprecated the method used for the attack contained within the letter.[25] The remainder of the meeting was rancorous. It was the task of the Treasurer Eric Koops to propose an increase in the subscription rate of almost 100% spread over a two-year period starting the following year, January 1972. Koops knew that a rise of this magnitude required careful explanation to members. At the Council's meeting in Keele at the start of its Spring Conference, weeks before the AGM at which the rise would have to be put to a vote, he had accordingly asked his colleagues on the Council 'to make a particular effort both in the time left at the conference and elsewhere to explain to members why it was essential that subscriptions should be increased as recommended'.[26] However, the postal strike reduced the attendance at the Conference, and it appears that many members arrived at the AGM ignorant of the subscription rises which Koops was proposing.

At the AGM Koops stressed that the increase in donations, which had improved the Group's finances, had been achieved on the understanding that the Group would seek to increase its subscription revenue and make itself more self-sufficient. But there was a significant enough body of unhappy members to ensure that his motion to institute the rise failed to attract the necessary two-thirds majority and was defeated. Instead, Leon Brittan suggested that the first stage of the rise – itself an increase of more than 50% for all classes of subscription – be approved. This motion was carried. But with the sharp increase came demands that the Group should do more. One further motion proposed that 'there should be no significant increase in subscription rates without a corresponding increase in the facilities and service offered to the membership.' Two further motions called for the new Council to commit itself to improving the Group's profile in the coming year. One was withdrawn in the light of Norman Lamont's statement that the Council intended to take action to enhance the Group's image; the other, probably for the same reason, was defeated.

It is difficult to assess how widely felt were the grievances articulated in 'Crisis at the Bow Group?'. Two hundred members would resign at the end of the year, unwilling or unable to pay the increased subscription which came into effect at the beginning of 1972. Howard implied in his own speech that the 'Crisis at the Bow Group?' letter reflected not a natural groundswell of opinion, but the surreptitious sponsorship of several members of his Council, though he did not identify them in public. But the fact that the Political Officer Norman Lamont had been pressured into investigating the Group's public relations, despite being the unopposed candidate for the chairmanship, implies that the concerns enjoyed a wider resonance or influential support. Lloyd recalls a sharp split in the Group between those who were involved – an inner circle – and those who were not, and he terms the moment the 'Peasants' Revolt'. 'You didn't get to know people unless you did something,' Lloyd believes, and it was hard to do anything unless you got to know other members. 'Then to have to pay more to be ignored,' says Lloyd, was the final straw[27]

There were additional reasons for concern: coverage of the Group was dwindling sharply. Figures from two years later showed that of relevant articles, the Monday Club received 60% of coverage, the Fabians 21%, while the Bow Group captured just 14%.[28] Independent scrutiny of the Group's press mailing list commissioned for an internal report on the Group's public relations revealed that it had been sending its work to 'people at too high a level'.[29]

A deeper insight into the situation was provided by one of the more vocal participants at the AGM, David Weeks, a young advertising executive. In a well-researched article in *Crossbow*, which demonstrated a strong understanding of the Group's historical development, Weeks attacked the Group for being pompous and reluctant to change, and serving mainly the ambitions of its Council.[30] 'Traditionally, the Bow Group likes to think that it eschews impact and publicity for their own sake but is influential in a C. P. Snow, lunch at the Club with the Under Secretary sort of way,' believed Weeks. 'Many members have a strong feeling that the lunches with Under Secretaries are being used less to promote well-researched policies and more to oil political escalators for the Group's leading lights to climb to power.' Weeks also highlighted the uncertainty over the 'no corporate view' policy and suggested that 'Chairmen of the Bow Group should curb their desires to be the only people allowed to issue press releases on behalf of the Bow Group.' Instead he believed that those who had a hand in writing a pamphlet should also have the opportunity of publicising it: a return to the more decentralised arrangement which had operated in the early 1960s. But his allegation, that the Group's publicity lay in the hands of a select circle, was corroborated in the same issue of *Crossbow*: the Editor, Christopher Bland, decided not to wait another issue before launching a robust attack against Weeks and other discontented members. 'This year's Bow Group annual general meeting veered between farce and tragedy; the usual backwoodsmen grumbling about the magic circle and the remoteness of the Council had something concrete to get their teeth into, in the shape of a proposal to increase the subscription.' Focusing on the potential cost of one of Weeks' solutions, which was to increase the support available to the Group's members, Bland observed that David Weeks' scheme did not 'marry well with resentment at increased subscriptions'.[31]

Christopher Bland's determination to get his retaliation in first – his own piece appeared at the front of *Crossbow*, Weeks' near the back – attracted an angry reply from the authors of 'Crisis at the Bow Group?', who identified themselves as Max Hanna, Eric Reynolds and Pamela Dyas in a letter to *Crossbow*.[32] They argued that they had been misrepresented: they had opposed not the subscription rise, but rather the manner in which it was put. Another letter in the same issue from Reg Simmerson also commented on the Annual General Meeting. Simmerson had been described in the previous edition as 'on the extremist fringe', since he had stood as an 'Anti-Common Market Conservative' at the recent Greenwich by-election. 'His continued membership of the Bow Group is inexplicable,' suggested 'Endymion', the anonymous author of the commentary page. Simmerson remarked that he could not remember an anti-Common Market Conservative addressing the Group in recent years. His letter went on to suggest that

> It is possible that, since the formation of the Monday Club, only left-wing Conservatives have been recruited by the Bow Group and

that this process has now gone so far as to justify your statement
that my continued membership is inexplicable. Certainly you seem
to imply that the political views of Bow Groupers now cover a
rather narrow band of the political spectrum; you also seem to
imply that you approve of this state of affairs. But political discussion is one of the main activities of the Group; will not this
discussion become sterile if right wing views are excluded?[33]

While Simmerson's political views were certainly very unusual for the
Group, it would seem that his point about the Group's breadth of views
– at least among its leaders – was not invalid in late 1971. There had
always been a temptation for the Council to pronounce on controversial
issues, but the fact that the Group's leadership was openly campaigning
in favour of Common Market membership, the coincident rise in
subscriptions and the wider discontent with the Conservative
Government from within the Bow Group brought matters to a head.

A few members of the Bow Group had good reason to feel let down
by the performance of their own party in Government. Controversy
surrounded John Davies, who had been Director-General of the
Confederation of British Industry, entered Parliament in 1970 and was
rapidly elevated to the front bench as Minister for Trade and Industry. It
was not so much what Davies himself said or did – he announced his
opposition to gearing policy to 'lame ducks' – but what happened around
him that aroused comment. No sooner had he made that commitment
than the Aviation Minister announced that the Government would lend
Rolls Royce £42 million, after Heath had cajoled existing private
investors to part with £18 million more. At the same time, the aero-
engine division was nationalised. It was sold into private hands a year
later. For Patricia Hodgson, a member of the Group who had been co-
opted onto the Bow Group Council as an assistant to the Political
Officer, the moment was a landmark disappointment. She had worked
with Nicholas Ridley on the issue of the nationalised industries at CRD
before the general election and believed that the Conservatives would
limit state intervention once in power.[34]

Although it is worth noting that Ridley had previously been attacked
in *Crossbow*'s 'Black Mark' column as 'ideological', it is clear that

Hodgson was not the only Bow Grouper alarmed by the Government's apparent change of heart; a clarion call for less Government intervention was repeatedly sounded in *Crossbow*. 'What our rulers ought to do is to cut down on the pep-talks and simply get off our necks,' believed Angus Maude.[35] Christopher Bland saw Europe as the means to strengthen competition and eliminate restrictive practices.[36] Although almost a fifth of the Group's members resigned as a result of the combination of the subscription increase and a growing sense of dissatisfaction with the Government, the Group's income remained strong. Alarmed by the turn of events, the British United Industrialists renewed their interest in the Bow Group's general support for market economics with the promise of a guaranteed income of £6,000 'over the next few years'.[37] It is notable that the BUI still regarded the Bow Group as the best channel through which to pursue its pro-enterprise objectives. More controversially, the Group also agreed to run a series of lucrative advertisements in *Crossbow* placed by the Rhodesian Government. English law prohibited *Crossbow* from encouraging emigration to Rhodesia, so the adverts obliquely invited readers to write to the Rhodesian Department of Information for more details on what the country had to offer. The combination of money from the Government of Rhodesia and the BUI meant that, by the Council meeting of 3 July 1971, it 'was agreed that the budget was too good to show to donors'.

The Government's deepening problems were to be graphically demonstrated to the Group during 1972. The Prime Minister, Edward Heath, accepted an invitation to speak at the Bow Group's 21st anniversary dinner in February 1972. But 'affairs of state' intervened. Heath had time to meet members of the Group at drinks before dinner, speak briefly, then depart to deal with an imminent crisis: the National Union of Mineworkers had decided to strike. The previous month, unemployment had broken the one million mark for the first time since 1957. To soften the news, John Davies used the consequent Commons debate on unemployment to announce a further injection of public money into the largely unviable Upper Clyde Shipbuilders consortium – in an attempt to halt further swelling of support for the Scottish Nationalists, but to further dismay among economic liberals. The events appear to have reinforced the conviction among some Bow Groupers that the Conservative Government was heading in the wrong direction, and that it was time for a radical change of policy.

Peter Lilley was usually to be found involved in encouraging the feeling that radical action was needed. As Research Secretary he regularly reviewed books for *Crossbow*. One of his reviews, published early in 1972, introduced *Crossbow* readers to the third edition of Alan Walters' IEA pamphlet, *Money in Boom and Slump*.[38] In this, Lilley admitted the incompleteness of monetarist analysis, instead stressing its topicality: 'Walters like many other monetarists introduces his theory by talking about the economic impact of a sudden increase in the money supply brought about by giving pound notes to everyone.' As the Group's Chairman two years later, Lilley would invite Walters to write a pamphlet for the Group demolishing the case for a new airport at Maplin. Although Walters was subsequently to join the Group, it was the first time an outsider had been commissioned to write. This first book review was an important indicator of the direction in which Lilley intended to push Bow Group policy.

This was a remarkably active approach from a man who just a few years earlier had been an outsider. Although, typically for a Chairman of the Group, he had studied at Cambridge, he described himself as 'not a very good activist' and he was not connected with the previous generation of Cambridge graduates, including Howard and Lamont (who had subsequently shared a flat on Harley Street), Gummer and Clarke. In other words, he was not a member of the inner circle whose seeming stranglehold on the Group's activities had caused so much friction the year before. But he 'eventually realised that if you put yourself into it, you can overcome diffidence'.[39] Even so, his rise to prominence within the Bow Group was almost accidental: at the time when he was elected Secretary of the Group – an organisational role – he was working for the UN in Tanzania, and had left it up to his friends to put him forward for the post. The first Lilley knew of the outcome of the vote was from a telegram advising him that he had lost. What did he expect, his friends asked, if he had tried to do his canvassing from an African jungle? Lilley heard no more until a call from the Bow Group's office. It was the

Group's administrator Patricia Sill Johnston, enquiring what the new Secretary wanted her to do. It transpired that John Butcher, the winner on the night, had taken the ballot papers home to destroy them, only to find on recounting them that Lilley, and not he, had won. Why he decided to conduct a recount at home remains unclear, but the following day he informed Peter Lloyd about the true result.[40]

But it was only during the following year when Peter Lilley succeeded Peter Lloyd as the Group's Research Secretary that his intellectual energy began to have an impact. He felt frustrated that his membership of the Group was held against him by the constituency parties he met while hunting for a seat: 'I would go along to interviews in safe Labour seats where Tory associations are very right-wing and they would imply that a "pinko" like me had nothing in common with blue-blooded Tories like them.'[41] In consequence, he recalls thinking that his first task was to make the Group open to the full range of Conservative thinking, believing that it had strayed from this basic tenet of its constitution. But care was needed. 'I did not want to replace a censorship of the left with a censorship of the right,' he adds, defensively.

Lilley was certainly willing to publish a number of pamphlets with which he disagreed, such as *Up, Up and Away*, the Group's support for the Vertical Take-off and Landing project and Laurance Reed's ideas for a participatory process in opening up the North Sea, in *Fish and Ships*. But the Group's most pertinent contributions had a tougher edge. Lilley himself wrote *Ulster – Do You Sincerely Want to Win?* in November 1972. The pamphlet was supposed to have been the fruit of a study group set up to investigate the options in Northern Ireland, but Lilley turns out to have been a proactive Research Secretary. 'It wasn't getting anywhere, so I took it over myself,' he remembers.[42] From then on, conducting the research for the pamphlet singlehandedly, Lilley met the commandant of the Londonderry Provisional IRA and future MP, Martin McGuinness, during a ceasefire. McGuinness had heard of the Bow Group but, Lilley believes, was expecting 'some trendy left-wing journalist'. If so, he was wrong.

The contrast between *Ulster – Do You Sincerely Want to Win?* and *Ireland: A New Partition*, written by Julian Critchley earlier in the year, could not have been more clear. 43 Whereas Critchley had unrealistically advocated the cession of the Catholic parts of Ulster to the South, Lilley argued that a political solution was not sufficient and that terrorism had to be suppressed by military force. Lilley believes that the pamphlet was the best thing he has ever written; he remembers Airey Neave describing it as his bible. Neave was later murdered in a car bomb attack by the Irish National Liberation Army in the shadow of Big Ben.

The associations which Peter Lilley made are perhaps as revealing as the Group's output. When Lilley stood for the Chairmanship in 1973, he had to beat Alan Craig, the previous year's Political Officer, to win. It was only the fifth time that the chairmanship had been contested in the history of the Group. Places on the Council that year were hotly contested so that its final make-up was less homogeneous than in previous years. Lilley described it as a mixture of the fringes of the Bow Group. Notably it included two of the three authors of 'Crisis at the Bow Group?', Max Hanna and Pamela Dyas, as well as David Weeks. Here was a Council comprising several of Lloyd's 'peasants'. But if many new Council members were united in their dislike of what had gone before, it was not clear that they shared Peter Lilley's favour of economic liberalisation and monetarism. Certainly Lilley did not believe so, a factor which may explain his decision to import Alan Walters to write on Maplin. While there is evidence to suggest that the broader membership of the Group was rattled by Lilley's style, he undoubtedly had supporters. One kindred spirit, Patricia Hodgson, succeeded him as Research Secretary. A sign of her own views on the Heath Government was provided in her conclusion to one article for *Crossbow*: 'Does not our present leadership combine, uniquely, the consistency of Disraeli with the glamour of Peel?'44

To some extent Lilley was building on his predecessor Peter Lloyd's views. When Christopher Bland resigned the editorship of *Crossbow* in the summer of 1972, Lloyd had deftly replaced him with a professional journalist, Leith McGrandle, who was the deputy City Editor of the *Sunday Telegraph* at the time. Working on a Sunday newspaper was consonant with the demands of *Crossbow*, but McGrandle also opposed Heath and seems to have agreed with Peter Lilley on many issues. The cover of McGrandle's first edition featured a cartoon by Richard Willson, depicting Heath wheelchair-bound, weighed down by an oversized broken leg, encased in a plaster marked STRIKES, INFLATION, ULSTER, MAUDLING and topped by a cluster of ranting trades unionists – which became a Willson trademark. But despite the hostile cartoon, the editorial pledged support to Heath, so long as he remained committed to reform.45 Amidst the criticism, the appointment of the Group's former Chairman, Geoffrey Howe, to the Cabinet as Minister for Trade and Consumer Affairs at the Department of Trade and Industry, went unremarked in *Crossbow*. In and out of Parliament between 1964 and 1970, Howe had been elected MP for Reigate in 1970, and was immediately appointed Solicitor General. Other Bow Group contemporaries recognised his promotion as a landmark. Among the letters of congratulation Howe received on the news of his appointment, was a short note from James Moorhouse, another of the Bow Group's earliest members. As an afterthought to his best wishes, Moorhouse added 'A great day for the Bow Group also.'46

To read the issues of *Crossbow* after January 1973, however, is to chronicle the Bow Group's orchestrated opposition to the Government in which Howe now shared responsibility. The most prominent sign of a change of heart came in the January 1973 editorial, where there were signs that the new management of the Bow Group regarded Britain's entry into Europe not as a triumph, but as a distraction from other issues. 'Much of the lack of the Government's grip noticeably last summer can be traced to the dominance of Europe in most Ministers' minds,' McGrandle argued in an editorial entitled 'We're in: Now What?' which revealed a considerably more lukewarm view of Europe than had prevailed before.47 McGrandle went on to criticise the President of the European Commission, Sicco Mansholt, for suggesting that a Prime Minister of the UK who sought to take Britain out of the EEC would find himself arraigned before the European Court of Justice. 'Nothing could have been more calculated to feed the suspicions of those who believe that the Common Market is little more than a bureaucratic and legalistic spider's web in which we are now hopelessly enmeshed,' he commented. By contrast Christine Stewart-Munro, writing in the same issue, believed that the same lack of democratic accountability presented the Group with an opportunity for research which was 'its biggest chance since it made its name with its research on African affairs. The institutions of the EEC have to be democratised, whole areas of Community policy are now in the melting pot, and the European Conservative and Christian Democratic parties will inevitably and slowly move towards common policies.'[48] However, the Group's leadership decided to put the new British European Commissioner, Christopher Soames, 'Under Fire' at the Bow Group's Party Conference fringe meeting in 1973.

The way was gradually clearing for the Group. In May 1973, *Crossbow*'s editorial analysed the disappearance of 'Selsdon Man', 'the tough confident Tory who would cut away the soft fat of Socialism and introduce a self-reliant realism to British industry,' noting, in an allusion to Shelley's tyrannical Ozymandias, that 'nothing of him remains.' It almost gleefully concluded that 'the collapse of the attitude and philosophy summed up in the "Selsdon Man" phrase has left a vacuum in Tory thinking.' Filling that vacuum would be the next task for the Bow Group because, by 1972, its main adversary, the Monday Club, had crippled itself in a well-publicised episode in which its South West London branch, led by Harvey Proctor, broke ranks and expelled its Bow Group members. Increasingly eccentric and in some cases extreme, the Club was vulnerable to criticism thereafter. Max Hanna wrote an article in *Race Today* claiming that the Club was 'in serious danger of becoming little more than a cockpit of uninformed bigotry and a breeder of demagogues'[49]. The Bow Group was becoming unchallenged once again. Peter Lilley did not believe that the Bow Group knew enough about what would come to be characterised as a 'New Right' philosophy to be able to write about it. No doubt aware of the power he had to introduce these new ideas to an influential group of young people, many of whom would become candidates and ultimately MPs, Lilley persisted with a programme designed to proselytise. He invited the Hungarian Tibor Szamuely to address the Group, since he regarded Szamuely's work – a powerful fusion of economic liberalism and traditional conservatism – as a 'touchstone of lucidity' worth emulating. Shortly afterwards, Szamuely died and Lilley took the opportunity to persuade CPC to publish a collection of Szamuely's writings under the title *Tibor Szamuely – Unique Conservative* in September 1973, six months into his chairmanship. John Ramsden describes the transformation Lilley had engineered: 'The storm-troopers of Tory progressivism had become the keenest advocates of the new economics, and as a predominantly youthful group they could also be seen as having time on their side.'[50] The Bow Group's influence was impressive: among its subscribers it numbered 50 Conservative MPs and, by October 1974, a sixth of all Tory candidates, all of whom received all the Group's publications.

At much the same time, triggered by the Government's impending financial crisis late in 1973, Lilley began to think that the Group should produce a manifesto. He remembers touring the Bow Group's study groups during the month leading up to the 1973 Party Conference garnering ideas which did not contradict one another.[51] But, judging by the reaction at the Council Meeting just one month before the Party Conference, he had not explained his plans clearly: 'The Chairman also revealed the "Alternative Manifesto" which he, the Research Secretary and the Research Liaison Officer had been working on: it was a paper telling the party that it would lose the election unless certain things were done.'[52]

The nature of the title and the secrecy with which the exercise had been conducted predictably caused concern within the Council. A Council member, Anthony Nelson, wondered what recommendations Lilley, Patricia Hodgson and Nigel Waterson had made, and questioned the implications of the title given that it had been written by just three people and the Group's commitment to having 'no corporate view'.[54] The minutes for the Council's meeting record that 'Peter Lilley agreed that Anthony Nelson's criticisms were very valid, but this publication in particular was to be produced reasonably quickly and secretly, which made advance consultation impossible.' Although he was a willing participant in the 'camaraderie, but also competition' between the Group's ambitious members, Nelson believes that there could be 'a degree of arrogance and intolerance about the Council meetings'. 'Peter [Lilley] had his own agenda,' he says today.[55]

In the introduction to the *Alternative Manifesto*, Lilley developed his idea that governments lost elections when they lost faith in their own distinctive direction and started trying to steal their opponents' clothes. Some of the themes developed in the manifesto were therefore traditional, including for example, a clean-up of pornography to 'create a decent society'. But other ideas were profoundly radical. Lilley advocated hiving off parts of the nationalised industries. He suggested the denationalisation of the Port of London Authority's dry docks, an example he chose mainly because he had done some work on the docks as a professional economist. Of course this particular idea had a blunt pertinence, given the Government's difficulties on the Upper Clyde during the previous two years. Laws to allow private enterprise to compete with nationalised industries, such as the Post Office, were also mooted. The Manifesto was most obviously a blunt warning that the Conservatives would lose the next election. It called for the amendment of Heath's 1972 Industry Act to prevent indiscriminate subsidies to industry and for competition to be brought into the public sector. It requested a Conservative pledge 'to keep monetary expansion from outstripping the growth in the economy'. And it warned that 'There is a serious danger that the Party may find itself faced with a General Election in the next 12 months without having ready a fresh, coherent electoral programme for the next five years.'

The Group never really refined the art of calculating how many pamphlets it would sell, and the Council significantly overestimated demand for the *Alternative Manifesto*. Ordering an extra 1,100 copies for sale, to bring the print run to 3,000, it managed to offload just 150 of those 1,100 to willing buyers. It is possible that, with an election in the offing, there was a limited appetite at the 1973 Party Conference for a critique of the Heath Government. The Group made a considerable loss on its attempt to broaden awareness of its new thinking.

The *Alternative Manifesto* 'made us thoroughly unpopular with the then Heath government', Waterson now recollects.[56] The simultaneously published Conference edition of *Crossbow* warned that 'the Government must show that having completed much of its 1970 programme it has not run out of ideas. This is why the Bow Group has produced an alternative Manifesto for the next five years.'[57] *Crossbow* also printed a spoof 'advance copy' of the Prime Minister's speech, written by one of the

Alternative Manifesto authors, Patricia Hodgson. 'We must say "Yes" to schemes of loss-making technology like *Concorde* and the RB.211. We must say "Yes" to vast public enterprises, costing the taxpayer millions, like Maplin. We must say "Oui" to President Pompidou,' were some of the words she inserted into the Prime Minister's mouth.[58] In line with *Crossbow*'s more sceptical tone, the *Alternative Manifesto* also took a tougher line on Britain's involvement in the EEC: it reaffirmed support for British membership, but asserted: 'We shall not hesitate to make Britain's interests clear to the rest of the Community. We are not prepared to pay a high price for entry into the EEC without the guarantee of concrete benefits now and in the future.'[59] 'Miss Hodgson', the *Daily Telegraph*'s diarist assumed, 'is not an aspirant for the Conservative Central Office list of prospective candidates.'[60]

The consequences of the *Alternative Manifesto* were to prove more immediately damaging to Peter Lilley's parliamentary ambitions. It was unheard of for a Chairman of the Bow Group to be excluded from the list of prospective candidates screened by Conservative Central Office, yet this was the position in which Lilley found himself by February 1974. Lilley remembers with some pleasure how rumblings came back that he was *persona non grata* with Heath. But at the time his isolation was highlighted by the fact that many other members of the Group had been selected as candidates. Among them was Alan Clark, whose name appeared on a list of Bow Group members who were candidates. Asked for his occupation, he had written 'Son of Lord Clark, CH KCB'.[61] Regardless of his own membership, Clark gave a typically acidic vignette of the Group when he recorded speaking to the Oxford branch of the Group at All Souls College, just after his selection, in November 1972.

> Yesterday I was in confident form. I had been invited to address a Bow Group dinner, black tie, good claret (or so I would assume), F. E. Smith in his early days. My apotheosis. But the Bow Group are just a bunch of arse-lickers really. Creepy little aspirant candidates who tremble at the thought, still less the sound of someone Right Wing. And they all have one thing in common, namely that they all want to enter Parliament. In the past they used to shun me,

probably on instruction from Central Office, but now here I am with, having been adopted for Plymouth Sutton, something of an *edge*.[62]

Wounded by his own failure to be selected, Lilley recalled the suggestion of his predecessor as Chairman of the Group, Peter Lloyd, that he should stay on for a second year. Lloyd was widely regarded as the most effective Chairman for several years, and his term in office, when he had tried to boost the Group's finances and its publications, had passed unremarkable in its efficiency. Lloyd discovered a crucial eccentricity of one of the Group's major patrons, Siegmund Warburg, when he came to ask him for money again during his year in office. 'Would I write him a letter in my own handwriting?' Lloyd recalls. It transpired that Warburg relied on a graphologist for advice, and it was only when Lloyd's script was deemed to display the right qualities that Warburg posted him a cheque.[63]

Lilley's decision to take his predecessor's advice gave the Group the continuity which an annual changeover of officers made difficult. There were more obvious political reasons than the smooth administration of the Group to take into account, however, and these were doubtless a factor in his decision to stand for the chairmanship again in 1974. Again he won, this time with no opposition. Only two previous Chairmen, James Lemkin and David Hennessy, had returned to serve a second year; after Lemkin, Lilley was the second Chairman to do so in consecutive years.

The Group stood still during 1974, though its opposition to the Conservative Government's economic policy intensified. The stasis was not the fault of its officers, but the logical consequence of the two General Elections which punctuated the year in February and October. Ninety-three members of the Group stood in the February election, of whom 46 were elected, a net increase of seven, although the election marked defeat for Edward Heath. There were just three editions of *Crossbow*, in January, June and December, and Council meetings assumed a perfunctory character. Nevertheless, the Group organised personal assistants for a number of MPs during the February election

and a team of 'wise men' to answer candidates' questions during the
October campaign, when 109 members stood for election. Having
eventually made the candidates' list, Peter Lilley fought and lost
Tottenham and Haringey to Norman Atkinson. He invited Atkinson to
address the Group in the spring of 1975 – the first Labour MP to do so
since Richard Crossman some five years earlier. Lilley tried to vary the
programme during his second year as Chairman. An eclectic group of
speakers included the historian Norman Cohn, whose book *The Pursuit
of the Millennium* Lilley greatly admired (and whose story of medieval
radicalism bears more than a passing resemblance to Lilley's own
ideological crusade) and the zoo-owner John Aspinall, whom Lilley had
met through Alan Clark. In his diary, Clark recorded that Aspinall's talk
had been 'only moderate'.[64]

Lilley did not allow the elections to force the Group to conform
throughout 1974. Although a paper on *The Next General Election*,
dated 4 January 1974, unsurprisingly declared the Group's strategy to be
to 'help the Conservative Party win as many seats as possible, our
members to get elected and our image to be protected in the Press and
within the Party as a result of this', Patricia Hodgson encouraged the
Group to compare the official manifesto critically with the Group's
alternative. Although several of its officers must have wanted to see
Heath gone, the Council planned a victory party if the Government
retained power. Of course the Government failed, there was no party,
and the June edition of *Crossbow* set out to examine what went wrong.
'Much thinking has already gone on within the party and this edition is
a contribution to it.' Gordon Pepper, who worked with Lilley, remembered how a Bow Group Conference at Magdalen College, Oxford,
quickly turned into a post-mortem after he gave a withering attack on
the prices and incomes policy to an audience in which the former
'Minister for Prices', Geoffrey Howe, was seated in the front row. Pepper
recalled how, after this first meeting, he was quickly invited to
contribute: 'The upshot was that Geoffrey introduced me to Sir Keith
Joseph and Robert Carr, the latter being the Shadow Chancellor. In
November Margaret Thatcher became Robert Carr's assistant
spokesman on Treasury matters and I soon met her.'[65]

Lilley tried to counteract the tendency of an impending second General Election to cause inertia by demanding a rethink in the Group's publication *Lessons for Power*. 'Conservatives must recognise that Trades Unions do not cause inflation. They may, by pricing workers out of jobs, create unemployment. But it is governments who create inflation, especially if they attempt to reduce unemployment by expanding demand. Such well-meaning attempts are in the end always unsuccessful.'[66] As Ramsden has observed, 'This was three months before Joseph's speech at Preston argued the same case.'[67] But the Conservative leadership was unmoved. To offer different policies to the electorate at a second election would be an admission that the party had been wrong in February. What thinking there was produced no new action.

The failure of the Tories to regain power in October turned the spotlight on Heath and produced perhaps the single most important editorial *Crossbow* had published to date. It appeared in December 1974, written by the new Editor, the former Chairman Peter Lloyd, who had succeeded Leith McGrandle. 'I changed *Crossbow* cheaply for the better,' says Lloyd, who pursued a 'ragged' style of 'the unresourced genius in the garret'.[68] Whereas it was decided in the aftermath of the February election that 'the Bow Group should not meddle in any "leadership crisis",'[69] later in the year the Group took a more active role. One consequence of the October election had been the postponement of the autumn edition of *Crossbow*, and it was with publication impending that Edward Heath appeared at the Group's annual cocktail party on 4 November. Two diarists described the scene:

> I had not realised what terrible trouble Ted Heath was in until I saw him this week at the Bow Group's annual party. To describe him as exuding bonhomie might be thought to be pushing matters a bit far: still, the fact remains that no fellow in the room was safe from being hailed as well-met.[70]

> Edward Heath did not stay long, perhaps put out by having to shoulder his way through the thick crowds. As he barged past me I heard him say to an aide: 'I'll just move around a bit and then I'll quickly disappear.' He was, no doubt, talking about his strategy

just for the evening, but the consensus among the Bow Groupers I
spoke to was that Heath should and would quietly disappear from
the leadership before long. The questions were whether he should
go now or later and, most crucially who should succeed him.[71]

Lloyd was recovering from fighting West Nottingham, and he was
relieved to be able to delay *Crossbow* for another five and a half weeks
while opposition to Heath began to crystallise. The press began to
speculate that the publication of an internal report by Alec Douglas-
Home setting out new rules for a leadership election might force Heath
to step down.[72] But what became clear was Heath's determination to
fight off any challenge. This dictated the tone of the Group's editorial.
Given the weight of opposition to Edward Heath, Lloyd today says he felt
obliged to write an editorial suggesting the Tory leader give way. But 'I
had absolutely no idea who should replace him.'[73] Either he or Lilley
decided to give the editorial the maximum effect by playing up the
Group's left-of-centre reputation, although neither of them fitted the
mould. On the day that Douglas-Home's report was published, a Bristol
regional newspaper mentioned that 'A broadside is expected soon from
the Bow Group which could normally be expected to support Mr Heath.
Instead it is expected to urge that he should stand down as an act of
statesmanship.'[74] By casting the Group in this way as a barometer of the
type of opinion Heath would have to convince, were he to retain the
leadership in a right-wing challenge, Lilley and Lloyd heightened the
impact of the editorial, which thus appeared to swing away from Heath.
The spectacle of a well-known sector of the Conservatives changing sides
caught the attention of the press.

'It is clear that the bulk of the Parliamentary Party are unhappy with
Mr Heath's continued leadership', and that activists 'do not look forward
to fighting the next election with him at their head,' Lloyd began. '. . .
The major argument against Mr Heath's continued leadership is not that
the Party with him at its head will find it much harder to win elections,
but that under him it has ceased to know where it is going and what it
stands for . . . It would . . . be an act of great statesmanship if Mr Heath
finally decided to stand down,' he argued, in a turn of phrase that was

widely picked up by the press. This argument revealed the widespread concern that none of Heath's potential challengers was willing or able to throw down the gauntlet. 'At the moment the spectacle of Mr Heath's potential rivals is like that of the English cricket team in Australia. All the best people are either in the wrong country, have retired hurt or have got themselves out by kindergarten strokes,' remarked *The Times'* leader for 18 December. It was in this context that the newspaper reported the *Crossbow* article as a call to Heath's opponents not to stand down. It is hard to assess how much the Bow Group's contribution mattered. The papers certainly interpreted one man's *Crossbow* editorial as a much broader shift away from Edward Heath; but this was happening anyway.

It is indisputable, however, that Lloyd's editorial was a withering attack on the Party Leader and it led directly to the MP Sir Anthony Meyer's resignation from the Group. 'I thought: "I may have done myself in",' Lloyd remembers, referring to his Parliamentary aspirations and his consequent summons to Conservative Central Office, where it became clear that he had been removed from the candidates' list. By that time, Heath had resigned, and Lloyd was asked whether he would like to be reinstated. 'Margaret Thatcher saved me,' he laughs today.75

But although, in a distortion of its 'no corporate view' position, the Group opposed Heath, it did not take sides in the contest which followed. Peter Lilley privately urged Geoffrey Howe to stand, and became his speechwriter and bag carrier for the duration of the campaign, really out of loyalty to him as a distinguished member of the Group, since he did not think that Howe should or would become leader. Howe enjoyed a similarly lukewarm endorsement from other former Bow Group members. He was 'the intelligent man's abstention', believed Ken Clarke, since 'he combined right-wing economics with left-wing social policy, the old Bow Group combination.'76

Lilley handled the coincidence of the leadership contest with the Group's annual dinner with care. Previous Bow Group Chairmen had tried to pick rising stars to speak at the Group's annual dinners. But Lilley did not ask Sir Keith Joseph to address the Group's annual dinner until it was clear that he would not stand in the leadership campaign. Given the timing of the dinner, he could have asked just about anyone to speak. By coincidence the dinner was held on the night of the second ballot. News of the result was brought to Lilley during the meal. 'The best man has won,' he announced. 'It was a simultaneously supportive and slightly cheeky' way to put Mrs Thatcher's victory, he says in retrospect.77 And it was a tacit admission that in public he felt obliged, at times, to recognise a greater diversity of views within the Group than he had accommodated during the previous two years.

———————

NOTES

1   Heath, *The Course of My Life*, p. 304.

2   Howard, interview, 13 April 1999

3   They were: Mark Carlisle, Christopher Chataway, Reginald Eyre, Michael Heseltine, Terence Higgins, Sir Geoffrey Howe, David Howell, Patrick Jenkin.

4   Londoner's Diary, *Evening Standard*, 26 June 1970.

5   Council Minutes, 6 July 1970.

6   Council Minutes, 6 July 1970, Appendix A: 'Research 1970/71'.

7   Nicholas Scott, 'Iain Macleod: Obituary', *Crossbow*, October 1970, pp. 8–9. Scott was MP Paddington South, 1966–February 1974; Kensington and Chelsea, October 1974–1997.

8   Shepherd, *Iain Macleod*, p. 527. Hayhoe was MP for Heston and Isleworth, 1970–74; Brentford and Isleworth, 1974–92. He was a Minister of State at the Treasury, 1981–85; Minister for Health, 1985–86.

9   Editorial, *Crossbow*, October–December 1970, p. 5.

10   Editorial, *Crossbow*, October–December 1970, p. 5.

11   Meyer entered Parliament after a career in the FCO. He was MP for Eton and Slough 1964–66; West Flint 1970–83; Clywd North West, 1983–92.

12   'Crosstalk', *Crossbow*, October–December 1970, p. 7.

13   *Sunday Times*, 20 September 1970.

14   Heath, *The Course of My Life*, pp. 457–8.

15   Bow Group Council, Minutes, 11 January 1971.

16   Nigel Ashford, *The Conservative Party and European Integration 1945–75*, Unpublished PhD thesis, Warwick University, 1983, p. 118. It is difficult to improve on Dr Ashford's detailed analysis of the Bow Group's role in the Conservative Party's European policy.

17 'Markeeters Carry the Rally on Shouting Power', *Times*, 7 June 1971.

18 Norman Lamont, *In Office*, London 1999, p. 449. It was Lamont's first public rally. President of the Cambridge Union and Chairman of the University Conservative Association, Clarke was elected MP for Rushcliffe in 1970. He was Minister for Health 1982–85, Paymaster General and Minister for Employment 1985–87; Chancellor of the Duchy of Lancaster and Minister for Trade and Industry 1987–88; Secretary of State for Health, 1988–90; for Education and Science 1990–92; Home Secretary 1992–93; Chancellor of the Exchequer, 1993–97. His Cambridge contemporary John Gummer was also President of the Cambridge Union and Chairman of CUCA. He entered Parliament as MP Lewisham West, 1970–February 1974; for Eye, Suffolk, 1979–83; for Suffolk Coastal since 1983. A Minister in various Government departments, he was Minister of Agriculture, Fisheries and Food, 1989–93; Secretary of State for the Environment, 1993–97.

19 Jenkins, interview.

20 Bow Group Council, Minutes, 22nd March 1970.

21 Christine Stewart-Munro, *Report to the Bow Group Council on European Liaison*, 12 June 1973.

22 'Mainland or Open Sea', *Crossbow*, July–September 1971, p. 5.

23 Graham Hallett, 'British Agriculture and Europe', *Crossbow* Supplement No.1, Spring 1961.

24 'You Too Can Enter Parliament', *Crossbow*, October–December 1969, p. 27.

25 The Bow Group, Minutes of the 20th Annual General Meeting, 29 April 1971.

26 Bow Group Council, Minutes, 28 March 1971. Koops unsuccessfully contested Wakefield in 1974.

27 Lloyd, interview.

28 Bow Group Council, Minutes, 5 February 1973.

29 Bow Group Council, Minutes, 21 April 1971, Appendix A: Report of the Publications Sub-Committee.

30 David Weeks, 'The Future of the Bow Group', *Crossbow* July–September 1971, pp. 40–3. Weeks was for many years a Westminster councillor.

31 'Annual General Fracas', *Crossbow*, July–September 1971, p. 7.

32 Letters, *Crossbow*, October–December 1971, p. 37.

33 Letters, *Crossbow*, October–December 1971, pp. 36–7. An indefatigable campaigner against European integration throughout his life, Simmerson died in 1998.

34 Patricia Hodgson, interview, 15 June 1999.

35 Angus Maude, 'The Land of Smiles?', *Crossbow*, April 1971, pp. 8–10.

36 Editorial, *Crossbow*, January–March 1972, p. 5.

37 Bow Group Council, Minutes, 10 January 1972.

38 Peter Lilley, Economic Fashions, *Crossbow*, January–March 1972, p. 43.

39 Lilley, *House Magazine*, 13 May 1991, quoted in Riddell, *Honest Opportunism*, p. 97.

40 The Rt Hon. Peter Lilley MP, interview, 13 April 1999. Lilley was MP for St Albans, 1983–97; Hitchin and Harpenden, 1997–. He was Economic Secretary to the Treasury, 1987–89; Financial Secretary 1989–90; Secretary of State for Trade and Industry 1990–92; for Social Security 1992–97.

41 Lilley, *House Magazine*, 13 May 1991, quoted in Riddell, *Honest Opportunism*, p. 97.

42 Lilley, interview.

43 Julian Critchley, *Ireland: A New Partition*, April 1972.

44 Patricia Hodgson, 'Peel versus Disraeli', *Crossbow*, January 1973, p. 15.

45 'Paying the Price of Reform', *Crossbow*, August–September 1972, p. 5.

46 Moorhouse to Howe, 9 November 1972. Moorhouse was MEP for London South, 1979–84; London South and Surrey East, 1984–99.

47 'We're In: Now What?', *Crossbow*, January 1973, p. 4.

48 Christine Stewart-Munro, 'Eurobowgroup', *Crossbow*, January 1973, p. 23.

49 Reported *Daily Telegraph*, 4 February 1972.

50 Ramsden, *The Winds of Change*, p. 419.

51 Lilley, interview.

52 Bow Group Council, Minutes, 3 September 1973.

53 Anthony Nelson was MP for Chichester October 1974–97. He was Economic Secretary, then Minister of State at the Treasury, 1992–95 and a Minister at the DTI, 1995–97. A Haringey councillor for several years in the 1970s, Patricia Hodgson gave up politics to concentrate on a career at the BBC. She was Director of Policy and Planning at the BBC 1993–2000; Chief Executive of the Independent Television Commission, 2000–. Nigel Waterson was elected MP for Eastbourne in 1992.

54 Anthony Nelson, telephone conversation with the author, 30 September 2000.

55 'Tories Could Face Defeat in Election – Bow Group', *Financial Times*, 9 October 1973.

56 Nigel Waterson, letter to the author, 22 April 1999.

57 'Now is the Time', *Crossbow*, October 1973, p. 4.

58 '*Crossbow* Exclusive', *Crossbow*, October 1973, p. 46.

59 Lilley, Hodgson and Waterson, *The Alternative Manifesto*, Bow Group, October 1973.

60 'Peterborough', *Daily Telegraph*, 4 October 1973.

61 *Sunday Times*, 24 February 1974.

62 Clark, *Diaries: Into Politics*, London 2000, p. 18. Undated entry in November 1972. Clark was MP for Plymouth Sutton February 1974–92, during which time he was Minister for Trade, 1986–89; Minister at the MoD 1989–92. After five years out of Parliament he was returned for Kensington and Chelsea from 1997 until his death in 1999.

63 Lloyd, interview.

64 Lilley, interview; Clark, Diaries: *Into Politics*, p. 62. Entry for Friday 17 January 1975.

65 Gordon Pepper, *Inside Thatcher's Monetarist Revolution*, London 1998.

66 A. Dalton et al., *Lessons for Power*, Bow Group, June 1974.

67 Ramsden, *Winds of Change*, p. 419.

68 Lloyd, interview.

69 Bow Group Council, Minutes, 4 March 1974.

70 London Diary, *New Statesman*, 8 November 1974.

71 Diary, *The Times*, 6 November 1974.

72 Under the old system the winner simply had to gain 15% more votes than the next best placed candidate. The Home formula required the incumbent leader to win 65%, making an outright win in the first round considerably harder. Rumours of this formula intensified the pressure on Heath to stand down, 'Pressure on Ted – "Stand Down"', *Evening Standard*, 16 December 1974.

73 Lloyd, interview.

74 'D-Day for Heath in Poll Threat', *Western Daily Press*, 17 December 1974.

75 Lloyd, interview.

76 Quoted in Ramsden, *The Winds of Change*, p. 451.

77 Lilley, interview.

Six

MONETARISM, BUT NO MONEY: 1975–80

Commentators believed that the Bow Group was in a strong position in the Conservative Party led by Margaret Thatcher. Shortly after Thatcher was elected, Peter Lilley retired as Chairman, to be replaced by his Research Secretary, Patricia Hodgson. Hodgson was Lilley's natural ideological successor, since she had been his close ally for the previous two years, although she was described misleadingly in *The Times* as 'a Tory romantic of an earlier – and congenial school'.[1] She was deeply dissatisfied with the Heath Government, and her support for Thatcher was well known. Allegations at the Annual General Meeting in 1975 that the Group had an increasingly anti-Heathite corporate view were fuelled by her uncontested election. Although Lilley reported that 'Several publications of conflicting views had been published' to defuse this protest, it was clear that the Group had moved against Heath, in terms of its public pronouncements on party matters: early in 1975 the *Economist* described the Group positively as 'a monetarist, free market only shrine'.[2] Anthony Nelson sees it in a different light, believing that the period saw efforts to 'railroad' the Group.[3] In the context of political developments following Thatcher's election, this was pragmatically recognised as being good for the Group and its members.

Whereas the Group could not have openly endorsed Thatcher's candidature without compromising its constitutional 'no corporate view', it became a vocal supporter of the new Party leader with friends in high places following the Shadow Cabinet reshuffle. Geoffrey Howe unexpectedly became Shadow Chancellor. Douglas French, who was first Secretary, then Research Secretary, of the Group, became Howe's research assistant, cementing the link between the Group and its most high-profile alumnus.4 Through French, Howe regularly picked the Group's brains for research during the following years. From September 1975, Christine Stewart-Munro, who ran the Group's Parliamentary liaison scheme, strengthened relations with the Parliamentary Party with a sophisticated scheme which paired MPs with Bow Group researchers. Group members were allocated specific projects and also drafted Parliamentary Questions for MPs. Among 19 MPs who benefited from the scheme were Norman Fowler, Kenneth Baker, Nigel Lawson, Nicholas Ridley and Michael Heseltine.5

The Group also made some play of the coincidence that women ran both it and the Conservative Party. This gave the Group the impression of being closely in tune with the leadership and, helped by numerous profiles of Howe which almost invariably mentioned his involvement in the Group in his youth, it was increasingly seen as an important barometer of political opinion. It was perhaps because of this that Margaret Thatcher accepted the Group's early invitation to speak at its 25th anniversary dinner in 1976. The Group quickly reciprocated with reinforced support for her in the September issue of *Crossbow*, which coincided with Thatcher's strong attack on the 'British disease' in New York. It was unusual for a politician, even in Opposition, to be so critical of domestic government to a foreign audience. The *Sun* described her speech as 'astonishing'. 'If the Leader of the Opposition has at last decided to stop pussy-footing around the major issues of the day, that is all to the good. She has been too cool for too long,' the *Sun* said: 'Critics inside the Tory Party say the same thing. *Crossbow*, magazine of the Tory Bow Group, yesterday came out with a call for the party to rally behind Mrs Thatcher's leadership. But how can they rally behind a leader who for so much of the time doesn't seem to be going anywhere?'6 The Group's decision to back Thatcher in print in September 1975 was followed up in October with a sympathetic interview conducted by Norman Lamont and published in *Crossbow*, in which Thatcher was able to expand her core ideas of personal and democratic freedom and an approach to the unions. 'I do not think it is advisable to seek head on clashes on great issues,' she told Lamont.7

The Group's public presence continued to grow, helped by Hodgson's formidable public speaking at the 1975 Party Conference, which was praised in public by Sir Keith Joseph and in private by Lord Thorneycroft. While there was little consensus on the solution to the inflationary crisis, there was increasing agreement that the state was unable to do better than society left to its own devices. The Bow Group benefited from being identified as part of a coalition advocating a position increasingly seen as common sense: a dilution of state power. 'Is it altogether surprising', asked a *Daily Telegraph* leader, 'if many politicians who cannot easily be classified as doctrinaire – Mr David Howell for instance – now seek to reduce the size of the State by selling off local authority housing? Or if the Bow Group is to be found alongside Mr Arthur Seldon, advocating charges for certain local authority services?'[8] The *Economist* portrayed Patricia Hodgson, and the Bow Group, as an important voice for the free market within the Conservative Party, although it observed that 'She is out of tune with her members only in being lukewarm about, if not actively against the Common Market.'[9] This was a notable sea-change from 1973, when the Group's leaders had barely questioned whether Britain should join the Common Market.

Patricia Hodgson's self-appointment as a missionary for the free market message put a severe strain upon the Group's finances. Considerable political capital had been invested by the Council into new thinking since the publication of the *Alternative Manifesto*, but it was not matched by sufficient funds and the *Alternative Manifesto* itself had registered a loss. The Council was forced to confront the consequences of its expansionary aims early the following year, when it was presented with two possible budgets. Budget A permitted expenditure of £9,575, while Budget B represented a significant expansion of activity costing £13,475, centred on more meetings, a more ambitious programme for the annual Party Conference and a large increase in expenditure on publications. It would be financed by a more aggressive membership drive, and increased fundraising. Michael Stern, then the Group's Treasurer, outlined the proposals: 'Budget A would involve a cut back in activities in order that the Group be maintained at roughly the same financial level as at present. Budget B would allow the Group to continue its programme of expansion, but would probably run the risk of the Group being in a serious financial position by 1976, probably requiring a substantial increase in subscriptions unless new sources of money could be found. He felt that if activities were cut back, the contraction of the Group would probably be permanent.'[10] Given the aims of the Council, a contraction was unthinkable. The Council agreed to expand.[11]

It is easy to see why this risky policy appealed, given the energy of the Group's decision-makers. Patricia Hodgson recalls 'a terrific feeling of crusade' within the Group at the time.[12] But the wider climate in 1974 did not favour the strategy. The Group traditionally lost members as the Tories lost power. This was as true in 1973–5 as it had been in 1963–4. The Council wanted to expand because it wanted to build support for an alternative to the Conservative Government's policies. But the same factor which motivated the Group – the Tories' failure to find a remedy to Britain's problems – also made it difficult to achieve the increase in the membership on which the Group's successful expansion depended. To bring in the subscription revenue it needed, the Group had to expand its membership by 100, to bring the total to around 1,020. Even at the time it should not have been surprising that it failed, given that a small-scale advertising campaign – the medium for the recruitment drive – had already proved a disappointment on previous attempts. The failure to attract more members spelled the beginning of serious financial problems for the Group, which began the following year and worsened, as Stern had predicted, in 1976.

Despite taking a risky decision, the Group fell victim to circumstances beyond its control. Its precarious finances were dealt a severe blow by a sharp increase in the rent on the Bow Group office at 240 High Holborn. The Group had moved to High Holborn in 1963 and since 1966, when the rent was first sharply increased, the office had been a growing liability. Nevertheless, the Group had rejected a plan to move to premises on Oxford Street and stayed put, renting out one of its rooms to make ends meet. By 1971, the Group's total expenditure on 240 High Holborn, including rent, rates and electricity, was £1,148, a sum which represented just under a quarter of the Group's income before donations.

Amid escalating inflation, protracted negotiations over the renewal of the lease and the rent between the Group and its landlord reopened in early 1974. The Group offered £1,000 for the following year. On 1 April 1974, the Council heard that 'the Landlords were being very tough on the new lease.' The landlords' final offer, of £1,900, represented a near doubling of the rental which the Group had to pay. This rise was the beginning of a series of rent increases, which the Group was able to escape only when it finally raised enough money to make good the premises, a condition which the contract stipulated, but which the Group was not able to meet for a further 20 years. For the time being it was forced to suffer the rent increases, because the state of dilapidation was too great to remedy. 'Dickensian it certainly was: not quite Hogarthian,' remembers one of the Group's administrators, Lynda MacKenzie:

> The electrical wiring would probably have put kinks in the hair of any health and safety inspector who could make it up the stairs. One day we discovered the ancient gas pipe in one of the cupboards was leaking. The gas company ordered 'No Smoking' until it could be capped. This made for one of the shortest and most fragrant Council meetings ever. There was panic when one latecomer, who had not received the fearsome warning at the beginning of the meeting, casually began to light up. At least four people were set to pounce on the cigarette lighter.[13]

Inflation, which led the landlords to shorten the lease to six months and renovate the common parts of the building, took its toll on the Group's finances. In a cunning, but desperate attempt to limit the scale of possible redevelopment – and so the justification for further rent rises – the Treasurer, Alan Bradley, applied to have 240 High Holborn Listed. His application was eventually rejected on the grounds that the property was 'not suitably historic'.[14]

The rise in rent was compounded by the effect of two election defeats in 1974, following which donation income was dramatically reduced. The British United Industrialists sharply reduced their support from the £7,000 they had given in 1973 to £5,000 in 1974. The only other donation the Group received that year was for £250, which left the Group substantially short of the £9,750 target on which it had based its budget. It escaped the consequences of its optimistic guesstimate because the General Elections sharply reduced its activity. That year it produced fewer pamphlets and one fewer edition of *Crossbow*, and saved any expense at the Party Conference, which was cancelled.

Though it can hardly be said to be the cause of the Bow Group's financial problems, the fact that the BUI had reduced the size of its donation was important. While the Group was surely wrong to antici-pate the sum it would get, never before had the amount the BUI had paid to the Group been reduced. Whether the BUI diverted money to the Conservatives to fight the election, or whether it simply withheld the money in opposition to the Heath Government's policies, is hard to tell. A comment which may suggest that relations between the Bow Group and the BUI had been somewhat frosty came at the end of 1975, when Bradley mentioned a recent 'improvement in our relations with our principal donor'. In 1975, the BUI gave the group £6,000, while other sources introduced to the Group by its patron John Baring contributed a total of £1,800.[15] But the underlying problem remained: the Group was not attracting enough new recruits, nor was a reduced programme of events enough to retain existing members. Despite the upturn in donations in 1975, the Group turned a £1,300 surplus in 1973 into a £1,886 debt that year.[16] The Conservative Party as a whole fared similarly, on a larger scale. By March 1975, the Party had accrued a debt of £1.2 million.[17]

None the less, Peter Lilley's political achievement in positioning the Group close to the centre of the 'New Right' provided some relief from the financial crisis. One of the perks of Opposition for the Bow Group was that it was much easier to get speakers from the Shadow Cabinet. The Group was sufficiently notable that not only did Margaret Thatcher agree to speak at the Group's 25th anniversary dinner, but Harold Macmillan, Alec Douglas-Home and Edward Heath all accepted invita-tions to attend. The event promised to offer a spectacular photo-opportunity, since it would be one of the first occasions at which Thatcher and Heath were both present in the same room since the leader-ship election.

This was no small achievement. Together, the two had launched the Conservative 'Yes' campaign to stay in the EEC in April 1975. Heath's pre-eminent role in the negotiations during the previous Parliament meant that even though he had returned to the backbenches inside the House of Commons, outside he remained an important national figure in the referendum campaign which ended on 5 June. Although his fall from office had been recent, his relations with Thatcher were cordial. This changed when Heath was openly hostile to Thatcher at the Party Conference in October 1975. By March the following year, the difficulty of ensuring that Thatcher and Heath would sit in the same room, let alone at the same table, seemed increasingly insurmountable. As a result Patrick Cosgrave, Thatcher's Political Secretary, was unwilling to admit the press to the dinner. When, on the morning of the dinner, Hodgson pushed again, Cosgrave threatened that Mrs Thatcher would pull out of the engagement. But luck was on Hodgson's side. At lunchtime on the day of the dinner, 16 March 1976, Harold Wilson announced his resignation. Mindful of the positive headline which an apparent rapprochement between Heath and Thatcher would now bring, Hodgson argued a final time for a photographer to be admitted: Cosgrave relented.[18] As the newspapers broke the news of Wilson's resignation the following day, the *Times* carried a unique picture of the three ex-Prime Ministers and Mrs Thatcher happily chatting together before the dinner.

But the evening started inauspiciously. Although Thatcher and Hodgson had agreed on what to wear so that there was no match, Hodgson changed her mind at the last minute. 'You said you'd wear blue,' were Margaret Thatcher's first words to her when it transpired that both had arrived wearing matching cream outfits. More worryingly, with minutes to go before dinner was due to begin, there was no sign of Heath. It was Christine Stewart-Munro who found the former Prime Minister, whom, it was later uncharitably suspected, had been biding his time in the cloakroom to upstage Mrs Thatcher, who was already nervous at the prospect of speaking in front of three previous Prime Ministers. On the high table, Heath was shouting criticisms of Mrs Thatcher at Macmillan, who had become quite deaf. 'I don't know how you can be so calm,' commented Thatcher to Hodgson as they ate. But there was not much conversation: Thatcher spent much of the dinner re-reading and altering the text of her speech. Afterwards she sent a note to Hodgson apologising for her preoccupation and inviting her for a drink in the Leader of the Opposition's offices inside Big Ben. Nerves had got the better of Thatcher that night; Patricia Hodgson's speech, recalled Nirj Deva, was, by contrast, a great deal better. Indeed, he cites the strong impression she made on him as one reason why he decided to throw himself wholeheartedly into the Group's activities.[19]

Hodgson was an important asset to the Group, not only for her striking public speaking ability, but for her connections with the developing free market network around Westminster, through the IEA in particular. This was important not least because of the foundation by Sir Keith Joseph and Margaret Thatcher of the Centre for Policy Studies. From one description of the CPS it is easy to see why it posed a threat to the Bow Group, whether intentional or not, since it impinged on the latter's territory. 'The aim of the CPS was to get at the fairly small number of people who influence the thinking of a nation. It was comparable to the Fabian Society.'[20] Although the CPS was principally seen as a threat to the dominance of the Conservative Research Department in policy matters, it was clear that any additional heavyweight body would exert a new gravitational force on the financial goodwill on which the Bow Group had relied to date. The issue of future funding was serious since the CPS, like the Bow Group, had to maintain the impression that it was not poaching money which might otherwise have gone to the Party: both organisations were thus reliant on similar sources. Moreover, from being a somewhat awkward onlooker in the Conservative policy hierarchy, the CPS was thrust to the centre of formal policy-making when Thatcher won the leadership election in March. Significantly, the CPS was a professional organisation. If its staff was small, and poorly paid, it none the less could make a full-time input where the Bow Group was a voluntary and, with the exception of its two secretaries, a part-time activity. In this respect, a pertinent illustration of the attractiveness of the CPS is the fact that it was a relatively unknown Bow Grouper, the 29-year-old Martin Wassell, who became, albeit briefly, the full-time General Director of the new think-tank.

It was not simply that the Centre for Policy Studies attracted money which might otherwise have gone to the Bow Group; it threatened to eclipse the Bow Group, as well as other parts of the Conservative Party. Most obviously affected was the Research Department, since the work of the Centre appeared to trespass on its broad free-thinking remit in Opposition. But in an institutional sense, the CPS did not encroach on the CRD's day-to-day work. Its task reflected that the thinking had largely been done; study groups convened by the Centre existed to explore the ramifications of the central market idea rather than different and competing ideas. But the CPS did place a question mark over the Bow Group's relevance. Like the Group, the CPS was conceived as a half-in, half-out organisation which was both independent and yet influential. But its existence reflected the fact that the Conservative leadership was set on a particular philosophy.

This put the Bow Group in a quandary, because much as Hodgson approved of the leadership, the Group was committed to 'no corporate view', and it was thus impossible for it to have the same single-minded purpose that the CPS had. Moreover, the search was now for method, and a strategy of dissemination, rather than further research. The Group was at a disadvantage, because the criticism of the CRD that it was unfitted to this sort of work, since it was staffed by young graduates with little, if any, experience of the commercial world, could be applied to the Bow Group, if to a reduced degree. Increasingly, older people with business experience were involved in developing policy-making and a strategy for Government.

That said, there was still room for the Group in the policy-making process, and Hodgson's connections ensured it was not overlooked. In a fit of forward thinking in the autumn of 1975, Sir Keith Joseph fired off three letters to the Bow Group requesting research on foreign aid expenditure by June 1976, help with speechwriting on housing policy (following his reading the Group pamphlet *Towards Freedom in Housing*, which he found 'full of useful material') and a report on the Post Office monopoly, copies of which he wanted delivered to himself and Michael Heseltine.[21] Hodgson replied to confirm that a Bow Group team headed by Peter Lilley could undertake the foreign aid work, but that 'On the Post Office I must be honest and say that David Alexander and Stephen Eyres of the Selsdon Group would have the expertise more closely at their fingertips than anyone else I can think of.' By being frank about the Group's strengths – Lilley had worked in Tanzania for the UN – and its weaknesses, Hodgson did not inflate expectations of the Group beyond what it could deliver.[22]

The Council discovered in May 1976 that no pressure group could hold a stall at the Party Conference later that year, though this was perhaps as much a reaction to the fractious behaviour of the Federation of Conservative Students at the time. Perhaps Ian Clarke, the incoming Chairman, seemed unduly optimistic when he said, in the same month, that the Bow Group had a good opportunity to influence the Party during the year ahead.[23] But events seemed to favour his belief. The papers made great play of his open letter to Thatcher, published on the eve of the 1976 Party Conference, which asked Mrs Thatcher: 'What would you do if the miners, railmen and dockers take you on?' A month earlier, the Group had demonstrated that it still had the power to shock, when it gained a lot of publicity for an open letter it wrote to David Ennals, the Secretary of State for Social Services. Coinciding with a Royal Commission which was considering the future of the NHS, the Group proposed a slimmer health service, in which ill smokers would be forced to pay for the cost of their treatment.[24] But it was unable to follow up numerous consequent bids for interviews, because all the authors were either away on business or too busy with work. The Council admitted that 'this cannot fail but give a very amateurish impression of the Group to the media.'[25] The lack of money was apparently compounded by a lack of organisation.

As these low-cost ambushes implied, the Group's ability to involve itself effectively in Opposition policy-making was severely limited by its shortage of money. Douglas French recalled how the Treasurer, Richard Simmons, had refused to countenance the addition of a card back cover to make Bow Group memoranda less flimsy on grounds of extra cost. The size of the financial problem was revealed at the Annual General Meeting in 1976, where Hodgson spoke for a motion raising the subscription by 50%, pointing out that the 'continuance of the Group was at stake'.[26] She had hinted at the consequences of the Group's financial problems in her annual report, in which she suggested that 'probably our most valuable work has been done through one-to-one contacts with Party spokesmen or in response to requests for specific projects.'[27] The financial crisis meant that *Crossbow* became erratic: the February 1976 edition was succeeded by 'Summer' and 'Autumn' issues. The Council mooted reducing *Crossbow* to a biannual publication in the spring of 1976, but it soldiered on through 1976 and 1977 with three editions in each year, although it became a thinner publication printed on considerably cheaper paper. But irregularity led to reduced press coverage; and advertisers became wary and withdrew their support. In the summer of 1976, the outgoing Editor Peter Lloyd, who was on the point of being selected for Fareham, hoped that his successor, Patricia Hodgson, 'may even be able to turn the magazine back from an occasional breakfast-time surprise into a regular quarterly'.[28]

The Group's failure to follow up press interest in its work hints that it was hindered by more than simply a lack of money. 'Things were at a much lower ebb,' recalled one member, Stuart Jackson, of the period between 1976 and 1978. Hodgson had tried to beef up the Political Committee, which, she reported at the end of her time as Chairman, 'now consists of most of those Bow Group members who are, or have been candidates', but the Council's minutes betray disorganisation, a loss of morale and mounting indifference to the Group from outside. The blame must lie with the Council itself. Standing Committees clashed; it was noted that many membership applicants failed to turn up to their interviews; and the Group's national essay competition received just four entries. 'It was the longest running essay competition in the world,' joked one anonymous member of the Office staff: 'the judges wrote more, cumulatively, in their many letters than did the entrants.'[29] The fundamental problem was summed up by Michael Stern, then the Group's Political Officer. He 'felt that we [the Bow Group] were living on efforts in past years at present and would get diminishing returns in successive years'.[30] A measure of how much the Group had lost standing was illustrated by a letter Douglas French, then Chairman of the Group, wrote to the *New Society* in September 1978, to complain about the magazine's failure to mention the Bow Group in a study of Tory political groups.

Below French's letter, the author of the piece replied that he had not mentioned the Group because 'its social function is of greater importance than its political function'.[31]

But despite being overlooked, the Group did not simply lie down and die. Patricia Hodgson took over from Peter Lloyd as Editor of *Crossbow* in late 1976. Whereas previous Editors had changed themes from issue to issue, Hodgson saw her editorship as an opportunity to drive forward a campaign for freedom. Her first editorial, in the spring 1977 edition, focused on the closed shop policy of the National Union of Journalists and its implications for the future of free speech. Edward Heath responded angrily to the thrust of her editorial policy. Speaking at the Group's annual dinner, he launched a personal attack on Hodgson saying that she was an 'antibody' who should be expelled from the body of the party. There was little sympathy for his views. Alan Clark recalled the riotous reaction: 'At the Bow Group dinner Heath rambled "down memory lane" then finally got into his theme about "... a realignment, moderate grouping of the centre" etc. *No!* people shouted. "Tripe!" I shouted from my traditional place at the end of the table.'[32]

Hodgson, meanwhile, was flattered that she had provoked such a reaction. Three further editorials written by her focused on the linked issues of freedom of speech and the closed shop. It was repetitive. Editing her final issue in the summer of 1980, she remarked: 'Some readers, I suspect, will be happy to be spared my constant editorials inveighing against the closed shop and the inadequacies of the new industrial relations law.'[33] But the technique worked because of the variety of the viewpoints into which Hodgson chose to put the message that Labour was eroding a basic human freedom. Russian dissidents and former Labour supporters, together with the staff of the CPS, put the case for freedom as an apolitical issue which the Conservative Party should champion. Journalists who had bucked the closed shop and George Ward – the businessman at the centre of the Grunwick dispute – were given space to describe their personal experience of coercion. The challenge, recalled Hodgson, was no longer in conceiving new ideas, but in 'giving them a shove'.[34]

The Conservative Party hierarchy seems to have agreed with Hodgson's assessment of the Bow Group's valuable function. The Group believed that 'There has been in the past an unwritten undertaking that we would not poach Party donors if the Party guaranteed our survival.'[35] In late 1976, Ian Clarke and Richard Simmons duly went to see the Party Treasurers, Lords Chelmer and Ashdown, to be reassured that Central Office 'would see that the Group did not go bankrupt'.[36] In part their lordships' willingness appears to have stemmed from their concern that the Group did not mount a public or private appeal to raise funds to counter the threat of nationalisation, an option which the Group had considered. By the end of the following year, the Group had received over £7,000 in donations. But it was not enough to avert a deepening of the Group's financial problems. As Ian Clarke drily put it, 'When I became Chairman, the Group was likely to have run out of money in April 1977. Thanks to various measures, nemesis has been postponed to December this year [1977].'[37]

In fact, it was the general upturn in Conservative fortunes which put the Group on a sounder footing. As victory in a forthcoming General Election looked more likely, the Group's membership recovered strongly, having fallen sharply after subscription increases were introduced in November 1976. The Treasurer observed that new subscriptions had generated £3,000 of extra revenue by March 1978.[38] *Crossbow* was restored to good health when the aptly named Richard Lazarus was appointed to restore moribund advertising revenue, which benefited, like the Group's wider reputation, from a return to regular issues of the magazine.

Restoring a more frequent *Crossbow* reflected a renewed sense of purpose lent to the Group by its new Chairman, Douglas French. Genial and intensely ambitious, French believed that it was time to reinvigorate the political meetings which were the Group's essential activity, and to redress its image as an intellectual grouping which was unwilling to get its hands dirty. By 1978 the Group was no longer attracting large numbers to its meetings. The problem was not apathy, but that the Standing Committees had developed a tendency to hold small meetings on specialist subjects which undermined the Group's central activities, causing poor attendance which discouraged further speakers. The Standing Committees were, perhaps, becoming too big for their boots. The select meetings they held to quiz individual experts may have held their own allure of influence, but they did the Group as a whole no good. French believed that attendance at meetings was 'a totem pole of the virility of any Group', so one of his first acts as Chairman was to ban the Committees from issuing invitations to speakers individually.[39]

Greater focus, and the access French had to senior members of the Shadow Cabinet through his work as a researcher for Geoffrey Howe, quickly improved both the calibre of the speakers and the numbers in the audience from week to week. There is no doubt that French set great store by speaker meetings: he even curtailed his honeymoon to ensure he could be back in London the following Thursday to chair a meeting with Chapman Pincher, the Defence Correspondent on the *Daily Express*. As the General Election loomed, many Conservative Shadow Ministers used the opportunity a Bow Group meeting provided to drive home their message to a much broader, national audience. Bow Group meetings were used in this way by both Keith Joseph, on the inability of Government to create jobs by direct action, and Margaret Thatcher, on the threat to the rule of law presented by arbitrary union action. Several members said after Thatcher's speech that it contained nothing new; but Bow Group meetings, which were once held behind closed doors, now became the platform for public statements which the national press scrutinised intently for signs of what a Conservative Government would do. The Bow Group benefited from the limelight.

One meeting deserves special focus, because it contained not a routine restatement of policy but a new idea which was to affect the landscape of many towns in the following 20 years. This was Geoffrey Howe's proposal for 'New Enterprise Zones', launched with the Bow Group's support at the Waterman's Arms pub on the Isle of Dogs on 26 June 1978. The Group's own affiliation with the area provided an appropriate link, but it had long been associated with the idea: 'New Industrial Zones' was one of three ideas on which Howe had asked the Group for help almost two years earlier.[40] Moreover, as Howe subsequently revealed, he had drawn some of his inspiration from a provocative article published in *Crossbow* in 1962, 'Wigan Delenda Est' ('Wigan must be destroyed') by Godfrey Hodgson.[41] Howe wondered what was needed to kick-start the regeneration of the decaying urban areas around Vauxhall which he saw each day on his drive to Parliament from his home in Lambeth. In a lunchtime speech to the Group he set out a radical plan to remove planning and employment controls, force the sale of publicly owned land, and exempt pioneering developers from rates and development land tax in areas which were derelict in Clydeside, Merseyside, the West Midlands and East London.[42] His hope was that the deregulated example which such zones would provide would raise pressure for much wider deregulation. As Howe observed, Margaret Thatcher was suspicious of the idea initially, partly perhaps because she saw it primarily as a matter of planning rather than enterprise, and it was not until his second Budget in 1980 that Howe was able to introduce it. It was, he later said 'the trail-blazer for several other policies of the 1980s'.[43]

As Lilley had done before him, French introduced a programme which ranged beyond Conservative politics, to ensure that the Group catered for 'catholic and diverse' tastes. The oddest meeting he arranged was for the playwright Arnold Wesker to give a recital. More controversially, both Tony Benn and David Owen addressed the Group early in 1979. French hoped that the Group would get to know its political opponents in the run-up to the General Election. The election also offered an opportunity to promulgate the idea that the Group were 'not just remote intellectuals but . . . prepared to go out and use a bit of shoe-leather,' recalled French.[44] The Group adopted Nick Scott, Paddington's MP, for the election. A Bow Group 'canvassing team' helped Scott return in 1979 with an increased majority. Such initiatives improved the Group's standing with London Conservative activists, and in turn its reputation, which remained based on well-grounded research work, not tramping the streets in search of votes.

As well as publishing the work of its own members, the Group published a collection of three speeches, released at the 1978 Party Conference. In *The Right Angle*, Margaret Thatcher, Keith Joseph, and Geoffrey Howe put the case for the Shadow Cabinet's new policies. The consequence for the Group was twofold. Not only did this cement the general perception that the Group was inextricably bound up with senior members of the Conservative Party, but, as French observes, the Bow Group became recognised once again as 'the sort of organisation through which the senior members of the Party would be happy to publish their words'.45 The selection of candidates in the run-up to the election seemed to confirm this: one in six candidates on the eve of the election was a member of the Group, and the *Economist*, in an overview of the first months of the new Conservative Government, described the Group as one of 'the party's three classical recruiting grounds (The City, the legal profession and the intellectuals of the research department and Bow Group)'.46 It was exactly this quasi-institutional status, as a training ground for would-be politicians, which the Group was so keen to achieve. It marked a sharp improvement of the Group's image, from social club to pillar of the Party's future.

With this sort of write-up, and because the stakes were raised by the General Election victory which returned the Conservatives to Government, it was not surprising that for a second year running the Group's chairmanship was contested. The candidates were the former Research Secretary, Richard Barber, backed by two previous chairmen, Hodgson and Clarke, and French's nominee, Donald Cameron. The AGM became somewhat acrimonious when it was questioned whether Douglas French had abused his position by writing 'to all new members suggesting that since they didn't necessarily know who all the candidates were, it would be best to vote for those proposed by him'.47 Whether or not this made a difference is hard to tell, but Barber won the ensuing vote.

In advance of the election *Crossbow* quietly canvassed all backbench MPs to ask them to nominate their ideal Cabinet. Sixty-two MPs replied seriously, a handful more said that it was not their prerogative to second-guess Margaret Thatcher, several others suggested joke Cabinets and 18 MPs, who worked together in Parliament's East Cloisters, nominated themselves, organised by Kenneth Lewis. 'I certainly think Mrs Thatcher should look to the East Cloisters when she is forming her first Cabinet,' wrote Lewis to the Editor, Patricia Hodgson. 'It might help her to make sure that she will actually form a Cabinet if some of the East Cloister

MPs were actually in her Shadow Cabinet.'[48] Of the East Cloisters 18, the only one who eventually reached the Cabinet was Malcolm Rifkind.

It is well known that Margaret Thatcher's eventual choice was conservative, even cautious. In retrospect, the aggregate of the replies from the 62 MPs who took the exercise seriously demonstrably confirms this. With one exception, Tom King, everyone who received more than 20 votes was invited to join Thatcher's first Cabinet. Pym, with 42 votes, and Howe, with 40, topped the table. In terms of what other MPs thought of them, Margaret Thatcher's most surprising choices were David Howell, who received nine votes but became Secretary of State for Energy, and Humphrey Atkins, who earned four but was made Secretary of State for Northern Ireland. Of those who were popular choices, but were not selected, the three who polled the most were Rhodes Boyson on 16, Teddy Taylor and Edward Heath, who both had 15 votes apiece.[49] The survey was not published until the spring of 1979, when victory looked certain. Even then, the Council minutes imply a degree of uncertainty about the Group's prospects with a Conservative Government. In April 1979, just a month before the General Election, which saw a record swing to the Conservatives, the Council took a little time at the end of its meeting to deliberate the question, 'Where Do We Go From Here?'. The debate was summarised by a bald and somewhat uncertain sentence: 'The position of the Group under a Conservative Government was considered and thought to be advantageous.'[50]

NOTES

[1]   George Hutchinson, 'The Worst of the Referendum Mischief May be Yet to Come', *Times*, 12 April 1975.

[2]   Quoted in Ramsden, *The Winds of Change*, p. 419.

[3]   Anthony Nelson, telephone conversation with the author.

[4]   French was MP for Gloucester, 1987–97.

[5]   Bow Group Council, Minutes, 12 January 1976. Kenneth Baker was MP for Acton, March 1968–1970; for St Marylebone, October 1970–1983; Mole Valley, 1983–97. He was Secretary of State for the Environment 1985–86; for Education and Science

1986–89; Chancellor of the Duchy of Lancaster 1989–90; Party Chairman 1989–90; Home Secretary 1990–92. Nicholas Ridley was MP for Cirencester and Tewkesbury 1959–92. He was Secretary of State for Transport, 1983–86; for the Environment, 1986–89; for Trade and Industry, 1989–90. He died in 1993.

6   'The Sun Says', *Sun*, 16 September 1975.

7   'Mrs Thatcher talks to Norman Lamont MP', *Crossbow*, October 1975, p. 23.

8   'Who Really Knows Best?', *Daily Telegraph*, 2 February 1976. Arthur Seldon co-founded the free-market Institute of Economic Affairs.

9   *Economist*, 17 May 1975, quoted in Ashford, 'The Conservative Party and European Integration 1945–1975', p. 341.

10   Bow Group Council, Minutes, 7 January 1974. Michael Stern was MP for Bristol NW, 1983–97.

11   Bow Group Council, Minutes, 7 January 1974.

12   Hodgson, interview.

13   Lynda MacKenzie, letter to the author, 2 June 2000.

14   Bow Group Council, Minutes, 12 January 1976.

15   Bow Group Council, Minutes, 8 September 1975.

16   Bow Group Council, Minutes, 1 March 1976.

17   Robert Blake, *The Conservative Party from Peel to Major*, London 1997, p. 328.

18   Hodgson, interview.

19   Nirj Deva, interview, 8 April 1999.

20   Morrison Halcrow, *Keith Joseph: A Single Mind*, London 1989, p. 66.

21   CPA KJ 2/1, Joseph to Hodgson, 14, 15 October 1975.

22   CPA KJ 2/1, Hodgson to Joseph, 13 November 1975.

23   Bow Group Council, Minutes, 10 May 1976.

24   'Tory Plan To Make Smokers Pay', *Sun*, 1 September 1976.

25   Bow Group Council, Minutes, 6 September 1976.

26   Annual General Meeting Minutes, 26 April 1976.

27   Chairman's Annual Report, 1975/76.

28   'Crosstalk', *Crossbow*, Summer 1976, p. 5.

29   'Notes on the Bow Group Office', written for the advice of future office staff, in the early 1980s.

30   Bow Group Council, Minutes, 11 October 1976.

31   *New Society*, 14 September 1978.

32   Clark, *Diaries: Into Politics*, p. 98. Entry for Wednesday 23rd March 1977.

33 'Crosstalk', *Crossbow* Summer 1980, p. 5.

34 Hodgson, interview, 15 June 1999.

35 Bow Group Council, Minutes, 11 October 1976.

36 Bow Group Council, Minutes, 8 November 1976.

37 Chairman's Annual Report for 1976/77, 15 March 1977.

38 Bow Group Council, Minutes, 6 March 1978.

39 Douglas French, interview, 21 December 1999.

40 Bow Group Council, Minutes, 11 October 1976.

41 Sir Geoffrey Howe, 'The Birth of Enterprise', *Crossbow*, Summer 1988, p. 6.

42 'Sir Geoffrey Suggests Inner-city Enterprise Zones Free of Red Tape', *Times*, 27 June 1978.

43 Howe, *Conflict of Loyalty*, p. 110.

44 French, interview.

45 French, interview.

46 *Economist*, 22 September 1979.

47 The Bow Group, Minutes of the 28th Annual General Meeting, 14 May 1979.

48 'Cabinet Making', *Crossbow*, Spring 1979, p. 12.

49 'Cabinet Making', *Crossbow*, Spring 1979, p. 12.

50 Bow Group Council, Minutes, 2 April 1979.

Seven

A CASE OF MISTAKEN IDENTITY?
1980–9

As *Crossbow*'s survey of MPs' own choices confirms, Margaret Thatcher chose a Cabinet which broadly reflected the Party's choice first before her own. But within her consensual approach there was a clear pattern to Thatcher's choice of whom she would give the key economic appointments in the Cabinet. Geoffrey Howe's position was confirmed when he became Chancellor of the Exchequer, John Biffen was chosen to keep a tight grip on spending as Chief Secretary to the Treasury, David Howell became Secretary of State for Energy, Keith Joseph took the Industry brief and John Nott, Trade. All but John Nott had been closely involved with the Bow Group: Howe and Howell had been its chairmen, Biffen a Librarian until his election as MP for Oswestry in 1962, while Joseph had advised *Crossbow*'s editorial team when the journal was in its formative stages.

When yet another former Chairman of the Bow Group, Leon Brittan, replaced Biffen as Chief Secretary to the Treasury in January 1981, he gave a copy of *The Conservative Opportunity*, the Group's 1965 collection of essays to which he had contributed, to the library in Number 10, in observance of a tradition required of all new Cabinet Ministers. Although a detail, this incident was a strong sign that Ministers remained proud of their involvement in the Group and even recognised the role which their membership had played in their subsequent political success. With several close associates of the Group in key political roles, Howe had good grounds to argue two years later that the Group 'had succeeded in capturing the intellectual commanding heights'.[1] In the same speech he made clear that he connected the Bow Group's earlier work with the new economic approach: 'the present strategy is the logical culmination of a tradition of thought which has been continuously developing within the Bow Group and elsewhere for 30 years.'

These firm believers in monetarism were not the only Bow Group alumni who made it into the Cabinet in 1979. Peter Walker at Agriculture, Fisheries and Food, Michael Heseltine at Environment, Patrick Jenkin at Health and Social Security, and Norman St John Stevas, the Chancellor of the Duchy of Lancaster (also responsible for the Arts), brought the Bow Group's 'total' to eight. While the Group's profile was certainly raised by being a common denominator of the political CVs of a substantial number of Cabinet ministers, it was to become closely associated with the 'wets' and increasingly viewed as a faction, a view which even its association with the monetarists and the 'no corporate view' could not prevent. One anecdote suggests how high this impression reached. When asked, years later, what his wife thought about the Group, Sir Denis Thatcher queried: 'Bow Group? Very left-wing isn't it?'[2]

'I don't think she ever identified with that activity at all,' explains Patrick Jenkin today about Thatcher's ambivalence about the Bow Group and its work.[3] In Opposition, Thatcher's dealings with the Bow Group were limited. That was why the Group was only cautiously optimistic in April 1979 that it would thrive under her. She had relied on the Centre for Policy Studies for research, and as Jenkin reflects, she was a conviction politician who had little time for the Group's intellectual excursions, preferring the finished product. There was a simple reason why an already ambivalent relationship became more tense: the Group was seen to have become increasingly embroiled in the factional atmosphere of the early 1980s.

'The main feature of our speaker programme was that four senior Ministers chose the Group as the forum in which to deliver major speeches on Conservative Party philosophy and its relationship to the politics of the Government.'[4] So Richard Simmons rounded up a tempestuous year for the Group in the spring of 1981. Nigel Lawson, David Howell, Sir Keith Joseph and Norman St John Stevas all used the Group as a platform to reach a much wider audience. For Ministers to approach the Bow Group, rather than the reverse, was a new development for which there were broadly two reasons: first, a growing split within the Cabinet, and second, the Group's evolution from an important influence on policy into an important constituency within the Party. The Group's problem was that it was ill-equipped for this role.

By accident rather than by design, the Group had found itself closely associated with the earliest signs of discontent within the Conservative Party in Parliament. The first was Julian Critchley, who was unmasked as the author of an anonymous article which described the Prime Minister as a 'she-elephant'. His association with the Bow Group, through which he had kept his political hopes alive 16 years earlier, was almost always noted. Another critic, whose views were reported in the context of him being 'a founder member of the Bow Group', was Keith Stainton, the MP for Sudbury and Woodbridge since 1963. He feared that 'the baby is in danger of being thrown out with the bath water' with the Tories' economic approach.[5]

Whereas the Group could in no way be held responsible for the thoughts of either Critchley or Stainton, there were signs that it wittingly began to court controversy later in 1980. Like Stainton, Norman St John Stevas had been a founder member of the Bow Group, attending the first meeting in Bow almost 30 years before in February 1951. As he became increasingly disillusioned with the Government's policy, he turned to the Group to vent his concerns. Speaking to the Group in June, he warned that the Government was in danger of giving the impression that its policies were 'part of a dogmatic crusade'.[6] The language Stevas used drew unmistakably on the 'wet' canon. 'It is no part of our purpose', he asserted, 'to recreate the two nations – North against South, rich against poor – which Conservative Governments have sought for a century or more to weld into one.' Stevas was not the first to enter the debate, but his contribution brought the Bow Group into the fray. Both *The Times* and the *Daily Telegraph* noted the contrast between Stevas' speech and one given also to the Group by David Howell the previous month.

But in case the divide was not apparent, the Group decided to give Stevas a further opportunity at the 1980 Party Conference. It was this speech, in the much higher-profile political atmosphere provided by the

Conference, that made the split clear. In a tacit attack on Nigel Lawson, the then Financial Secretary, who had just published a pamphlet on the monetarist philosophy of 'New Conservatism', Stevas appropriated Sir Keith Joseph's phrase to say that indeed, monetarism was 'not enough'. Instead, he made it clear that if the Government was 'to counter the socialist projection of our party as the paradigm of hard-faced selfishness and callousness, our monetary policy has to be set squarely in the wider setting of traditional Tory social concerns and traced to its roots in moral values'.[7] The newspapers extracted a clear message from Stevas' barely concealed criticisms. 'The deep philosophical differences within the Government were brought out into the open again yesterday with a speech from Mr Norman St John Stevas [which] . . . amounted to a complete rejection of the "New Conservatism" advocated by some of his colleagues,' reported the *Financial Times*.[8] The ructions that resulted from his speech were long-lasting: eight months later, in his end-of-year report, Simmons noted that Stevas' speech 'has, of course continued to attract attention'.

It might have looked as if the Bow Group was simply fulfilling its constitutional requirement to have 'no corporate view'. But this was hardly the case. The Chairman, Richard Simmons, appears to have been sympathetic to a relaxation of Government economic policy. Just as he invited Stevas to address the Group at Blackpool, he simultaneously urged Thatcher to ease the Government's strict non-interventionist policies on industry in his open letter to the Prime Minister, also published at the Party Conference. When Stevas became the first reshuffle victim in January 1981, he referred back to his June speech to the Bow Group in a subsequent statement which warned Tories not to become associated with 'a single technique for managing the economy'.[9]

There is no doubt that the publicity which the Bow Group gave to Stevas alarmed some of its Council members. Even so, the Council resolved to stick to its guns, believing that the media recognised it as a 'responsible organisation', for allowing dissent. But there were signs at the Council Meeting immediately after the Party Conference that many Council members were keen to retreat from platform politics to the safer ground of research in order to show that responsibility.[10] It appears that many senior members feared for their own political prospects if the Group became too strongly associated with dissent. Just as Margaret Thatcher declared that 'the Lady's not for turning', it appeared that the Group, by entertaining a prominent dissident like Stevas, fitted into the category of those who could turn if they wished. The glory in which the Group had basked as its members took places in the Cabinet turned out to have a sour aftertaste when they began to fall out in the deeply divided atmosphere of 1980–1.

The real catalyst of the debate into which Stevas had entered was not the apparent ineffectiveness of monetarism, but the alarmingly rapid progress being made up the polls by the Social Democratic Party. The spotlight remained on the Group, because as the SDP surged ahead to a level of public support twice that of the Tories, it seemed that not only was the Bow Group an important constituency of Conservative opinion, it comprised exactly the sort of Conservatives the SDP was most likely to attract. This image was enhanced by the defection to the SDP of an earlier Bow Group Chairman, the MP Christopher Brocklebank-Fowler. In its examination of why no other sitting Tory MP followed Brocklebank-Fowler's lead, the authors of the definitive history of the SDP note that 'The only other group of any significance to join from the Conservatives were a number of senior Young Conservatives who later stood as SDP parliamentary candidates.'[11]

In the run-up to the local elections that year, the Group gained a number of unwanted additions to its archive of press cuttings as it transpired that more than one SDP candidate had previously been a member of the Bow Group. One of these was Jeremy Hardie, once a member of the Bow Group's speaker panel, who contested Norwich South.[12] Such was the growing climate of mistrust that when Nirj Deva, the Group's new Chairman, invited Roy Jenkins to speak later in the year, it was assumed that the group was wavering not fact-finding.[13] This impression was helped by a report of the meeting which was leaked to the *Guardian*'s diary. According to the diary, Jenkins' 'views went down among the assembled "wet" Tories uncommonly well. "I must say that I have a good deal of sympathy with what you say . . .", began questioner after questioner. The cracks in the mould continue to widen,' concluded the diarist, in a reference to Jenkins' phrase that the SDP would 'break the mould' of British politics.[14]

With the Bow Group seemingly giving way, ministers made a concerted effort to maintain its support for their policies. Thinking that it would be an essentially favourable forum in which to mount a defence of Government policy, Sir Keith Joseph himself approached the Group to ask whether it would stage a speech he wanted to give on 'A Mid-Term Industrial Strategy' at short notice.[15] Addressing the Group on 1 April 1981, he insisted that the Government had a coherent industrial strategy, and defended the subsidy of British Steel, British Leyland and ICL. At the end of the same month, Geoffrey Howe also spoke to the Group, directly attacking Roy Jenkins' alluring policy of deferred monetarism as 'mañana monetarism'. As if to defuse the Bow Group's concerns, Howe was also keen to suggest that the Group had intellectual ownership of the Government's strategy.[16] If this was a subtle attempt at flattery, it failed. In a strongly worded *Crossbow* editorial Richard Barber lashed out at Joseph, and by June, the Bow Group was described by the *Times* diary as 'reviled . . . within the Prime Minister's inner sanctum'.[17]

In fact, Barber's attack was anything but 'wet'. In the summer edition of *Crossbow*, published on 26 May 1981, he attacked Sir Keith Joseph for giving in to pressure to prop up industry with Government money. It was, he argued, 'a fitting irony that the most persistent critic in opposition of government aid to lame ducks – Sir Keith Joseph – was the Minister called upon to rise in the House of Commons and announce an aid programme of £5.3 billion for B.S.C. [British Steel Corporation]'.[18] That Joseph was on the receiving end was a little ironic, given that it was he who had advocated that *Crossbow* take 'a controversial editorial policy' at the third meeting of the journal's Board in 1958.[19]

Barber went on to suggest that Joseph had been 'by universal consent . . . the most dismal disappointment of this administration'. Although *Crossbow*'s coverage in the press had dwindled because it was, once again, published erratically, this attack was shocking and made a useful peg for the ongoing story of the ideological battle within the Cabinet. *The Times* gave the story a front-page splash, inferring from the unexpected outburst a much wider shift in Conservative opinion – but in the opposite direction from Barber's own standpoint.

> The Bow Group, whose membership of 63 MPs includes eight Cabinet ministers, says the failure to curb the public sector has made the economic sacrifices over the past two years 'almost worthless' . . . Although the Bow Group never expresses a collective view it is known that the opinions expressed in today's article headed 'Sliding to defeat?' are gathering increasing support among members.

The article went on to name the Cabinet ministers who were members of the Bow Group. The inherent paradox of the story, in which a 'dry' attack on the Government was used as evidence of a strengthening of 'wet' anxieties, led to *The Times*' decision to run the piece being criticised: the *Daily Telegraph*'s leader the following day dismissed the Group's fusillade as inconsequential, noting that there was 'weightier Conservative opinion than the Bow Group' which had as yet remained silent.[20] As Editor of the *Spectator*, Alexander Chancellor poured similar scorn on the story. 'The prominence *The Times* gave it,' he said, 'is what is known as creating news rather than reporting it.'[21] The Chairman of the Bow Group, Nirj Deva, was horrified by the impact the story had had. He hastily wrote to *The Times* in praise of Joseph's denationalisation of British Aerospace and British Telecom, and described him as 'a good friend of the Group', thereby disowning Barber.[22]

Although Norman Tebbit also sprang to Joseph's defence, expressing his regret that '*Crossbow* should have got itself into such a muddle by publishing a superficial and misleading article', which, he added, failed 'to discriminate between restructuring and featherbedding', it was too late. Not only had damage already been done to the reputation of Sir Keith Joseph – who later complained that he had felt personally wounded by the attack – but the Group found itself under attack from two sides. Other parts of the Conservative Party said it was out of touch, while the regional press thought it was as hard-line. It was clear that the episode had an effect, though commentators were divided on what that effect was. Some believed that the exposure had stiffened Thatcher's resolve;

others thought that the episode made it plain to Margaret Thatcher 'that the man on whose ideas she still leaned was himself becoming a political lame duck'.[23] Sir Keith Joseph's departure to the less exposed Department of Education at the reshuffle in the autumn of 1981 seemed to confirm the latter view.

The Bow Group was clearly becoming more fractious, but the complexion of its views was hard to characterise. Francis Pym was despatched at the Party Conference to pour oil on troubled waters. Soothingly, he painted a Conservative approach which 'has flowed as a slow broad stream throughout the centuries'.[24] In a move designed simultaneously to cool the calls for monetarism and console other members unhappy for the opposite reasons with the Government's economic policy, he urged the Group to beware an over-reliance on economics. 'The Conservative Party embraces ideals and imperatives far wider than the quest for sound money.' But the following day Geoffrey Rippon addressed the Group. He demanded Howe's resignation. 'We are in a monetarist rut,' he believed, 'The only difference between the rut and the grave is that the rut is longer.'[25] Again, the Group's leadership appeared to concur. In the Chairman's open letter to the Prime Minister published in *Crossbow* – by now a traditional fixture of Conservative Party Conferences – Nirj Deva advocated intervention by raising taxes to take the pressure off high interest rates.

The controversy surrounding the Group's activities did not help its financial predicament. Deva wrote to Pym after his speech, making it clear that although he would like to publish it, funds were not available, and that he hoped Pym would approach CPC. Printing costs had shot up, with the consequence that the Group's output had to be cut back. Perhaps the acidity of Barber's editorials was the result of his frustration at the lack of publicity *Crossbow* attracted when it lost its regularity. By March 1981, *Crossbow* was described as existing on a 'hand to mouth basis'.[26]

Once again, the Group's financial problems arose from an over-reliance on donations. Following the retirement of Colonel Hobbs in 1976, the Bow Group's fruitful relationship with the British United Industrialists had waned. Potential donors were either too discouraged by the Tories' handling of the economy to open their wallets, or actively straitened from doing so by the effects of the recession. The cause of the crisis was all too clear to the outgoing chairman in 1981, Richard Simmons. He commented on how the suddenness with which the financial crisis unveiled itself had caught the Group exposed:

> This year, because of the difficulties being generally faced in raising money for political purposes, our donation income failed to materialise at a level sufficient to meet our commitments. This development came too late in the year to avoid running into substantial deficit, since the only cost reductions we could have achieved at the time would have so seriously curtailed the activities of the Group as to undermine its entire future.[27]

In fact, in 1980, income from donations had halved from the total of £10,330 received in 1979, while the Group's expenditure had increased from £27,261 in 1979 to a projected £31,700 in 1980. By the end of that year Simmons predicted that the Group would be in deficit to the tune of £20,000 before any donations were set against this figure. The likelihood of donations covering the shortfall was remote: as a *Financial Times* survey of the problem in July 1981 noted, the value of donations – often for symbolic round numbers – had failed to keep up with rampant inflation. The newspaper selected *Crossbow* as a vivid illustration of the consequences:

> *Crossbow*, the quarterly magazine of the Bow Group, is now down to two issues a year . . . Each issue costs about £1000 net to produce. Nowadays the money is just not there. You do not have to be a Tory to regret this lessening of group's contribution to the political debate. On the other side of the fence, the magazine *Socialist Commentary* disappeared because of lack of funds some years ago. Its loss is still felt.[28]

Ten months earlier, *Crossbow* had nearly gone the same way. 'The day of the political quarterly was over,' proposed one Council member in a polemical paper on the future of *Crossbow* which was put before a crisis meeting of the Council in October 1980.[29] The story told by the magazine's finances tends to reinforce this opinion. The Group had always subsidised *Crossbow*, but the deficit per issue rose dramatically from £399 in 1975 to £1,140 in 1979. Strong sales of advertising in the late 1970s kept the problem at bay. But because many of the adverts were really political donations which could be discreetly paid out of companies' advertising budgets, advertising went the same way as the Group's donations in 1980, down from a high of £750 for each of the three 1977 issues to £145 for the Spring 1980 edition. Though the deficit on the first issue of 1980 narrowed slightly to £1,051, this was unsustainable for any length of time. The dilemma was that though 'it was felt that *Crossbow* was the most important and widely read of our publications, on the other hand . . . it was a financial millstone and scarcely read at all.' But the thought of losing what publicity *Crossbow* did generate hurt the Bow Group Council too much to ditch its 'flagship'. Instead, future issues of the magazine were halved in length to cut printing costs.

At much the same time the Council reviewed three strategies to put the Group back on course. Of the three, two involved cutting staffing levels and reducing the Group's level of activity. Both were anathema. Instead the Group reduced its staffing and resolved to increase membership to 1,200, raise money from pamphlet sales and social events, and simultaneously launch an appeal for donations to coincide with the Group's 30th anniversary. The target was to raise £25,000 by the end of the year and obtain pledges to guarantee the Group's future for the following three years. Measured by the terms of its aim, the appeal was not a success. Current members and alumni proved just as unable as companies to find money to spare. By March 1981 the appeal had raised £2,000 of which £250 was a donation made by Richard Simmons to start the ball rolling. It was a boost to the Group, but it did not address the size of the deficit.

Nirj Deva vividly recalls his thoughts when he took over the chairmanship in June that year: 'I went into the office and looked at the figures and realised I had a severe problem.'[30] He had only narrowly made it to the top of the Group by beating the fiery Joe Egerton in the election to run the Council. Although the Group's patron, John Baring, again came to the rescue, the fact was that the Group was becoming almost completely beholden to Conservative Central Office. Amid the severe shortage of money affecting all political parties and their satellites, CCO had successfully attempted to secure overarching control of all available donations to Conservative causes and had acquired powers to redistribute what it did not need to maintain its own functions. It gave Deva's predecessor Richard Simmons notice that it intended to phase out the subsidy it now gave to the Group over a two-year period.

As a result, the following year Deva found himself having to ask the Party's Deputy Chairman, Alan Howarth, out to lunch in Pimlico in order to extract £5,000 from Party funds for the Group. The Group could take some comfort in the leverage it could apply by calling on old friends like the Chancellor of the Exchequer to intercede on its behalf.[31] But its financial subservience to the Conservative Party was not good for it during this period. Begging funds from Central Office gave rise to 'a very uncomfortable relationship', believes Deva, which affected the Group's intellectual independence.[32] Nicholas Perry, later a Chairman of the Group, recalls that the rumours of the Group's lack of funds attracted offers of what he describes as 'tainted money' from the Israelis and the South Africans, among others, which was offered with the hope that the Group would lobby support for them. It was, he now believes, a miracle that the Group did not succumb to one of these overtures, which would have had devastating consequences on its reputation.[33]

With very little money, and finding the political friction at home uncomfortable, it was perhaps not surprising that the Group's focus shifted overseas. Contacts made at summer political drinks parties where members mingled with MPs, Ministers and foreign Ambassadors had a way of crystallising into invitations to travel abroad. Michael Stephen, who had been the secretary of the Bow Group's Foreign Affairs Committee for many years, provided a wealth of contacts which opened the door to a series of international escapades undertaken by members of the Group with MPs during the early 1980s.[34] But here too, there was great potential for controversy. Whereas the Group felt rightly unable to take foreign donations, support in kind, in assistance on foreign trips, was certainly within limits. Certain governments proved very willing to fund overseas trips and there was debate on whether the Group should take advantage of the opportunities this opened, but not always on moral grounds. There is a sense that some members opposed the trips largely because they had not been invited to participate. The argument came to a head at a meeting of the Council on 5 February 1980 when Kingsley Manning, a brilliant and colourful Council member, proposed that the Group should abandon a planned trip to South Africa. He failed to muster a majority, but as one of those who did go out to South Africa, Lord Onslow observed on his return:

> The South African taxpayer paid out approximately £2500 for me with 15 other members of the Bow Group to tour around Rhodesia, South Africa and Namibia. This alone tells us quite a lot about South Africa. What country would spend £40,000 on showing three undistinguished peers, two members of the European Parliament, one Conservative MP, 10 sundry Bow Groupers [around] . . . unless it was desperately worried about its image![35]

It is difficult to rate the political value of these tours, though undoubtedly they have provided a host of amusing stories. Michael Lingens remembers one trip to East Germany where 'we were guided by a Stasi female guide who was so attractive that it changed our minds about communism.' He has 'hilarious memories of Nirj [Deva] running the taps in his bathroom to talk to me in case we were overheard'. In turn, Deva – who is Sri Lankan – jubilantly recalls the horror of his hosts as he made a point of using the whites-only toilets in the South African Parliament. From South Africa, the Group took an ageing South African Air Force Dakota – minus its side door – to Namibia where they landed at Windhoek. When the time came to leave again, one engine refused to restart. Deva, who had read aeronautical engineering at university, claims the credit for climbing on to the wing and finally getting it going. But the tension had been too much for another fellow passenger, and muttering about the inadequacy of his insurance cover, Bill Cash decided he preferred two days on Windhoek's airstrip to a perilous onward journey into Angola, and jumped out of the plane on to the tarmac.[36]

The fully funded adventures the Group enjoyed at the beginning of the 1980s unsurprisingly made these trips 'a very popular aspect of the Group's foreign affairs activities', as Nigel Waterson acknowledged in a review of the Foreign Affairs Standing Committee's work several years later. But he did have doubts: 'However, there does seem to be an inverse relationship between the availability of subsidised foreign visits and the attractiveness of the regime involved. Clearly stable democratic non-repressive Governments have no need to subsidise visits by Bow Group members. It could become noticeable (if it is not already) that we tend to go to places like Chile.'[37] Not only did the Group visit Chile in 1983 to question all parties about the political process, but its members met General Pinochet and his staff for dinner at the Moneda Palace in Santiago. Michael Stephen recalls an illuminating query made by his military neighbour at dinner on this occasion: 'Tell me,' he was asked, 'how many years do you have to serve in the British army before you can become a Member of Parliament?'[38] Though the trips were controversial, Stephen argues that they had a significant function. As he points out, 'the Group could often speak to people with whom the Government could not be seen to be associated.'[39]

Nevertheless, there was a feeling that the Foreign Affairs Committee did not make the most of the opportunities for more than a select bunch of the Bow Group's members. Midway through 1981, a chance contact with Fred Kellogg of the Republican Ripon Society in London gave the then Political Officer, David Shaw, the idea and initial impetus to launch a Trans-Atlantic Conference between the Ripon Society and the Bow Group, to be held early the following year. Both groups shared a similar outlook: indeed, it had been the publicity given to the Bow Group around its tenth anniversary in 1961 that had stimulated the creation of the Ripon Society in Cambridge, Massachusetts the following year. With the decision to hold a conference early in 1982 began a chain of fortuitous events which put the Group at the centre of the Falklands Crisis. As Fred Kellogg puts it today: 'Our planning was impeccable, including the occurrence of the Falklands crisis at the time of the conference, for which David [Shaw] was entirely responsible.'[40]

Not least to increase his own popularity within the Group, Shaw was determined to ensure that the trip was open to any member who wished to go. The onus was on him to raise the sponsorship for the trip which would enable this to happen. One of the younger members of the Group who took advantage of the cheaper flight and Conference, before continuing on a debating tour, was William Hague. The Ripon Society provided about £2,000; Shaw arranged some commercial sponsorship; but the most interesting source of funding was to come through Ed Williams, an American friend who worked for the State Department at the US Embassy in London. Williams introduced Shaw to Charles Wick who, as well as being a close friend of Ronald Reagan, was the Director of the US International Communication Agency. The USICA funded radio stations to broadcast anti-Communist propaganda to Eastern Europe. Williams portrayed the Bow Group as a bastion against Communism in Britain and Wick signed the cheque.[41]

There were good grounds for a Conference which would stress the Atlantic connection of the USA and the UK in 1982. Relations between the Conservatives and Republicans were not strong, partly because the friendship between Thatcher, in power for two years, and Reagan, in the Oval Office for just one, had yet to develop. In any case the substantial all-change which accompanies a change of President in the United States at that time moved the balance firmly in favour of Reagan's Californian supporters, who filled posts which were usually the preserve of East Coast technocrats. At the same time, reflecting the Californian outlook, the focus of US foreign policy swung towards South America. There were some in both London and Washington DC who felt that this new emphasis came at the expense of the 'special relationship'.

For the Bow Group in particular, perhaps the choice of a Trans-Atlantic Conference also represented its search for political companionship outside Europe after its branches on the continent had been wound up. Shaw visited Washington several times in the run-up to the Conference, developing interest in a ten-day trip in September 1981 and building anticipation for the British visit just before the Bow Group arrived in 1982. Through the combined influence of Wick and Senator John Tower, the Bow Group secured Caspar Weinberger's involvement in the Conference. Tower was a friend of Mark Carlisle, one of the MPs who took part in the Conference, and Chairman of the powerful Senate Defence Committee. From Britain, the Secretary of State for Defence, John Nott, had promised to attend. But there was only so much Shaw's contacts and organisation could achieve, important though they were. It was luck and timing which turned a well-run but run-of-the-mill conference into an opportunity that gave the Group a strategic role. On 2 April 1982 Argentina invaded the Falklands. David Shaw felt at first hand the urgency of the discussions which immediately began between London and Washington. A fortnight after the invasion, Shaw was making a transatlantic call on the free US Embassy tie-line, wrapping up the arrangements for the Conference, when the operator interrupted. 'The President would like to speak to the Prime Minister. Is your call essential?' an amazed Shaw was asked.[42]

If the Group was not yet privy to the British strategy, it quickly became so. Out of the blue, John Nott personally telephoned Shaw to tell him that he would not be able to attend the Conference, but intended to send the Minister for the Armed Forces, Peter Blaker, instead. From then on Shaw was kept abreast of both the British and US Governments' views. 'I remember thinking it would be a help,' Sir John Nott says now, about the significance of the Bow Group's visit to Washington at such a sensitive time.[43] Since the Government appeared to face an uphill struggle on Capitol Hill, the Group's coincidental visit appeared to be a bonus.

Jeane Kirkpatrick, the American Ambassador to the UN, had pointedly kept an invitation to a banquet at the Argentinian Embassy on the night of the invasion, and the American Government was determined to appear neutral in public. The proponents of Reagan's Latin American foreign policy opposed support for any British military action which, if successful, might weaken General Galtieri and encourage Communism. Yet, as Britain's military strategists made clear, the UK Government had to create a favourable political climate by 1 May if a military strike were to have a chance of success.[44] To achieve this, the British Government adopted a forked strategy: to prevaricate enough to highlight the Argentinians' intransigence but also to portray the US response to the crisis as the first major test of the NATO alliance. Both elements of this message were visible in Peter Blaker's reply to Caspar Weinberger's address at the Bow Group's Conference on 22 April. He was quoted as saying that 'Britain could look to open support from the United States if the present negotiations failed because of Argentinian intransigence.' He added that 'every member of NATO will regard the decision of the United States Administration as relevant to its own position and the future of NATO.'[45] Of course, the US Government had already given Britain its tacit support, but the British Government was keen to encourage any initiative which might strengthen American public opinion enough to force the Government into an open declaration in favour of the UK. The Bow Group's Trans-Atlantic Conference was just such a forum.

Republican opinion in the Senate was strongly pro-British, so the Bow Group found no shortage of speakers to address the Conference, sometimes with television cameras rolling in the background. In a deliberate attack on Reagan's strategy in South America, Congressman Jim Leach told the Group that there was more US support 'for British policy on the Falklands than for American policy towards El Salvador'.[46] Other speakers included Congressmen Jack Kemp and Tim Petri. Through them, the Bow Group met the Wednesday Group, senior Republican Congressmen who represented all strands of opinion within the Party, days before the Senate voted by 79 votes to 1 in favour of supporting the UK. When on 30 April the Argentinians finally rejected US Secretary of State General Alexander Haig's three-day-old proposal, the groundwork for the British plan was complete. Supportive public opinion enabled Haig to state openly that the United States could not condone use of unlawful force to resolve disputes and that the President had declared that the United States should respond positively to requests for material support for the UK. Reports of the Conference in the British press spurred Alan Clark who decided to catch Concorde to join in on the last day:

> When we arrived at the Dirksen building, a sort of American Norman Shaw, full of Senators' offices, where the [Trans-Atlantic] Conference was being held, it was twenty-past four London time .
> . . But in Washington it was twenty-past ten and a bright sun

blazed down on the blossoms. Our guide repeated his earlier
suggestion that we should go to a hotel room and relax a bit.

'I do not want to "relax",' I snapped. 'I want to go to the
Conference'.

. . . On the sixth floor we found the Conference. Crawling with
candidates, both English and American, a smattering of Senators.
Two very big MPs, Mark Carlisle and Peter Emery, were booming
away.47

At no time in its previous existence does the Group appear to have
become so integral to any Government tactics, certainly not at such a
crucial moment. 'Everyone was high,' remembers Shaw. The bubble was
burst only when he failed to be elected Bow Group Chairman on his
return. Six months' preoccupation with the Conference had limited his
ability to cultivate the Group's membership in London.48

However, the euphoria generated by the Trans-Atlantic Conference
could not disguise the Group's continued financial problems, which
caused increasing friction among the Council members involved in
research. The Group's output dipped sharply as recession bit into its
activities. From a high of 21 pamphlets and memoranda in 1980, the
Group published just nine in 1981 and 11 in 1982. As the Group's
finances became more strained, memoranda, which were often no more
than several sides of paper stapled together, became a more realistic
vehicle for ideas than pamphlets, which were costly. This carried an
important political consequence: successive Research Secretaries found
that their power to influence the direction of the Group's research was
reduced as the cheaper memoranda had traditionally been the Political
Officer's responsibility. As a paper agreed by the new Political Officer
and Research Secretary implied, this change had been the source of
'unhealthy competition and discord' between the two officers.49 To end
this tension, the Political Officer, Michael Lingens, and Research
Secretary, Simon Mabey, sought to make a clearer definition between
'papers' and 'memoranda'. Papers were to address perennial issues
through careful analysis, with the purpose of leading to principles and
recommendations. Memoranda were to be more polemical in style, time-
critical and designed to appeal to specific interest groups by

recommending specific action. A new committee of four 'wise men' was set up to assess the merits of each research paper, while memoranda, as befitted their urgency, required the approval of just two people: the Chairman and the Political Officer.

But the underlying economic problems which had brought the issue of control of publication to a head did not recede quickly, although economic growth resumed in the UK in 1982. Consequently, the Group's ability to publish remained restricted. Of the limited output, two publications were particularly notable. The first cut across the lines drawn by Lingens and Mabey by being both extensive and topical. *Playing at Peace*, by Keith Best, was a 120-page study of international peace movements jointly researched and published by the Bow Group and the Konrad Adenauer Stiftung, which had gained the impression that the Bow Group was a 'gilded path' to the top of politics with which it was worth maintaining contact.[50] With a foreword written by the Prime Minister, *Playing at Peace* was launched in London in March 1983 by Michael Heseltine – who had replaced John Nott as Defence Secretary – as an opening shot in his campaign against CND during the run-up to the General Election later that summer.[51] At much the same time Nirj Deva and Michael Lingens conceived the idea of a pro-nuclear deterrent lobby group, Women and Families for Defence, run by Olga Maitland out of the Bow Group's office. Bruce Kent, CND's general secretary, spoke to the Group later in 1983, though he freely admitted at the meeting that only a fraction of a percentage of Conservative supporters favoured unilateral disarmament. On an entirely different note was Philip Goodhart's *Stand on Your Own Four Feet*, which merited discussion in a *Times* leader.[52] Goodhart tried to address a problem which some believed the expected economic recovery would uncover: a higher natural rate of unemployment caused not by the structure of the labour market, but by the advance of electronic technology, which tended to replace human labour. To counteract this trend, until greater productivity boosted profits and wages, he suggested job sharing, on the basis that for the young and old especially half a job was better than a life on social security. The Group saw other ways to exploit information technology, pioneering a conference aimed at companies wanting to supply Government departments.

This was not the Group's first attempt to commercialise itself. Falling revenue from donations had spurred the Group to consider marketing itself as a 'political updating service' as early as March 1980, asking an annual subscription of £500 from firms interested in keeping up to speed with political developments. The scheme, however, attracted no one. But whereas the Group failed to appear capable of providing a professional service because it was seen as a part-time enterprise, it could succeed in mounting occasional conferences, where it could offer its contacts on a one-off commercial basis. Until 1983, even in the case of the Trans-Atlantic Conference, the Bow Group had organised conferences with its own members in mind. The Council overlooked the commercial potential of Bow Group conferences until it realised the Conservatives' extended majority after the 1983 general election would sustain them for at least another term in Government and that, with many of its former members occupying Cabinet posts, it could use its connections more profitably. Even so, 'we stumbled into this conference game', remembers Nigel Waterson, a long-time member and later Chairman.[53] It dawned on the Council that it was in a position to court the wide audience of firms hunting Government contracts with the Ministers it could attract to speak. Had the Conservatives not been in power, this lucrative formula would not have existed for the Group and in time income generated by conferences became a source of revenue on which the Group relied. By the mid-1990s, when it became clear that the Conservatives would not win another term, the Group's dependence on these conferences would become a serious concern.

Though in future years the Group came to specialise in conferences on defence procurement, in the early 1980s IT was the natural place to start. The Group's conference in March 1983 built on the substantial contacts of one member, Philip Virgo, and gained from the access he had to the membership database of the National Computing Centre, where he worked. The Group persuaded two alumni, Patrick Jenkin, the Secretary of State for Industry, and Tony Newton, then Parliamentary Under-Secretary at the Department of Health and Social Security, to discuss the role of Government in promoting IT and its own computer technology needs. John Wakeham, as a Minister at the Treasury, was asked to talk about the computerisation of PAYE. The leaflet announcing the conference – which, incongruously, had been produced on an old-fashioned typewriter and duplicated – made it clear that 'discussion time' would 'be available for delegates to put their views to ministers'. Members of the Group or the National Computing Centre were entitled to half-price tickets at £50. About 100 businessmen attended, who paid the full price.

Even with this auspicious start, the Group's finances remained in serious deficit, which was due in part to its disorganisation. Again, donations had failed to match expectations, and the previous year's 30th Anniversary Appeal had reduced the Group's ability to make a widespread demand for money. But when David Shaw became Chairman in May 1983, he discovered not only that the Group had built up a deficit of over £5,000 by December the previous year, but that since the beginning of 1983 that deficit had continued to increase by £1,000 a month.[54] The Group's lowest ebb had come upon it almost unobserved.

The financial problems were symptomatic of greater drift within the Group, characterised by too many meetings, which attracted embarrassingly small audiences, a trend which, as Douglas French had observed several years earlier, quickly damaged the Group's reputation. By the time he took over, Shaw believed that the Group was weeks away from insolvency. To add to his problems, Barber had again used his editorial in *Crossbow* to attack a Cabinet Minister, this time the Home Secretary Willie Whitelaw, who was faced with rising crime statistics. Barber urged the Prime Minister to replace Whitelaw with a more 'abrasive' character, and while it was suggested that his view mirrored an existing feeling on the right of the Conservative Party, it was clear that, as in his attack on Sir Keith Joseph, Barber was vehemently opposed within the Group. When asked at the Group's Annual General Meeting whether he had seen the editorial in advance of publication, the outgoing Chairman, Colin Coulson-Thomas, said that he had not.[55] Deva and Lingens, aware of the damage they feared Barber could do to their own parliamentary aspirations, attacked him through the letters page of *The Times*, describing his criticisms as unjustified at the start of a four-paragraph paean to Whitelaw and his record.[56] Shaw, the new Chairman, inherited the problem.

It was perhaps unsurprising, amid this heated atmosphere and impending financial crisis, that the Group's office staff resigned. There was simply not enough money to pay them, and the deteriorating conditions in which they worked were no incentive to stay. As Shaw put it: 'our administrative and financial systems had completely broken down, some 90 overseas visitors from the United States and Germany were due to arrive seven weeks later and a General Election campaign was in progress.'[57] The Conservative Party was again persuaded to help the Group with a donation of £5,000, after Shaw met the Party Vice-Chairman Michael Spicer and explained how close the Group was to extinction. Shaw also persuaded Lynda MacKenzie to return to the Group as its administrator, and embarked on a programme designed to steer the Bow Group away from bankruptcy towards profitability. Publications were put on hold, the ball was postponed until the autumn and a system of management accounting was instituted to allow constant monitoring of the Group's income and expenditure. 'It became a much slicker operation,' believes Nigel Waterson.[58] Within three years, the Group's financial relationship with the Conservative Party was to be reversed: it was then the Group that would lend the Party money. Although his self-confident manner did not endear him to every member of the Group at the time, there is little doubt that during his year as Chairman David Shaw laid the foundations for this turnaround.

The circumstances helped: the Tories' overwhelming victory in the 1983 general election boosted morale, and it was reported by September that new members were 'coming in thick and fast'.[59] But there were other factors. The Group's publications had almost broken even in 1980, but it was under Shaw that, for the first time, they made a net profit for the Group. This was the first dividend of the work which Nicholas Perry, the Research Secretary between 1983 and 1985, put into constructing an effective and systematic approach to publicising the Group's published work. Perry formulated eight criteria to ensure that political impact became a touchstone for would-be authors; he identified early media coverage as the single most important requirement to make civil servants and ministers interested and generate sales.[60] Lynda MacKenzie recalls how 'The Today Programme in particular became a marker for how much debate each paper was going to generate.'[61]

Relevance and originality earned the Group financial and political reward. Nick Perry remembers his strategy for the first paper, on the sale of British Gas, which was the first published by the Group after its self-imposed moratorium. He invited just about the most controversial author he knew, Rodney Atkinson, to propose a bit by bit auction of the company's field interests to enable small exploration companies to penetrate the market.[62] At first, Perry produced only enough papers to go with the initial press releases on the Bow Group's photocopier. Only when publicity achieved by this mailshot led to further demand did Perry make more copies, also on the photocopier.[63] It was laborious work, but not only did this short memorandum raise the Group over £250 within a short time, but the plan it mooted came to be known as the 'Bow Group option' in Government circles, one of four possible ways to privatise the company and the route which the Government largely followed.[64]

A healthy turnout at the second Trans-Atlantic Conference, held in Britain, also suggested that the Group's fortunes were improving. The second Conference capitalised on the success of its Washington predecessor, attracting 200 delegates including a seventy-strong contingent from the United States and almost 20 Germans from the Konrad Adenauer Stiftung. One measure of the reputation which the Conference had gained from the previous year was the fact that three British Cabinet Ministers, Geoffrey Howe, Norman Tebbit and Tom King, addressed the Conference. Most importantly it made the Group a profit of £1,000 on a turnover of about £15,000. The Group's November ball, organised by Cheryl Gillan, attracted a record attendance of 450 from whom the Group made a profit of £4,400.[65] David Shaw, who launched his own venture capital company specialising in small firms late in 1983, saw the Bow Group's future being as 'a networking and conversational club where ideas could be developed' and believes that business relationships did develop through the Group.[66] This was a new direction for the Group. Businessmen featured prominently in Shaw's speaker programme; during his year as Chairman both Sir Alex Jarratt and Kenneth Durham, the chairmen of Reed International and Unilever respectively, addressed the Group.

Having turned its publications into a profitable activity, the Council turned its attention to *Crossbow*. By the autumn of that year Bow Publications, the arm of the Bow Group which published *Crossbow*, had signed an agreement with Millbank Publications to produce the magazine on a commercial basis. Behind the scenes there were concerns that the administrative burden was too great for Nirj Deva, who had replaced Richard Barber as Editor of *Crossbow*. Publicly, this gripe was glossed over, and *Crossbow*'s readers were informed that the deal had been concluded to widen *Crossbow*'s market substantially 'so that it becomes a major national policy quarterly'.[67]

Though in fact the deal with Millbank was eventually to fall through, by the end of 1983 the idea that *Crossbow* could become a major policy journal was becoming a plausible aspiration. In terms of its membership, the Group had probably reached the apex of its influence. One in four of those Conservatives elected in June that year were members of the Group, a total of 92. This total reached 100 during the Parliament. MPs constituted more than 10 per cent of the Group's membership. The finances improved dramatically: Shaw's connections brought £11,000 in donations; the deficit of over £5,000 for 1982 was turned into a surplus of £5,000 by the end of 1983. By late summer the following year, the Group had sufficient funds to do up its dilapidated offices, which, the Council was told, 'had not been decorated for 13 years'.[68]

This rapid turnaround had a positive impact on the Group's political profile. Awareness of the Group's activity had increased: on air, the presenters of Radio 4's *Today* programme expressed their admiration for the Group's output and the quality of its members' thinking.[69] The Group's international standing was sufficient to attract Jacques Chirac, then Mayor of Paris, to speak to a packed Committee Room 14 in the House of Commons. Saying that he had come to Britain to learn, Chirac praised Margaret Thatcher's programme of privatisation before dining with the Group. He left at midnight for what he termed a special engagement, which caused David Shaw to raise an eyebrow. The Group's most telling coup, however, was to persuade Clive Jenkins, the General Secretary of the Association of Scientific, Technical and Managerial Staffs, to come to talk on 'Unions in the Future'. A few years earlier he had declined, on the grounds, one contemporary member recalls, that 'he did not speak to organisations outside the labour movement'. A mixture of commercial success – achieved through the stringent financial control which had previously been lacking – and an eye for the politically salient topic had won the Group significant status once again. Yet the Group's reputation was threatened by the furore which erupted over Michael Lingens' remarks as Chairman at the Party Conference later that year.

Lingens' vehicle was the annual 'Open letter to the Prime Minister', published in the Party Conference edition of *Crossbow*. 'The Bow Group chairman's open letter to the PM had become a bit of an institution (and a bit boring – the PM never replied except to send a brief acknowledgement)' recalls Lingens; '. . . [it] had got diluted by many years of sycophancy as successive chairmen did not want to be too controversial or rude in case this affected their selection chances.'[70] He decided to reverse this trend: 'One year into the Government's second term of office, a dismal picture of missed opportunities emerges. Key policies have run out of steam and political enthusiasm.'[71] Criticism much stronger than this had become a feature of *Crossbow* in the years in which Richard Barber was Editor, but the allegation that the Government was running out of steam hit a raw nerve. It was not the first high-profile criticism of the Government that week immediately before the Party Conference; the Archbishop of Canterbury, Dr Robert Runcie, had entered the debate on the miners' strike, questioning the Government's policies in the light of high unemployment and poverty. The Group also called for policies to ensure that poverty was eliminated. To add insult to injury, the Bow Group's pre-briefing of its letter to the political lobby had obscured the announcement that David Young, the Minister without Portfolio, would head a new jobs taskforce, an emblematic move designed to show the Government's determination to cut the jobless total. That this was allowed to happen was strange since Number 10 apparently knew of the existence and the content of the letter before they received it. The *Sunday Times*' report, written on the eve of the ill-fated Brighton Conference, suggested that Stephen Sherbourne, who was then Thatcher's Political Secretary, was the first person to receive news of the Group's plans.[72] Whereas Dr Runcie could not be attacked, the Bow Group was a legitimate and obvious target and Mrs Thatcher seized the opportunity.

With warning of the Group's intention, Thatcher's office was able to write a detailed rebuttal of the Group's allegations, to appear as the Group's own letter was released on the Sunday afternoon for publication in Monday's papers. The *Daily Telegraph* printed her response in full in its story. Thatcher centred her reply on the Bow Group's most sensitive allegation that Conservative enthusiasm for privatisation was petering out: citing the examples of companies transferred from public to private sector ownership, Thatcher stated that her Government's policies had led to 'the transfer of around 150,000 jobs to the private sector'.73 On top of this, Thatcher added, the Government was about to embark on 'the greatest ever act of de-nationalisation: that of British Telecom . . . To dismiss all of this, including the privatisation of BT as "cautious" and "defensive" is crackers'. 'Like you,' she rounded off, 'I am making public the contents of this letter.' Commentators believed this rebuke to be unprecedented; although Lingens' letter did reflect wider concerns that the Government was insensitive to the problem of rising unemployment, his decision to open the debate to include a critique of privatisation was badly judged.

Weakly, Lingens replied to Mrs Thatcher: 'If opinion polls are any guide, the country is behind you. Our Party Conference will show the country that we have the courage to do what we know to be right.'74 Lingens believes the episode had a positive long-term effect. 'I remember many MPs and former chairmen being very complimentary at the time – not because they necessarily agreed with what I said (though many did) but because there was a feeling that the Bow Group was doing what it should be doing, namely stirring things up and being radical without being partisan or factional. It certainly put us "back on the map" in that the press gave much more publicity than before to subsequent papers and letters to the press – and the effect lasted a few years.'75 The strength of the criticism levelled at the Group reflected its influence but revealed its inability to defend itself from attack from the Government. If it was an unfair contest for the Prime Minister to pick a fight with the Bow Group, there was no question that Mrs Thatcher was anxious to stop the Group's criticisms from escalating. Her resolve to continue 'full steam ahead' was seemingly confirmed by her determination to continue the Conference after the IRA's bombing of the Grand Hotel in Brighton later that week.

One incontrovertible point which Michael Lingens did make in his letter was the need for the Conservatives to develop a clear environmental policy. A string of environmental issues – the encroachment on the green belt and Sellafield's contamination of the Cumbrian coastline, to name two – had already been seized upon by the Alliance as it tried to establish itself as the greenest political party. It was ironic, Lingens suggested, that 'a Tory Government which represents a party linked to the countryside, dithers about policies for the environment.' Lingens had identified natural Bow Group territory: the environmentalist Jonathon Porritt had been a member of the Group briefly during the late 1970s and in the mid-1980s several members of the Group were passionate enough about environmental politics to set up the 'Tory Green Initiative'.[76]

Interest in the politics of the environment was reflected in the Council's decision to invite the Chairman of the Council for the Protection of Rural England, David Aster, to speak to the Group around the time of the Party Conference in 1985. The Bow Group had a close link to the House of Commons' Environment Select Committee: Marie-Louise Rossi, the Bow Group's Treasurer, was the daughter of the Select Committee's Chairman, Sir Hugh Rossi MP. It was unsurprising, then, that Hugh Rossi submitted a clear memorandum to *Crossbow* which set out the abilities and limitations of the Committee. Rossi's candid note was published in the 1984 Conference edition at the same time as the Bow Group tried to colonise what it saw as crucial electoral ground with a radical paper, *Conservation and the Conservatives*. This paper was designed to coincide with the Government's rethink of the 1981 Wildlife and Countryside Act. Its author, Tony Paterson, advocated the creation of a Conservation Minister of Cabinet rank, a 'Clean Air' Act to address the problem of acid rain, and cuts in the use of nuclear power. *Conservation and the Conservatives* was a well-timed, pioneering piece of political analysis, which generated significant sales. Three years later the Prime Minister would grasp the issue in a lecture on the future of the planet to the Royal Society. The Bow Group was discovering that well-timed, good ideas could be controversial but profitable as well.

More profitable still were the conferences which the Group continued to organise. These conferences ignored the intricacies of policy debate and honed an agenda which quickly arrived at the commercial opportunities available from Government procurement needs. The Bow Group revisited defence procurement as the subject of several of its conferences during the mid-1980s. This was an acknowledgement that the Group's best interest lay in acting as a forum for ministers and representatives of the defence industries to meet. The scale on which the first defence procurement conference was organised was unprecedented: a budget of £27,000 was proposed and accepted by the Council. The exact profit the conference made is not clear, although it was described in the Minutes as 'highly successful . . . both in political and financial terms'.[77] Subsequent conferences on the Strategic Defence Initiative in February 1986 and again on defence procurement in May the same year, in association with Panmure Gordon, were both highly profitable, making gains of around £5,000 and £3,000 respectively.

Again, it was a member of the Group with a commercial interest, Dexter Jerome-Smith, who worked for GEC, who generated the impetus for these conferences. Having aroused the interest of the US Embassy, the Group had relatively little difficulty encouraging US politicians to come across the Atlantic at the Group's expense to speak. At the SDI conference, William Schneider, an Under-Secretary at the State Department, outlined the US Government's intention to sign several specific research contracts with foreign companies to develop the SDI. Lieutenant-General James Abrahamson, the Director of the Strategic Defence Initiative, spelt out the commercial opportunities, saying: 'We want, by providing money for your own people to work here in their own areas, to nourish your own technology in your own gardens.'[78] The event was unexpectedly enlightened by an attempt by the Russian military attaché, Victor Kuslov, to gatecrash the conference 'brandishing a fistful of fivers'.[79] Such was the attraction of rubbing shoulders with defence procurement ministers that by April 1986 it was acknowledged in the Council that there was 'no risk of a financial loss on this [the second defence procurement] conference . . . the reality is that Defence Conferences are successful because companies cannot afford to miss them.'[80] But it was felt by some that the commercialism harmed the Group: as a previous Chairman, Richard Simmons, scathingly put it, '*pace* Bow Group conferences SDI was always generally regarded as either dangerous or nonsensical over here, excepting the lucrative contracts implied.'[81] It is hard to avoid the conclusion that the Group simultaneously published the pamphlet, *Why Yes to SDI?*, written by Jerome-Smith, simply to maintain the hype on its conference, rather than to support the controversial SDI project. The revenue from these three conferences paid for a great deal of the Group's day-to-day political activities, a renewed attempt to develop a better-based relationship with the media in a series of lunches.

One beneficiary of the Group's newly found financial stability was its new Chairman, the precocious Nicholas Perry, who as Research Secretary had been one of the architects of the business-like rebuilding of the Group during the previous two years. Before he had even assumed the chairmanship, Perry invited controversy. In response to the announcement by Francis Pym of a new grouping within the Parliamentary Party, Conservative Centre Forward, Lingens and Perry had written to *The Times* in an attempt to dissuade Pym from launching his group.[82] A week before a vote had been cast at the Bow Group's 1985 AGM, Perry, who was the uncontested candidate for the chairmanship, signed the letter off as 'Chairman-elect', since he had already faced down his major potential challenger, Nigel Waterson, who waited another year before becoming Chairman.[83] It was 'slightly presumptuous', he admits today, a view shared by Bow Group members attending the Annual General Meeting the following week.

In their letter, Perry and Lingens registered their alarm at Pym's creation, the purpose of which was to take a collective view and vote en bloc on economic and other issues – in effect a party within the Tory Party. 'We sympathise with Mr Pym's concern about unemployment. We deplore his methods,' they concluded, and were attacked for supporting the party line the following day by the MP and historian Robert Rhodes James. But it seems that Lingens' and Perry's decision to speak out was significant in causing the failure of Conservative Centre Forward. One member of the new group's steering committee, Tony Baldry MP, announced his resignation from the faction apparently as a result of reading their views. Baldry's departure, together with that of Jerry Hayes, led the newspapers to describe Conservative Centre Forward as cracking up, barely 24 hours after it had begun.[84]

This was perhaps the most exciting moment of Perry's chairmanship, and it happened before he was even formally Chairman. As he himself said in his annual report at the close of his term of office, 'Consolidation is not an invigorating business. Inevitably it involves an element of bureaucratic endeavour which does not appeal to the more buccaneering instincts.'[85] Much of that consolidation had already been done under his predecessors, Shaw and Lingens: 'I was in the happy position of picking up something which was firing on all cylinders,' remembers Perry. But he saw the need to create a systematic approach to running the Group, one which was both idiot- and politician-proof. 'The Group's democratic processes do not dictate that election should be on the basis of business competence: nor, in an essentially political organisation, should they ever do,' was his belief.[86] Like Douglas French before him, Perry pruned the Group's meetings back to one a week. Two years earlier, two and sometimes three meetings each week had attracted dwindling audiences. Care was taken to avoid clashes between the Group's activities. The Group formalised its existing and new arrangements through contracts, and Perry reaffirmed the central 'no corporate view' mantra by drawing up a model disclaimer, following the furore of his own making which had erupted at the AGM. The Group took on a part-time book-keeper, and the Council was able to call on an up-to-date snapshot of the Group's finances as a result. An extra part-time administrator, Helen Pender, was recruited, and for the first time in over ten years, the Group enjoyed a high level of administrative support. The ongoing conferences demanded and in turn financed this expansion.

The Group's inner vigour was symbolised with a few flamboyant gestures. Though the Council decided not to undertake some of the serious renovation of which its office was now in desperate need, it did put up a brass plaque advertising itself by the front door at 240 High

Holborn. This advertised the address as the registered office for Bow Functions Ltd and Bow Publications Ltd. Passers-by would have been forgiven for thinking that the Bow Group was a commercial consortium rather than a political organisation any more. Perry concluded his year with a glossy ten-page report, copies of which were provided for all members at a total cost of £6,000, in which he exuberantly chronicled his year's notable achievements, and to cap it all, the Group offered the Conservative Party a loan of £15,000 out of the surplus it had built up. This, Perry grins, 'was done out of sheer amusement' – but Conservative Central Office took up the loan.

As the minutes of the meeting in February 1986 at which the loan was discussed make clear, other members of the Council wondered whether the Group could curry favour by making the loan. In the wake of the Brighton bombing, security at the 1985 Party Conference was sharply tightened, and the number of passes allotted to the Group was cut from 12 to two. When the loan was agreed it was mentioned that the Group should seek a commercial stand in return, presumably as a means of gaining entry for more of its Council members.[87]

It was not until Perry stepped down as Chairman that he had the opportunity to speak out more forcefully about Government policy. Unlike many of his colleagues, he had no aspirations to a Westminster political career, and so felt more able to make his opinions known. His chance came when Richard Bacon, who had succeeded Nirj Deva as the Editor of Crossbow, resigned to go to America. Perry took on the job in the summer of 1986, and says he 'thoroughly enjoyed' being outspoken. Under his editorship, Crossbow gained a somewhat incongruous motoring section. Nissan and Rover became regular advertisers, possibly as a result of the column, but more probably because of the prominence of the Party Conference issue and the Group's links with the Government.

Since he was not interested in a career in national politics Perry also felt he could be blunt. He attacked a rumour that the Government intended to extend tax relief on mortgage interest payments from £30,000 to £35,000 as 'buying votes' before the General Election. The Daily Mail praised Perry's radicalism; the Sun attacked him for arguing that an increase in the threshold of MIRAS might have an inflationary effect. 'Where have these pale blue gents been these past 20 years?', the *Sun*'s editorial demanded to know, 'All property prices have been soaring . . . It is taxes, still far too high after seven years of Tory rule, which are the engine of inflation.'[88] The Bow Group maintained the pressure on the issue, awarding first prize in its reinvigorated essay competition to an examination of 'Tax Relief and Home Ownership', which argued that MIRAS was both 'highly regressively distributed', and the result of 'haphazard' Government planning.[89] In the issues after the 1987 general election, Perry focused on social issues. During his editorship *Crossbow* was to provide a regularly cited critique of the new Government's policy. Particular targets were the Tories' policies for the inner cities and education. But even his tone was clipped, however, by the general election imminent by 1987.

The election brought a halt to the Group's routine activities, remembers the then Chairman, Cheryl Gillan. But there was an excellent political and economic dividend when victory followed. Group members had formed last minute 'hit squads' targetting the North Westminster, Hampstead and Highgate constituencies, and helping to ensure the return of the Conservative MP in both. Fourteen members of the group were elected for the first time, including Ann Widdecombe, for Maidstone. The year also saw the retirement of a number of Conservative MPs. 'We had a great problem' recalls Gillan: 'no fewer than seven out of 13 of the MPs chairing Bow Group standing commit- tees retired'. A rush to fill the places followed. The Bow Group's Victory Ball was a sell-out generating a £10,000 surplus, which helped increase the Group's overall fund to over £22,000 by the end of Gillan's term of office in Spring 1988. In the period which followed the Election, the Group was able to trade heavily on its connections with the Government. A conference on 'Town Hall Tenders' was organised at which Nick Ridley, Paul Beresford, the leader of Wandsworth Council, and Christopher Chope spoke.

That Autumn, Cheryl Gillan wrote a broad open letter to the Prime Minister, recommending an increase in Government expenditure on research and development, a longer term outlook in the wake of the stock market crash, reform of tax on married couples, the abolition of inheritence and capital gains taxes and suggested, for the first time, a separate department for culture, media and sport, on the grounds that such an important aspect of public life deserved a less fragmented political approach. Her suggestion was later taken up.

The benchmark for *Crossbow*'s assessment of the new Government was an interview in the journal with the Prime Minister which was published four days after she had requested the dissolution of Parliament in 1987. Here she stated that 'We will not hold on to our achievements simply by coasting.' Before the election it had been reported that the Group had warned its members of 'the need to rein in our usual outspokenness in what could be an election year'.[90] But, after an election campaign which revealed the limitations of the Conservative Party's machine, Perry felt able to launch an attack on several fronts against Party policy, which was widely reported, since it came in the summer 'silly season', when the Group had previously enjoyed heightened coverage due to a lack of competing political news. Moreover, as the *Guardian* observed, 'the editorial is the first public election post-mortem to come from within the Tory camp.'

Perry concentrated his fire on the workability of two Government policies. He argued that there was little chance of Conservative policy for the inner cities succeeding along the lines of the model provided by the London Docklands Development Corporation. Perry was also sceptical whether the Government's threat to take over poorly performing local authorities could work. 'All of Whitehall put together would not have the manpower or ability to run half a dozen cities from London.' He was similarly scathing about the opt-outs envisaged by the Conservative Government for schools and council tenants. 'The idea of whole schools opting out convinces no-one; nor will it until the details are clear . . . It should be obvious to anyone with a working knowledge of the state school system that the type of schools likely to muster the initiative to opt out are going to be those which have an excellent PTA and parent governors. In short they will be schools where there are no problems to begin with.'

The *Times Educational Supplement* looked upon the Bow Group as a crucial influence at this time, since it believed that 'it is only

Conservative criticism which is likely to bear fruit in Mr Baker's consultations.'[91] As for privately run estates, Perry asserted that private landlords would only be interested in taking on idyllic estates: 'For each estate which finds a way to opt out [of local authority control] there will be dozens which cannot.' In summary, Perry called on the Government to abandon 'the trite, unhelpful stand point that unemployment and adverse social conditions do not cause crime. Because for all practical purposes, they do.'[92] The *Independent* saw this statement as confirmation that 'the concept that unemployment is not linked with crime' was 'steadily being eroded'.[93] At a political level, Robin Oakley, then *The Times*' Political Editor, suggested that *Crossbow*'s shot was 'an early warning that this year's Tory Party Conference may not be an altogether self-congratulatory affair'. Perry had succeeded in taking some of the shine off the new Government.

Not that the Bow Group had been reduced to the sole function of critic. At a time of substantial criticism from Labour and the unions about the state of the National Health Service, *Crossbow* devoted itself in Spring 1988 to healthcare, with the Secretary of State for Health and Social Security, John Moore, paying tribute to the institution of the NHS, but describing the changes which its internal market reforms had brought. Other contributions were more buccaneering: John Redwood aired the possibility of giving tax rebates to people who had taken out private health insurance, and David Green of the IEA proposed a voucher scheme for health. Sir Gerard Vaughan MP argued that it was the length of the waiting list, not the public/private argument, which mattered most, while Eammon Butler, the Director of the Adam Smith Institute, advocated scrapping health authorities altogether, replacing them with 'Health Management Units' which would compete among GPs to provide medical services for their patients. New thought of this kind enabled the Group to restore its separate subscription service, which provided non members of the Group with every new pamphlet for an annual fee.

Throughout the 1980s, the Group had been strongly involved in advocating greater competition and increased private provision, sometimes in line with the Government, sometimes going beyond it. In January 1980, the Group had issued a strong call for the reform of building societies, arguing that demutualisation would bring greater competition, and reduce the queues for mortgages by creating competition on interest rates. Although the Group believed that this would be good for savers and reduce mortgage queues, the Achilles' heel of *Building Societies – The Case for Reform* was that, as the authors acknowledged, interest rates would certainly go up as a result. In *North Sea Giveaway*, Peter Lilley called for Department of Energy to auction off offshore sectors to the oil companies, instead of allocating them as was the norm at the time. But perhaps the most brilliant plan, in terms of its impact and populism, was the proposal made in July 1980 by Tim Eggar, Jocelyn Cadbury and David Shaw to privatise British Gas, and give shares in the company worth £20 to everyone over the age of 18. 'The Bow Group scheme is not harebrained because it bears strong similarities to one already being studied by the government for [the] British National Oil Corporation,' reported the *Sunday Times*.94 Both this pamphlet and the later contribution by Rodney Atkinson which Perry had laboriously photocopied set out the Group's credentials as a key player in the debate over British Gas and an advocate of mass share-ownership.

In 1986, the Group attracted widespread interest with a scheme to allow UK companies to issue bonds to raise capital for long-term investment. 'Employment Bonds', the Group argued, would significantly reduce unemployment by stimulating industrial investment. The following year, in *Programme for Reform – A New Agenda for Broadcasting*, Toby Horton, the former Managing Director of Radio Tees, called for the licence fee to be scrapped and the BBC to be partly privatised, to allow greater commercial competition. Under his plan, the BBC would receive public money only to fund its external services and a new television World Service.

But if, with occasional exceptions, the Bow Group was largely in favour of the Government until 1988 and proactive in its policy-making, this attitude began to change during that year. Nick Perry turned his attention to the Community Charge – which, significantly, the Group had never defended – arguing that it was 'only a semi-regressive hybrid', by which he meant that it was not a truly neutral charge for services provided by the council, because the tax would also fund some social security and education spending. Instead, Perry argued that central Government should levy additional tax to cover these items, leaving the services supplied by local authorities to be covered by a Community Charge. In the same issue Rodney Atkinson re-examined his commitment to the market economy in the light of recent takeovers. His faith, he said, had been shaken by the pre-eminent role a few fund managers and arbitrageurs, and not the consumers, had in determining the outcome of takeovers. 'It cannot be the aim of the Conservative Party to replace State socialism with a laissez faire agnosticism – such careless licence is likely to rebound and lead to a resurgence of State tyranny. Where will those who have misunderstood and dangerously exaggerated market economics take us next?'[95] Almost as an aside, in the last paragraph of his article, Atkinson noted 'the first signs of a serious challenge to the present leadership'. During the next three years, the Bow Group was to act as a platform for one of the strongest contenders.

In June 1988 Geoffrey Howe laid claim again to the Enterprise Zones which he had developed as an idea first in the late 1970s, with the Bow Group's help. It published both his 1978 address announcing the idea and a follow-up speech made aboard the ship *Celtic Surveyor* that year.[96] By 1988, the fruits of the combination of deregulation and tax reliefs could be seen most vividly in Docklands, where Howe had made his 1978 speech to members of the Group. Notably, Howe referred to Heseltine's role in the execution of the policy, saying that he had 'committed himself with vigour to implementing the concept as a key part of his overall policies for reviving the inner cities'.[97] The *Guardian* reported that the speech would be seen as a significant reminder of Howe's role 'against the background of recent difficulties with Downing Street'.[98] The figures Howe quoted spoke for themselves: 'Employment in the Isle of Dogs zone rose from 641 people in 1982 to 3,700 at the beginning of 1987 . . . The number of firms located here in 1982 was 105, by the beginning of 1987 it had risen to 270 – a growth of 157%.' He concluded: 'The Bow Group was there at the creation. Ten years ago today we set out together a future vision of economic revival which accepted as first base the benef-icence of the capitalist system. Ten years later, the sight we survey exceeds our wildest dreams. The future we saw then is successfully at work.' But more interesting than the speech was the timing of its subsequent publication. Howe held it back from the Group until the late summer, so that the piece, which was effectively an advertisement for himself, appeared not in the midsummer lull but at the height of the political season in the Party Conference edition of *Crossbow*.

In the same issue of *Crossbow* the new Chairman of the Group, Marie-Louise Rossi, welcomed the Education Reform Act, but believed that the Conservatives' education programme was weakened because it did not include nursery education.[99] Nick Perry, the first member of the Bow Group to consider writing its history, unveiled the results of his early investigations in an article which traced the Bow Group's roots back to the East End and the Bow Constitutional Club, where the Group had first met. The article neatly tied in with Howe's speech:

> Right alongside the Bow Bells [the pub across the road from the Club where the Group had held its first annual dinner] . . . is a halt on the Docklands Light Railway Line, glorying in the name of Bow Church Station. And just up the road is a perfect example of what Sir Geoffrey in his "Enterprise" speech called the "meat counter effect"; the Bow Triangle Business Centre, a neat development of small business units just being completed on old Railway Board land, which could hardly have been contemplated were it not for the Docklands-led boom in the East End.[100]

The Bow Group championed the redevelopment of brownfield sites and it appeared to be a guardian of the green belt to the Secretary of State for the Environment, Nicholas Ridley. Faced with a ring of MPs around London, all of whom opposed further house building, in typically forthright fashion Ridley chose the Bow Group to make the case for building more homes in the South-East. The speech, on 10 May 1988, was at first billed in *The Times* as an 'attack on the rural lobby', but the reaction during the day before forced him to soften his tone: the *Daily Telegraph* expected Ridley to 'try to pacify backbenchers when he makes a keynote speech to the Bow Group of Conservative MPs'.[101] In the event Ridley tried to tread a line which placated his own Home Counties MPs by using the expansion of the green belt under successive Conservative governments to justify more housing. Nevertheless, it was for this speech which Ridley coined the term 'Nimby' – 'Not In My Back Yard' – to describe those who refused to countenance such development, even though they would directly benefit. This stance attracted criticism: *The Times* leader a week later noted the gaps in Ridley's discussion, and argued that a *laissez-faire* approach could not satisfy anyone. 'Far better – but out of character – would be for Mr Ridley (and his colleagues, for this must be a Cabinet affair) to be positive about growth and attempt, in some measure, to plan it.'[102] By the time of the Party Conference, Ridley again faced having to justify his decision, in a two-stage strategy. Following his endorsement of a pamphlet which celebrated 40 years of the green belt, Ridley again spoke to the Bow Group. 'It is not necessary', he argued, 'to go back to living in caves, to hair shirts and peat fires and to a minimal organically grown diet, for mankind to survive as a species. We can safely reject appeals to "repent for the end of the world is nigh".' But the tide was turning against Ridley's own laconic dismissal of the environmental lobby's claims. Coincidentally, as Ridley addressed the Group, a former member of the Bow Group, Jonathan Porritt was speaking to the Friends of the Earth. 'Government action has been nowhere and nothing,' he believed. That was an approach of which Ridley probably approved. But the Bow Group remained unconvinced: as well as Porritt, it invited Virginia Bottomley, David Bellamy and Sir Hugh Rossi to its Oxford Conference the following year, to suggest a way for the Conservative Party to 'rise to the challenge and become the "green party"'.

By the beginning of 1989, having enjoyed several unusually healthy financial years, the Bow Group yet again had more mundane financial concerns: and the lease on the High Holborn Office was the cause of its undoing. A succession of Chairmen had ignored the Group's require-ment to share the costs of repairing the building, which by the late 1980s was in a state of serious disrepair. Two contrasting events had taken a heavy toll on the Group. The stock market crash early in the autumn of 1987 had a significant effect. Although Norman Lamont, then the Financial Secretary to the Treasury, announced at a meeting of the Group shortly afterwards that there would be no stop to the Government's privatisation programme in the wake of the crash, the Group itself was exposed as the bottom briefly dropped out of the commercial conference market, on which the Group had become, with hindsight, over-reliant. Though the Council failed to spot the change in business interest quickly enough to avoid burning the Group's fingers with a number of agreed commitments, it was a second, opposite, factor which proved decisive. This was the property boom in the late 1980s. 240 High Holborn changed hands twice, before finally being sold early in 1989 to a developer who had every intention of renovating the property before resale.

Marie-Louise Rossi, then the Chairman, remembers the sinking feeling as she arrived at 240 High Holborn one day to find workmen erecting scaffolding around the building.[103] Due to the repairing clause in its lease, the Group suddenly found itself responsible for a substantial cost of the improvements. After some negotiation, the Group agreed to pay a sum of around £30,000 towards the work. At a stroke, the efforts of the previous six years in putting the Group on a firm financial footing seemed to have been erased by the decision of the new owner to refurbish the building. In fact, the Group's financial circumstances had been misleading, since the massive potential liability represented by the repair clause of its lease agreement on the dilapidated building did not have to be included in the accounts. David Harvey, then the Group's Political Officer, remembers the immediate effect of the settlement: 'There was no money for publishing, no money for staffing, no money for nothing.'[104] The Group went to the lengths of debating whether new computer software meant that it could dispense with central London premises and run a virtual office from then on. In the autumn of 1989 the Group was forced to leave 240 High Holborn for less central and altogether more basic accommodation at 92 Bishop's Bridge Road, Paddington.

In a Group in which there had usually been no shortage of willing candidates for places on the Council, suddenly there was a dearth. Without administrative support, the pressure of running the Group fell squarely on the shoulders of its Council members. Moreover, the threat of bankruptcy acted as an additional deterrent, since if the Group went bankrupt, the Council was liable for its debts. 'Lots of able political people looked at it and decided it wasn't worth the effort,' believes Harvey today. Ian Donaldson, the successor to Marie-Louise Rossi, 'became Chairman almost by default', comments Nick Hawkins, who was later Chairman himself.[105] Donaldson's quiet and studious air concealed his main business interest as the part owner of a night-club on the Kings Road in Chelsea. It was widely believed not to be a success. 'One got the impression that Ian got tied up in the night-club's financial worries,' recalls one contemporary. The strain of running the Group was possibly exaggerated by the dominance of former members of the Oxford University Bow Group, who formed an intimidating bloc within the London Group's active membership at the time. Given his own ambition to run the Group as a significant political force, Donaldson was disappointed that he spent much of his time as Chairman 'firefighting'.

As the Group's financial worries again caused hiccups in the publication of *Crossbow*, the Group's effort became increasingly focused on the Party Conference. In the annual 'Open letter', in the 1989 Conference issue of the magazine, Donaldson concentrated on the unexceptional aim of extending share ownership, but caught the eye of the press with his suggestion that pensioners should be given free shares from the water and electricity privatisations to improve their standard of living and reinforce the share-owning democracy. The Group's financial problems were to make this *Crossbow* the last regular issue until February 1994; in between the Group would make do with a single issue each year, published for the Conference. Outwardly, then, the Group maintained its usual presence; but clearly its ability to exert influence was limited by its shortage of money. During these years, the Group concentrated its efforts on hosting high-profile events during the week of the Conference.

For two years running, in 1989 and 1990, Geoffrey Howe was without a place on the Party Conference platform: in his new role, as Leader of the House and Deputy Prime Minister, he was not responsible for any area of policy. Significantly, in both years, Howe agreed to speak to the Bow Group: in 1989, when he accepted the invitation from the new Chairman Ian Donaldson in April, he could not have known what would happen later in the year. As it transpired, following the reshuffle, his address to the Group became his 'most conspicuous engagement', because even as Deputy Prime Minister there was no slot for him on the Conference platform. With perhaps more than a sideways glance at the Prime Minister, Howe began by noting the revolutionary connotations of the 200th anniversary of the French Revolution and urged the Conservatives to 'think afresh about the direction of British politics', and not to rest on their laurels. The 1990s, he argued, would be 'the quality of life decade', in which the Conservatives' primarily economic agenda would need to broaden, but not lose sight of its liberal precepts. It was more of a 'talk', as Howe himself later described it, than a speech. But it was also a gently worded warning of the perils of both being out-of-touch and using assertive, instead of explanatory language. 'We will need to be cautious about superlatives, hyperboles and absolutes,' he said.[106] His words were taken to refer to his view of Margaret Thatcher's stridency on Europe. The *Evening Standard* that afternoon portrayed Howe's speech as an expression of his 'growing concern'.[107]

His speech the following year was in a similar vein, though by now Howe's difference of opinion with the Party leadership could barely be concealed. The speech covered similar ground, with Howe again making predictions about the character of politics in the future. Again Howe cautioned against stridency, this time with a sly reference to another Tory grouping: 'no turning back', he quipped, was not the same as 'bash on regardless'.[108] Again, Howe emphasised simple communication as the key to future fortunes: 'We need to leave people in no doubt that our aim . . . is not upheaval for its own sake but the achievement of rising standards . . . Our central purpose is not to privatise but to humanise.' It was only when Howe resigned on 1 November that the press returned to pick, almost forensically, over the wording, the semantics of which had assumed a crucial importance in the light of the events which followed. With this hindsight, but in advance of Howe's resignation speech, the *Guardian* was to call his speech to the Bow Group his 'final political testimony'. The newspaper concluded that 'Sir Geoffrey's differences with Mrs Thatcher went wider than mere doubts about her style and tone on Europe.'[109] These messages were barely noticed on the day of the speech. That day, it was Howe's message about Economic and Monetary Union that excited the interest of the media. While the new Chancellor of the Exchequer, John Major, was playing down the likelihood that Britain would join the European single currency, Howe was emphasising its importance. While the rest of the country was considering the quality of its life, the Tories were to spend the next decade considering the issue of Europe and the euro.

NOTES

1   Geoffrey Howe, Speech to the Bow Group, 28 April 1981.

2   I am grateful to Jeremy Bradshaw for this remark.

3   Jenkin, interview.

4   *Chairman's Annual Report for 1980/81.*

5   *Daily Mail,* 26 February 1980.

6   'Tories Must Win Public Support Says Stevas', *Daily Telegraph,* 10 June 1980.

7   'Stevas Hits at Hard-line Monetarism', *Financial Times,* 9 October 1980.

8   'Stevas Hits at Hard-line Monetarism', *Financial Times,* 9 October 1980.

9   *Guardian,* 17 February 1981.

10   Bow Group Council, Minutes, 19 October 1980.

11   Ivor Crewe and Anthony King, *SDP: The Birth, Life and Death of the Social Democratic Party*, Oxford 1995, p. 537n.

12   *Eastern Evening News,* 25 October 1982. Hardie went on to be the Chairman of W. H. Smith.

13   Nirj Deva was MP for Brentford and Isleworth 1992–97. He was elected an MEP for the South East region in 1999.

14   'Dripping Wet', *Guardian,* 30 October 1981.

15   Bow Group Council, Minutes, 26 March 1981.

16   *Times,* 29 April 1981.

17   *Times,* 10 June 1981.

18   'Sliding to Defeat?', *Crossbow,* Summer 1981.

19   Bow Publications Ltd Board Meeting, 26 January 1958.

20   'Warning Bells of Bow', *Daily Telegraph,* 27 May 1981.

21   *Marketing Week,* 1 September 1981.

22   *Times,* 1 June 1981.

23 *Times Educational Supplement*, 25 September 1981.

24 The Rt Hon. Francis Pym MC MP, 'The Conservative Case', 14 October 1981.

25 *Manchester Daily Star*, 16 October 1981.

26 Bow Group Council, Minutes, 2 March 1981.

27 Chairman's Annual Report for 1980/81, 31 March 1981.

28 'Coming to the Financial Aid of the Parties', *Financial Times*, 3 July 1981.

29 The paper was written by Peter Hardy, and dated 18 September 1980. Special Meeting of the Bow Group Officers and Council, 19 October 1980.

30 Nirj Deva, interview, 24 October 1999.

31 Nicholas Perry, interview, 28 January 2000.

32 Deva, interview.

33 Perry, interview.

34 Michael Stephen was MP for Shoreham, 1992–97.

35 *Guardian*, 17 March 1980.

36 Deva, interview.

37 Nigel Waterson, Report to Council, Minutes, 26 October 1984.

38 Michael Stephen, interview, 24 October 1999. The party comprised Ivan Lawrence, Jim Lester, Baroness Hooper, Michael Stephen, Nirj Deva and Michael Lingens.

39 Stephen, interview.

40 Fred Kellogg, email to the author, 31 December 1999. David Shaw was MP for Dover 1987–97.

41 David Shaw, interview, 25 November 1999.

42 Shaw, interview.

43 The Rt Hon. Sir John Nott, interview, 25 October 1999.

44 Admiral Sandy Woodward, *One Hundred Days*, London 1992, pp. 93–4.

45 *Daily Telegraph*, 23 April 1999.

46 'The Guns Fire Live Shells Too', *Daily Telegraph*, 4 May 1982.

47 Clark, *Diaries: Into Politics*, p. 326. Entry for Tuesday 4 May 1982. Carlisle had been MP for Runcorn since 1963. In 1983 he was elected for Warrington South, which he held until 1987.

48 Shaw, interview.

49 Lingens and Mabey, 'Bow Papers and Bow Memoranda', 4 October 1982.

50 Perry, interview. Best was MP for Anglesey, 1979–83; for Ynys Môn, 1983–87.

51 'Kremlin will be Watching, Heseltine Warns CND Protesters', *Daily Telegraph*, 29 March 1983.

52   20 September 1982.

53   Nigel Waterson, interview, 19 May 1999.

54   Shaw, interview.

55   The Bow Group, Minutes of the 32nd Annual General Meeting, 9 May 1983.

56   *Times*, 9 May 1983.

57   Bow Group, *Chairman's Report,* 1983/84.

58   Waterson, interview.

59   Group Council, Minutes, 12 September 1983.

60   Political impact was chief among the criteria. Report published in the Council Minutes of 11 June 1984.

61   Lynda MacKenzie, letter to the author, 2 June 2000.

62   Rodney Atkinson is a prolific author of pamphlets and books.

63   Perry, interview.

64   Bow Group Council, Minutes, 11 July 1983.

65   Cheryl Gillan has been MP for Chesham and Amersham since 1992. She was Parliamentary Under-Secretary of State at the Department for Education and Employment, 1995–97.

66   Shaw, interview.

67   *Crossbow*, Autumn 1984, p. 2.

68   Bow Group Council, Minutes, July 1984.

69   Bow Group Council, Minutes, 13 March 1984.

70   Michael Lingens, email to the author, 31 October 2000.

71   'Taking the Long View', *Crossbow*, Autumn 1984, p. 4.

72   'Why the Tories Are Worried', *Sunday Times*, 7 October 1984.

73   '"Full steam ahead", Vows Thatcher', *Daily Telegraph*, 8 October 1984.

74   '"Full steam ahead", Vows Thatcher', *Daily Telegraph*, 8 October 1984.

75   Lingens, email.

76   Jonathon Porritt was Director of Friends of the Earth 1984–90. He stood as a candidate for the Ecology Party in Local, General and European Elections between 1977 and 1984.

77   Bow Group Council, Minutes, 4 June 1985.

78   'How UK Can Gain from Star Wars', *Guardian*, 18 February 1986.

79   'Peterborough', *Daily Telegraph*, 18 February 1986.

80   Bow Group Council, Minutes, 17 April 1986.

81   Richard Simmons, 'Why I Would be Voting Dukakis', *Crossbow*, Autumn 1988, p. 40.

82   *Times*, 14 May 1985.

83   Perry, interview.

84   Perry, interview. Baldry has been MP for Banbury since 1983. Hayes was MP for Harlow, 1983–97.

85   Bow Group, *Chairman's Report*, 1985–86.

86   Bow Group, *Chairman's Report*, 1985–86.

87   Bow Group Council, Minutes, 12 February 1986.

88   *Daily Mail*, 26 August 1986; 'The Sun Says', *Sun*, 27 August 1986.

89   Simon Davies and Christopher Bailey, 'Tax Relief and Home Ownership', *Crossbow*, Autumn 1987, pp. 34–6.

90   *Independent*, 19 March 1987.

91   *Times Educational Supplement*, 21 August 1987.

92   'The Fruits of Victory', *Crossbow*, Summer 1987, p. 6.

93   'Struggle to Curb Crime and the Fear of Crime', *Independent*, 19 August 1987.

94   *Sunday Times*, 13 July 1980. Eggar was MP for Enfield North from 1979 to 1997. Cadbury was MP for Birmingham Northfields from 1979 until he committed suicide in 1982.

95   Rodney Atkinson, 'A Chocolate Challenge', *Crossbow*, Summer 1988.

96   The Rt Hon. Sir Geoffrey Howe QC MP, *Enterprise Zones and the Enterprise Culture*, Bow Group, 1988.

97   Sir Geoffrey Howe, 'The Birth of Enterprise', *Crossbow*, Summer 1988, p. 6.

98   'Howe Enterprise Architect', *Guardian*, 27 June 1988.

99   Marie-Louise Rossi is Chief Executive of the International Underwriting Association.

100   Nicholas Perry, 'Bow Road Revisited', *Crossbow*, Autumn 1988, p. 13.

101   *The Times*, 9 May 1988, *Daily Telegraph*, 10 May 1988.

102   'Sour Grapes in the Green Belt', *Times*, 17 May 1988.

103   Marie-Louise Rossi, interview, 29 March 2000.

104   David Harvey, interview, 9 March 2000.

105   Nick Hawkins, interview, 27 October 1999.

106   Howe, *Conflict of Loyalty*, p. 602.

107   *Evening Standard*, 11 October 1989.

108   The Thatcherite No Turning Back Group was formed by MPs who had first been elected in 1983.

109   *Guardian*, 3 November 1990.

Eight

EUROPE AND BEYOND

The origins of the Group's renewed debate on Europe can be traced back to its annual Oxford Conference at Jesus College in March 1988, the subject of which was the Single Market and '1992', a date which had acquired an epochal significance for the consequences it was expected to bring to businesses in Britain. Fresh from negotiations at the EEC's February 1988 summit, Francis Maude, the then Minister for Corporate and Consumer Affairs, predicted a radical change in the business environment after trade barriers had been lifted. Broaching the issue of qualified majority voting, the instrument by which the single market would be agreed, Maude made an early warning of the danger 'if the European Commission was tempted to bring forward proposals under the article providing for qualified majority voting when other articles requiring unanimity might be more appropriate'.[1]

Early in 1989 *Crossbow* focused on Europe. In answer to her self-imposed question, 'What Sort of Europe?' the new editor, Joanna Bogle, concluded that

> A truly united Europe – a 'Europe of hearts' – is an ideal worth holding. But what it should mean is a spiritual and cultural unity-in-diversity, buttressed by a common prosperity, secured from common enemies, conscious of a common mission, open to new responsibilities and challenges. A federated bureaucracy, easily controllable by one faction or another, lacking a sense of history and shorn of any sense of limits on its own importance, is a notion from which every sane European retreats with a shudder, and rightly.[2]

In the following issue, a federal Europe was debated, with Professor David Regan taking up the case against and Dr Lutz Stavenhagen the arguments in favour.

The same issue of *Crossbow* announced the formation of a European Standing Committee. It was a sign that interest in European affairs had rekindled: the previous European Affairs committee, then chaired by Robert Jackson, had been mothballed in September 1984 after it was agreed that European considerations infused UK politics so much that they could be debated within individual domestic policy groups.3 Dudley Fishburn MP agreed to chair the new European Standing Committee, and Ian Taylor MP became its vice-Chairman. The politicians the committee invited give some idea of its collective political outlook. They included Malcolm Rifkind, Tristan Garel-Jones, Sir Edward Heath, Roy Denman and Lord Cockfield, all of whom at that time held a broadly favourable view of closer European integration.

Barely one page of Sir Geoffrey Howe's speech tackled the issue of Europe when he addressed the Bow Group on the Party Conference fringe just before his resignation in 1990, but in doing so he gave the press the story it wanted. Howe's words were only read to the extent that they fulfilled the media's appetite for a 'Tory split' story; the remainder of the text was ignored. Alastair Campbell, who began the decade as the Political Editor of the *Sunday Mirror* and ended it as the new Prime Minister Tony Blair's spokesman, is an apt observer of this moment:

> No sooner had he [Major] sat down, than mysterious figures in Labour-style suits were whispering at us to look at the inside back page of Sir Geoffrey Howe's speech to the Bow Group. 'Wow' we said. The dead sheep had risen in the name of Jacques Delors. Here was a Euro split . . .4

Within an hour of John Major, the Chancellor of the Exchequer, saying that 'Joining the ERM does not mean that we are on a road leading inexorably to a single currency' in an attempt to settle a restless party, Howe had endorsed the single currency as Britain's only option:

> Europe is no longer peripheral to British politics . . . We will see
> Europe as . . . the basic vehicle for Britain to shape events on the
> wider international plane . . . If we in Britain are to punch
> beyond our weight, we have to be part of a team. Leadership
> cannot be exercised in a vacuum, not least if you lack economic
> or military dominance. Whether we like it or not, the process of
> European integration is proceeding by the day. We cannot afford
> to be passive bystanders or armchair critics; or least of all, to
> opt out emotionally from the club . . . We need to play a defining
> role in the next stages of integration. The next European train is
> about to leave, for a still undefined destination but certainly in
> the direction of some form of economic and monetary union.
> Shall Britain be in the driver's cab this time? Or the rear
> carriage?

This was the first of what was to become a genre of transport metaphors, all of which were calculated to play on British fears of being left out of Economic and Monetary Union. Britons, Howe seemed to suggest, should hurry aboard the train first and check the destination only when it had gathered speed. There was a sharp contrast with the abstract manner in which Howe dealt with Europe in his speech to the Group the previous year. Then he had concentrated on the benefits of membership, which had acted as a 'beacon of freedom' and catalysed political change in the Eastern Bloc.

The vivid quality of Howe's advocacy in 1990, and the manner in which the relevant excerpt was briefed to the lobby journalists, shows a more pro-active, yet perhaps a more despairing approach. Its language was reflective, perhaps, of Howe's marginalised position on the fringe and a subtle preview of his decision to resign. His words were resonant, however, and the Group was to reverberate to the European debate for the rest of the 1990s. As Michael Lingens remarks, 'Many friendships in the Party have been broken because of the wretched European question and I'm sure the Bow Group would have proved more susceptible to this division than other pressure groups that had clearer ideologies.'[5] It was, then, precisely because the Group had no corporate view that it became, as in the early 1980s, the battleground of competing ideologies. And again the Group again found itself in demand as a platform for political opponents within the same Party.

The more instant concern for the Group at the beginning of the decade was money. David Harvey used the coincidence of the Group's 40th anniversary in 1991 to launch an appeal, in the hope of providing a sinking fund to cushion the Group in its current and subsequent rough patches. But given the suddenness of the Group's financial failure, the Group had to conquer a certain amount of suspicion from potential donors that it would not simply waste funds given to it. A hint that there were doubts about the way in which the Group had been run in recent years came in Harvey's immediate decision to form a panel of Bow Group trustees to whom the Council would report on a regular basis. A year's fundraising began with an appeal from Christopher Bland to give 'the odd five hundred, five thousand, fifty thousand or even just five pounds if you're only an MP'. There was also a successful ball, a forum of members of Mrs Thatcher's first Cabinet chaired by the former Tory MP and *Times* journalist Matthew Parris, at which Howe, Carrington, Jenkin, Walker, Howell, Biffen and Fowler all spoke, and two conferences. Together these events made the Group around £50,000. This was a substantial sum, but not even a tenth of the £750,000 target which the Group had set itself. The Group's new and cheaper office in Paddington clearly did not appeal to the Council. During Dexter Jerome-Smith's year as Chairman, Council meetings were held at his home in Slough, with his wife taking the minutes of the proceedings. Impractical though this arrangement was, it contributed to a severe cut in the Group's costs, and between 1991 and 1993 the Group drastically reduced its debt.

The turning point in the Group's financial fortunes came when Nick Hawkins became Chairman. As MP for Blackpool South he was the first Chairman to be in the House of Commons at the same time. The Group benefited from having a full-time politician at the helm, not least because Hawkins' long-suffering researcher was able to carry out some of the administrative tasks and take the pressure off other members of the Council. Being an MP 'was a huge help', remembers Hawkins, because it gave him added credibility when negotiating with its bank over its £15,000 overdraft, and from access to other MPs in the lobby it was not difficult for him to persuade his colleagues to speak to the Group. By encouraging his colleagues to lean on the Pairing Whip who could allocate them time off the evening's vote, Hawkins was able to secure a higher turnout of MPs at a dinner in January 1993 hosted by Nuclear Electric than a Chairman outside Parliament might have. Even so, Hawkins regards the ball as the highlight of the year, at which those present had the chance to see Michael and Sandra Howard opening the dancing to music provided by the Crickets.

But it was the rising salience of Europe as the major political issue within the Party that raised the Group's profile once again. Edwina Currie, who had been at the forefront of the Birmingham Bow Group, and Michael Spicer argued the future of the European Union on the eve of the 1992 Party Conference in a debate which was televised by the BBC television programme *Newsnight*. European Commissioner Leon Brittan addressed the Group during the Conference. The signs of the confrontation that would grip the Conservatives during 1993 were already apparent in the Group's literature. The MP who would galvanise the Maastricht rebellion later in the year, Bill Cash, had powerfully put the arguments against closer European integration in a Bow Group pamphlet in 1990, *A Democratic Way to European Unity – Arguments against Federalism*. With the Group acting as a forum for debate within this increasingly tense climate, Hawkins believes that he was justified in saying that it was 'neither right nor left, just influential'.

When internal political controversy had kindled in the early 1980s the Group had been very willing to act as a platform for the key protagonists. Its reward had been a close – sometimes too close – association with the factional atmosphere of the first Thatcher Government. In 1993, after the mauling the Government received at the hands of the Eurosceptics during the ratification of the Maastricht Treaty, Norman Lamont approached the Group to ask whether he could speak at its fringe meeting at the Party Conference that year. In the light of his critical resignation speech, and given the timing of the fringe meeting, accepting Lamont's request offered the possibility of considerable publicity. But in contrast to his predecessors of ten years earlier, the Chairman in 1993, David Campbell Bannerman, naturally shied away from hosting a speech by the ex-

Chancellor. The first sign that Lamont was planning to unburden himself came on 23 August in the *Mail on Sunday*: 'Lamont to stitch up Major at Conference', predicted the newspaper: 'The ex-Chancellor will make a blockbuster speech' warning that the Prime Minister would be ousted unless he showed more leadership. The story worried Campbell Bannerman: 'I had to find out whether he was going to damage the Party,' he says today. Although 'to increase The Bow Group's political impact' was at the top of the list of his priorities in his manifesto for the chairmanship earlier in the year, he was equally determined that the Bow Group should not be seen as an accomplice to an event which would fuel the ongoing story of Conservative divisions, no matter how much impact it might have.

But the Bow Group Council was nethertheless keen to host what promised to be an important political event. Campbell Bannerman decided to try to compel Lamont to speak on his terms. He wanted the former Chancellor to concentrate on the broader issues of management of monetary policy rather than on an assault on Britain's membership of the Exchange Rate Mechanism, the exit from which had fatally wounded Lamont. Worried that the Party's hierarchy would press the Council not to run the event at all, the Group warned Norman Lamont that it would cancel the event if Lamont intended to use the Group's fringe meeting as a platform from which to damage the Party leadership. Members of the Council also approached Charles Lewington, the *Sunday Express*'s Political Editor, and persuaded him to run a story warning Lamont not to criticise John Major. Lewington obliged, writing a faintly disguised shot across Lamont's bows on the front page under the headline 'Lamont Gagged'.[6] Asked to 'confirm' whether they were on the brink of banning Lamont from speaking, the Group said that it would be seeking assurances from the ex-Chancellor that he would be restricting his remarks to 'Government policy, not personalities'. Prominent was a quote by Campbell Bannerman: 'I cannot condone any personal attacks made on the Prime Minister.' Behind the scenes, the Council threatened to pull the plug on Lamont, who was forced to reveal the contents of his speech to defuse mounting speculation when the *Mail on Sunday* alleged that he was considering challenging Major for the Party leadership.[7]

The advance hype ensured that the Bow Group's was the 'main fringe story of the Conference', believes Campbell Bannerman. Norman Lamont, speaking from behind an array of microphones and the Bow Group's prominent logo, was pictured during his speech the *Financial Times* the following day. Yet his speech proved to be mild compared with the rumours that he would unveil a critique of the Government's European policy. Like many other former Chancellors, his address revealed that he had become an advocate of an independent Bank of England. He also supported further spending cuts, he said, as well as reforms to Capital Gains Tax and the privatisation of the Royal Mail. His bitterness presented itself only in a brief joke on the state of the economy. 'Recession is when your neighbour loses his job,' said Lamont, 'Depression is when you lose your job. Recovery is when the Chancellor loses his job.' Sensing an anti-climax, the press rapidly dispersed, but the Council breathed a sigh of relief. Despite the publicity, some members of the Council had been rattled by the experience of being at the focus of intense media speculation.

There was a postscript to this episode. The following year, Lamont again asked the Group – forcefully, in the opinion of some of its members – whether he could speak at its fringe meeting. 'I remember a very difficult . . . Council meeting when we had to decide how best to tell him that we did not want to provide him with a platform,' remembers the then Secretary of the Group, Katherine Bowes.[8] The Chairman, Alexander Nicoll, did not want to turn Lamont down; but other members, with an eye to possible sponsorship, preferred a current, not a former Government Minister, and the Council again faced pressure from Conservative Central Office not to host the event. It was left to the Political Officer, Simon Elliott, to inform Lamont that he was not wanted. Rebuffed, Lamont wrote, in the words of one Council member, 'a stinking letter' in which he announced his resignation from the Group 'forthwith'. Lamont had regularly sponsored the Bow Group's events inside Parliament by booking rooms for it and he undoubtedly felt put out, though the impact of his resignation was limited by the fact that he forgot to cancel his standing order to the Group. He gave the speech, in which he suggested that Britain could leave the European Union, to the

Selsdon Group instead. In his memoirs he makes no mention of the incident which led this to happen.

Whereas the Group had shared the limelight when it organised equally controversial meetings in the 1980s, it barely merited a sub-clause in newspaper reports of the Lamont speech it staged in 1993. Lamont's own membership of the Bow Group – which was probably a factor in his decision to ask to address them – was seen as irrelevant to the story in 1993; nor was the Bow Group mentioned except in passing as the sponsor of the event at which he spoke. In the 1980s the Bow Group had been a label for a particular Minister or an important, if contrived, peg for a story; by the 1990s it was as if the Bow Group was no longer relevant to the narrative. David Campbell Bannerman remembers the impact this anonymity had on members of the Group. By the time he became Chairman in May 1993 there were, as he puts it, 'fundamental discussions going on about whether the Bow Group had a future'. The Conservative Party's open divisions were a factor in this uncertainty. But Campbell Bannerman believes that there was an identifiable deeper trend. 'There was an undertow to it all,' he says today, describing the Government's move away from think-tanks during this period to what he believes was an over-reliance on the Civil Service.[9] By 1995, the *Guardian* described the Group in passing as 'fading in influence'.[10]

None the less, David Campbell Bannerman tried to make the most of this unpromising situation. He organised sponsorship for several of the Group's events. The line-up that he was able to muster for an evening conference on the future of Social Security funding in February 1994 – Frank Field, the Labour Party's expert on welfare, Alan Duncan and Peter Lilley, the Secretary of State for Social Security – goes a long way to explaining the continuing readiness of companies (in this case Allied Dunbar) to sponsor Bow Group events. The Group revived its association with Oxford to hold a Conference at Exeter College in March 1994 to explore the means to a solution in Northern Ireland. Among the speakers were the Secretary of State for Northern Ireland, Sir Patrick Mayhew, Ken Maginnis and Colin Parry, whose son Tim had been killed in the Warrington bombing the year before. This conference was significant enough to ensure that the Irish Prime Minister John Bruton spoke to the Group later in the year.

By early 1994, in the second half of Campbell Bannerman's chairmanship, the Group was receiving a healthy income, with functions and profits from its Conferences the two major sources of income after subscriptions. Donations, once the staple of the Group's continuing existence, now accounted for just £500 of the Group's income of £45,341 for the first half of 1994. In particular, a Conference on Public/Private Sector Partnerships held in March 1994 earned the Group a profit of over £6,700, matching speakers from construction, healthcare and transport with politicians with a substantial stake in the programme. Virginia Bottomley, the Secretary of State for Health, and Stephen Dorrell, the Financial Secretary to the Treasury, both addressed a hall packed with hopeful businessmen, while Alastair Morton, the Chief Executive of Eurotunnel, Sir Brian Nicholson of BUPA and Sir John Egan of the British Airports Authority put the business case for the partnership. As defence procurement had done for the Group during the Cold War, so the substantial budgets which Government departments had to encourage public/private partnerships provided a lucrative source of revenue for the Group in the 1990s, provided it did the organisation. And here lay the rub.

During the 1980s, conferences had at first been organised by members of the Group – often interested or involved in the subject matter – with all the profit going to the Group itself. Although the reward was considerable, the burden of administration was significant, and by 1986 the Group employed three part-time staff to deal with the workload generated by the conferences and functions it ran. As the Group ran into financial trouble once again at the end of the 1980s, it faced a tough choice: by reducing its staffing level, it would be unable to cope with the lucrative conference organisation which represented a key route back into the black. In stopping the Group's decline, Hawkins had been significantly helped by the fact that the Group's administration had been shared by his own Parliamentary researcher and Terry Bowers, a long-time member who had heroically provided voluntary assistance to the Group for several years.

Once shrunken, however, the Group's administrative arrangements remained piecemeal: as late as 1995, the Group's staff was described in a guide to political groups as 'one volunteer plus interns'.[11] Campbell Bannerman had set out a possible solution to the problem in his manifesto for the chairmanship and when elected, he contracted out the task of organising the Bow Group's conferences to a specialist company, City and Financial, which was run by a member, Maurice Button, a long-term member of the Group and then Chairman of its Trade and Industry Committee. Campbell Bannerman's decision to contract out the Bow Group's services reflected his manifesto commitment to keep the Group's overheads low by passing the burden of organisation away from the Group on to commercial partners. But in sponsored conferences, there was a fine line between the Group choosing a topic for a conference, and a lobbying company asking the Group to hold a conference on a subject of its choice. The Bow Group's relationship with City and Financial tested this to the limit.

'It was in many ways so welcome,' recalls Jeremy Bradshaw of the professionalism which City and Financial brought to the Bow Group's conferences. In support of a more commercial policy, the Group's membership, which had been in decline, began to rally. But Bradshaw believed there were inherent dangers in an overly close relationship between the Group and City and Financial. More widely, he felt that there was a 'general fatigue, lack of originality, lack of imagination' in the way that the Group was run.[12] Like Bradshaw, the trustees were also concerned. During the period when Alexander Nicoll was Bow Group Chairman, they began to warn that the difference between the Group and Button's company was becoming blurred. Demanding clarification of the handling of the Group's commercial conferences, they were disturbed to receive a note from City and Financial in reply: 'The receipt of this note from City and Financial,' they warned Nicoll, 'instead of one from the Council would appear to be symptomatic of what we would consider is a badly managed relationship between the Council and a contractor.' The letter continued: 'we are concerned to see Maurice Button also writing as "Chairman of the Bow Group Trade and Industry Committee" to advertise one of the Conferences.'[13] The trustees were worried that the Group was in danger of using up goodwill from ministers, some of whom were allegedly unaware that the Group was making money from their appearance. As a result, City and Financial quickly wound up its contract with the Group.

Months later, in the final year in which he was eligible to do so, Button decided to stand for Chairman at short notice. An outsider to the Group's formal hierarchy, his candidacy immediately upset Simon Elliott, the Political Officer in Nicoll's year as Chairman, who had hoped he might take the chairmanship unopposed. 'I decided to introduce an element of competition to what otherwise had been Buggins' turn,' says Button today.[14] He was supported by other senior members of the Group, who believed that a series of uncontested chairmen could be a recipe for lethargy in the Group; whereas in the early part of the decade there was no one willing to shoulder the burden of the Group's financial problems, in the better climate of the mid-1990s this had suddenly changed.

Elliott's disappointment that he suddenly had a challenge to fight off was exacerbated by the lavish and well-organised campaign which Button rolled out. He unveiled a slate of candidates subscribing to a detailed plan for the Group's development inside an impressive manifesto titled *Building on our Strengths* and covered in the pale blue by then closely associated with the Group's corporate image. Whereas undoubtedly candidates had helped one another in previous Bow Group elections and often tried to arrange the succession, a formal slate was a new departure, and it was unveiled in a way which riled some who felt that it was inappropriate in a group which put emphasis on individual views and prided itself on gifted amateurism. The Trade and Industry Committee threw a 'totally polished' drinks party in the Cabinet War Rooms, which Button's opponents claimed was in practice a launch party for his bid.

Simon Elliott decided that the funding of Button's campaign was the ground on which it was best to fight. His own, nondescript, mailing stated: 'I do not offer you a glossy brochure, I do not offer a free reception. What I offer is the guarantee that through sheer hard work, the creation and nurturing of new ideas and talent and the willingness to stand up and be counted, the Bow Group will over the next two years, be the cutting edge.' The problem was that, away from the metropolitan hothouse which the Group had become before the election, members intending to vote by post viewed Button's manifesto more favourably. To these people, whom Maurice Button had carefully targeted, he had cleverly made it look as if he was the ready successor, and Simon Elliott the unprepared pretender to the throne, when in fact Elliott had been nominated by a previous Chairman, Nigel Waterson MP, and the then Chancellor of the Exchequer and former Birmingham Bow Group member, Kenneth Clarke MP.

Elliott supplemented his campaign with a series of attacks planted in the Peterborough column of the *Daily Telegraph*, in which the agenda of the Cabinet War Rooms reception was questioned and Button's intent to commercialise the Group was alleged. Button himself was anonymously described as 'looking as if he shaves three times a day'.[15] But the mud did not stick. Button won because his campaign was both professional and credible: it demonstrated to a sizeable majority of the members who voted that he already had the skills to run the Group. Simon Elliott appealed to the Trustees, but his contention that the election had not been properly run failed simply because the Group's rules on electoral procedure did not cater for a campaign on this scale. The problem was that the ill-will unleashed by the election was to plague the Group over the following two years.

This latent discontent did not preclude a successful year for Button's Council. The Research Secretary, Fiona Buxton, and the Treasurer, Philip Walker, worked for Button at City and Financial. The Group's finances continued to improve, with the surplus carried forward at the end of 1995 totalling a record £36,894.[16] Increasingly the vehicle for politicians' rather than members' articles, *Crossbow* was apparently to be found on the Prime Minister's bedside table at the Party Conference. Although Button's manifesto target of 2,000 members in the long term was very optimistic, for the second year running the Group increased its membership by 10%, a substantial achievement given the Tories' wider misfortunes. But dissatisfaction persisted. Jeremy Bradshaw, who helped with the Group's press operations, and who had raised the issue of the conflict of interest between the Bow Group and City and Financial, was particularly strongly opposed to the regime.

When it appeared that Maurice Button was pushing strongly for Simon Hoare to follow him as Chairman, Bradshaw surprised other members of the Group by standing at short notice. A strong Eurosceptic who chaired the Group's European Standing Committee, Bradshaw was deeply concerned about the Group's evolution, and believed that it had become a ladder for not just political, but also personal careers. For a second year running, there was a bruising election, this time between Hoare's slate and Bradshaw. Bradshaw used similar tactics to his predecessor, holding a drinks reception on the House of Commons terrace overlooking the Thames, and constructing a slate of his own. Crucially, he mustered a wide-ranging number of MPs, among whom he encouraged concern about Hoare's colourful background as a student politician in Oxford and about the general direction of the Group. Bradshaw raised the profile of the election so much that he received unexpected support up to the last minute: Jonathan Aitken had his vote for Bradshaw couriered to the Carlton Club in support – the only problem being that his membership had expired some years earlier so that he had no right to vote. Very narrowly, Bradshaw beat Hoare. The atmosphere was poisoned by the election campaign, however, and the new Chairman found a hostile and uncooperative reception within the Council, where almost every other member had been elected as part of Hoare's slate. Vikas Agrawal was one. His letter to Fiona Buxton, shortly after the election, revealed the drawbacks of electoral slates in an organisation which, at the time, had relatively few who were keen to run it: 'I will endeavour to live up to the faith that you and the other senior officers placed in me by accepting a relatively unknown person onto the slate.'[17]

The election of a successor to Jeremy Bradshaw, Nicholas Green, seemed to heal the rift, but it coincided almost exactly with the defeat of the Conservatives in May 1997. Under Tony Blair, the Labour Party had successfully stolen the Tories' clothes and presented themselves as a safe and better alternative to John Major's ailing Government. How this was achieved remains the subject of fascination among politicians and commentators alike. Paul Johnson drew an interesting analogy: he twice described the future Prime Minister as a potential member of the Bow Group. Blair was 'a One Nation, Bow Group Conservative', he told

Spectator readers. 'Blair is the perfect late 20th century Conservative. He has Bow Group written all over him,' he wrote in the *Daily Mail* two months later.[18] It is interesting that Johnson chose to use the Group's reputation to classify the character, relative youth and successful image of Blair soon after his election as Labour leader, a galling indication of the continuing power of the Group's brand. This type of image was exactly what Blair needed to inspire past Tory voters to trust him.

After the defeat, many former MPs left the Group, leaving a total membership of about 700.[19] In his first term-card, Nicholas Green argued that 'When the Conservative Party is in Opposition, the Bow Group plays a very different role to that when our Party is in Government. We become much more policy-orientated and speaker meetings become a genuine forum for the exchange of ideas.' Under Green, the Group almost immediately began to have an impact on the plans of the new leader, William Hague, to modernise and revitalise the Tories. In *Members' Rights*, by Philip Gott and John Penrose, which argued for the introduction of one member, one vote, for the Conservative leadership election, the Group was once again instrumental in proposing a new method for electing the Party's Leader. The Party's appointed moderniser, Archie Norman MP, subsequently introduced a system which would put future candidates to a ballot of all the Conservative Party's members; the Group's thoughts on the subject were said to have influenced the final choice of mechanism.

Hague welcomed the Bow Group's programme of events in the autumn of 1997, saying 'I want to encourage an intellectual renaissance in the Conservative Party and the Bow Group has an important role to play in that process.'[20] By 1998, the Group was in a stronger position to play this role. The legacy of the previous years' conferences had left the Group in robust financial health. The acrimonious atmosphere of the previous two years was rapidly forgotten because the annual changeover of the officers meant that the mid-1990s were barely remembered by those newly involved in the day-to-day management of the Group. After the defeat, some of the Group's work was inevitably retrospective or investigative. How should the Tories tackle the Government? One man who had been at the centre of the debate on how the Conservative

Government should portray 'New' Labour was Maurice Saatchi. He offered a thought-provoking analogy of this problem as a game of chess, inviting the Bow Group to look over its 'opponent's shoulder'.[21]

Green's successor as Chairman, Nicholas Edgar, commissioned the history of the Group to be published to coincide with the Group's 50th anniversary, itself a remarkable symbol of survival. The decision to commemorate the past itself reflected the essentially healthy state of the Group's membership and finances, a far cry from the situation at both the 30th and the 40th anniversaries. The membership picked up, rising from 800 at the beginning of 1998 to perhaps as many as 1,100 by the end of 2000, and in the meantime the Group was able to improve its accommodation, moving to 1A Heath Hurst Road in Hampstead to share an office with Hampstead Conservative Association, whose Chairman, Andrew Jones, was then the Group's Political Officer.

Through branches at Oxford, Cambridge and Durham the Group also secured a presence in its traditional recruiting grounds. By contrast, every other regional branch was long since defunct; the Birmingham Group's dormant bank account was finally closed in 1999.

Under Andrew Jones, Nick Edgar's successor as Chairman, the Group made two strategic decisions: to ally itself more closely to the formal policy-making apparatus in the Party, and to colonise areas for research that were not closely associated with the Tories. By choosing themes such as electing more women MPs (an issue which the Group's rival, the CPS, only addressed a year later), charities' accountability, human rights and ethics in foreign policy, the Group made a deliberate move from the issues already swarming with think-tanks to areas where Conservatives had seemed to fear to tread.[22] Timing a pamphlet on reforming the NHS to coincide with the annual winter beds crisis and the Christmas news lull, the Group achieved widespread exposure and a front-page splash across the *Daily Mail* with its arresting comparison of the 300 extra deaths a day from the three major diseases in Britain, compared with continental mortality rates, with similar daily casualty rates of the Second World War.[23] In his speech to the Group's annual dinner in 1998, Hague had identified institutional childcare as a national disgrace. Prompted by his vivid experience of the problem during his time as Welsh Secretary, two years later the Group published a new approach to institutional childcare, *The Worst Parent in Britain*, by Rachael Bolland, a senior nurse in a leading children's hospital, and Mark Nicholson, an accountant. The Group kept a close eye on the signs that it was influencing current thinking: today Guy Strafford proudly notes that Hague had quoted from Bow Group research on health in July 2000, and from the childcare pamphlet two months later describing both as a 'very impressive contribution to our Party's thinking'.[24] Coverage in the *Economist* and the specialist press suggested that the Group's research was having an impact not only within the Party but also beyond it.

For both Andrew Jones and Guy Strafford, who followed Jones to run the Group, the major challenge was to remain prominent in a crowded market and to make the most of new technology. Careful financial management and loyal donors enabled the Group to spend more on presentation to match the quality it hoped to achieve by publishing fewer pamphlets. The cost, but also the quality, of *Crossbow* consequently increased. The magazine continued to be dominated by the writing of current rather than future politicians, but it was once again a consistently produced magazine, helped by the fact that it once again had longer-serving editors, Andrew Hicks and Gary Meggitt. By 2000, a team of as many as ten people were helping Meggitt's successor, Jocelyn Ormond, in the design and editing process. Although the pamphlets remained a traditional pale blue colour, an *Ideas Book*, edited by the Group's Research Secretary Damian Hinds, departed from the traditional format. The book included a range of suggestions from 'outlawing gazumping' and 'giving free stamps to OAPs at Christmas' to 'bringing back navy-blue passports'.[25] Unlike the *Alternative Manifesto* of 1973, the tone of which was critical, the *Ideas Book* was not only positive but accessible. The Tories' Shadow Transport Minister, Bernard Jenkin MP, gently floated another of the thoughts, permitting traffic to turn left at red lights when possible, shortly after the book was published.

The Group also experimented with the opportunities offered by the Internet. With a number of the Group's active members involved in the Internet boom at the end of the 1990s the potential of a website to spread the Group's ideas in a new dimension was recognised. Its first attempt was unsuccessful, and showed the signs of being a static advertisement for the Group rather than a changing entrance into the Group's latest research. With this failing in mind, the Group reopened its redesigned and more ambitious site late in 2000. It also began to offer advice on e-commerce and e-government to policy-makers within the Party.

The traditional forums have remained important nevertheless, not least because the Group appeared to be enjoying its own renaissance. From abroad, New Jersey's Republican Mayor Bret Schundler, and Lesley Noble of Canada's Progressive Conservatives, offered views on new policy and political strategy. There were signs that the Group was becoming a resurgent forum in domestic politics. In 1999 it allied itself firmly with Michael Portillo's campaign to present himself as a more compassionate figure than he had cut as Defence Secretary in Government, by inviting him to return to a political platform for the first time to speak on education. The Group enjoyed substantial media coverage for its 'exclusive'. Again in 2000, now as Shadow Chancellor, Portillo's only appearance on the Party Conference fringe was at a Bow Group event on e-commerce. To rebut a growing impression that the Conservatives were becoming increasingly intolerant, the Shadow Foreign Secretary, Francis Maude, deliberately sought out the Group to host a speech in which he acknowledged the contempt in which politicians were held and called for a drive 'to restore honesty and integrity to this country's political debate':

> We must make a relentless honesty the first and abiding hallmark of the modern Conservative Party . . . we must insist on the highest standards of accuracy and probity in what we ourselves say. . . we must conduct ourselves in our public and political lives with a rigorous integrity . . . we have to be big enough to admit it when we have got things wrong, and to apologise . . . our political activities must always reflect an unerring commitment to political principle and conviction . . . The last component in bringing honesty back to politics is a forthright candour about the limitations of government and politics in the network age.[26]

He urged the Party to 'show a welcome home to anyone who shares our beliefs and show that we are a tolerant and inclusive party for all the people'. That Maude approached the Group to give this message was an indication that, fifty years after its creation, the Bow Group still retained its hallmark as a thoughtful and forward-looking group of future leaders of the Conservative Party.

———————————

NOTES

[1]   *Financial Times*, 21 March 1988.

[2]   'What Sort of Europe?' *Crossbow*, Autumn 1989, p. 1.

[3]   Council Minutes, 3 September 1984. Jackson has been MP for Wantage since 1983. He was MEP for Upper Thames, 1979–84. Fishburn was Executive Editor of the *Economist* before becoming MP for Kensington in July 1988. Since 1997, when he left Parliament, he has been Chairman of HFC Bank.

[4]   *Sunday Mirror*, 14 October 1990.

[5]   Lingens, email.

[6]   'Lamont Gagged', *Sunday Express*, 19 September 1993.

[7]   'I May Stand as Leader', *Mail on Sunday*, 3 October 1993.

[8]   Katherine Bowes, email to the author, 10 February 2000.

[9]   David Campbell Bannerman, interview, 15 February 2000.

[10]   30 June 1995.

[11]   *PMS Guide to Pressure Groups*, 1995.

[12]   Jeremy Bradshaw, interview, 29 April 1999.

[13]   Butcher, Watts, Smart, to Nicoll, 14 March 1995.

[14]   Maurice Button, interview, 14 December 2000.

[15]   Peterborough, *Daily Telegraph*, 15 May 1995.

[16]   Bow Group, *Chairman's Report for 1995–96*.

[17]   Agrawal to Button, 26 May 1996.

[18]   *Spectator*, 1 October 1994; *Daily Mail*, 12 December 1994.

[19]   Bow Group, *Chairman's Report, 1999/2000*, p. 3.

[20]   24 September 1997. Hague was elected MP for Richmond (Yorkshire) in February 1989. He was Secretary of State for Wales 1995–97; Leader of the Opposition 1997–.

21   The Lord Saatchi, *Looking Over Your Opponent's Shoulder*, Bow Group, 1998.

22   On these issues, the authors were Fiona Buxton, Guy Strafford, Aidan Rankin and Michael Grenfell.

23   C. Philp, *Making the NHS Better*, Bow Group, 2000.

24   Guy Strafford, interview, 13 December 2000.

25   *The Bow Group's Ideas Book 2000*, edited by Damian Hinds.

26   The Rt Hon. Francis Maude MP, speech to the Bow Group, October 2000.

Nine

'THE BOW GROUP GENERATION'

T he extraordinary fact about the Bow Group is that it has survived in its original guise. Run by an annually revolving series of young people and thus prone to rapid changes of fortune depending on their ability, it has nevertheless managed to evade numerous financial crises, factional squabbles, General Election defeats and the gradual crowding of what was once an open market for new ideas. It has spawned several imitators and competitors: the undergraduate founder of Pressure for Economic and Social Toryism (PEST), Michael Spicer, wrote to the Group in the 1960s to ask for advice on setting up a new group and ideas about fundraising: the Group decided not to help him out. PEST metamorphosed into the Tory Reform Group many years later. The Monday Club was set up by young Conservatives to counteract the influence the Bow Group seemed to have on Party policy on Africa. Once an organisation several thousand strong, today it is a frail shadow of its former voluble self. Of the professional think-tanks closely associated with the Conservative Party, the Centre for Policy Studies and a recent arrival, Politeia, both compete genteelly with the Bow Group. Neither has managed to build a brand in the way that the Group remains closely associated with youth, earnestness and a philosophy of promoting facts over ideology, a brand which has been reinforced not only in fact, but in fiction.[1] The Group survived its early fragile years, faction and financial crisis in the meantime, and so far, fierce competition in the market for ideas today.

Beyond that simple observation, conclusions about the Group are harder to draw. That is principally a reflection of the importance of the people running the Group, and the extent to which they have been able to set and push a particular agenda. In this, the Group's constitutional mantra of having 'no corporate view' is misleading. Although the opinions of its members are as varied as they are numerous, individual Chairmen and Editors of *Crossbow* have been able on many occasions to promote particular views with impact, partly because they appeared to have the endorsement of the Group as a whole. Moreover, with changes in the Group's personnel, these changes could occur extremely rapidly.

When both the Chairman of the Group and the Editor of *Crossbow* have shared a similar view, the effect has been pronounced. Peter Lilley and Leith McGrandle moved against Edward Heath during the second half of his Government. Lilley and Peter Lloyd, months after the second General Election defeat of 1974, provided what has been viewed as the most cogent articulation of the problem the Tories had with Heath by that date. Michael Howard and Christopher Bland together produced a strongly pro-European slant to *Crossbow* at the time, though it was a view with which few in the Group disagreed. One was Simon Jenkins. His editorial view of Heath's Government took a very different tone, before he passed *Crossbow*'s reins to Bland.

At another time, the uneasy cohabitation of Chairman and Editor produced internal fireworks. Richard Barber's acerbic editorials about Sir Keith Joseph and Willie Whitelaw in the 1980s gained considerable coverage, to the consternation of Nirj Deva, the Chairman at the time. Without the restriction of the 'no corporate view' policy which inevitably restricted Chairmen, and often without the political ambitions which tended to enforce orthodoxy, Editors often had more power to influence the Conservative Party immediately. The Group's influence, whether wielded by the Chairman, his Council or the *Crossbow* editorial, existed most importantly inasmuch as other people believed it to exist. Regardless of the reality, which was often rather less than either the Group's officers would admit or its critics acknowledge, perceived influence in the 1960s led to the formation of the Monday Club and forced Ministers to take notice of what the Group was saying, after Bow Group pamphlets attracted significant coverage and became handy disarming material for the Opposition to use in the House of Commons.

The Group's occasional political surprises might have caused some of the Party's senior MPs and officials irritation, but this did not evolve into outright hostility because the Group enjoyed the support of some of the Party's most influential members. Seeing the Group as a useful tonic to his own and the Party's image, Harold Macmillan willingly helped the Group, a sponsorship which undoubtedly protected it when outrage over its statements on Africa grew at the beginning of the 1960s. R. A. Butler and Iain Macleod also recognised the value of the Group, both as a discriminating forum in which to test ideas and presentation, and as a useful satellite for testing policy before the Government made a formal announcement. Inside Conservative Central Office, Sir Toby Low, later Lord Aldington, proved a vital supporter of the Group's interests against general scepticism among the Party's National Executive. Involved in the Group from the first publication of *Crossbow*, Sir Keith Joseph recognised its value as a dependable, prompt provider of accurate research during the 1970s. Geoffrey Howe is the best-known, but far from the only alumnus of the Group who has taken a keen interest in recent years. He saw a dual social and political value when he was discussing the evolution of 1980s Conservative policy: 'In more than one way, today's Conservative Government represents the Bow Group generation.'[2] It was both the group of friends and the forum in which policies of the 1980s were first articulated in the 1960s.

The goodwill nurtured by the Group was an identifiable but intangible asset which enabled it to call in financial support both in times of expansion, as in the late 1950s, when *Crossbow* was lifting off, and in the periodic financial crises of the 1970s and 1980s. Perhaps most importantly, the continuing interest and involvement of many of the Group's members after they have left office partly compensated for the annual change of officers and age limit on office-holding. This continuum of loyalty has clearly been one of the Group's enduring strengths and it was very apparent during the research for this history. As Lynda Mackenzie, the Group's administrator for many years, puts it:

> One thing that has become very clear over the years is that the Group is a place where strong friendships and networks are

generated. There have been deep rivalries and enmities, too, but my impression is that the camaraderie is greater and outlasts the arguments. The Bow Group generates a lot of goodwill; the friendships extend beyond the political arena.[3]

The loyalty flows not least from the fact that the Group was instrumental in raising the profiles and so advancing the careers of a series of aspiring Tory politicians. Illustrating the 21st anniversary issue of *Crossbow*, published in 1980, the cartoonist Richard Willson depicted the magazine as a springboard off which David Howell, then Geoffrey Howe, and a number of other former Editors were seen taking the plunge.[4] But none of these could have made the splash they did, had it not been for the Group's corporate weight, as a fundraiser and as a publisher. While it is clear that these ambitious young men would have found other ways to enter politics had the Bow Group not existed, the fact that it did gave them the chance to propel their views into print at an early stage of their careers. Aspiring politicians like Julian Critchley or Leon Brittan clearly recognised the value of their association with the Group, which had a formidable reputation. The Group's brand, which was only fully recognised for its commercial significance in the 1980s, was already adding credibility to the views of its active members two decades earlier.

The recognition of the Group's intrinsic value came early. The first signs of political success among the Group's early members, such as John Biffen's election in Oswestry in November 1961, galvanised the Group into a clearer political hierarchy for which there was strong competition. From being an organisation in which there was a 'turn and turn about' approach to office-holding (with two Chairmen returning later to serve a second term to provide continuity), the Group became highly competitive. Although Chairmen tended to groom successors and the person holding the post of Librarian – which evolved into Research Secretary – was often seen as the Group's Chairman-in-waiting, there were more challengers happy to try to upset the succession. For two years in 1961 and 1962, all the four major positions on the Council were contested (Chairman, Research Secretary, Librarian, Treasurer). The role of Political Officer was created to formalise the competition between the officers managing the Group's research and public profile, and after 1964 it was contested in eight out of the following 12 years. In the background, two General Election defeats shook up the Parliamentary Party and opened the way to a new generation of younger candidates to apply for seats.

Challenges in the early 1970s also fed off mounting discontent with the way in which the Group had been run by people like Michael Howard, Christopher Bland and Christopher Brocklebank-Fowler. New outsiders grappled for position with the self-appointed successors of previous Chairmen, and three out of four of the main posts were contested in the Council elections of 1971, 1972 and 1973. Two years later in 1975, all four posts were contested. Through the 1980s, elections were more sporadic, although there was more frequent, but largely amicable, competition for the chairmanship in the early part of the decade. Nirj Deva and Joe Egerton fought one another in 1982; David Shaw and Simon Mabey in 1983. Deva is quick to note that Egerton was generous in defeat. It was only when financial crisis enveloped the Group at the end of the 1980s that the Group's members lost their appetite for power. Disappointingly, but perhaps revealingly, there were no incidences of subsequent Cabinet Ministers standing against one another for the chairmanship, and only a single example of two subsequent MPs, Julian Critchley and Hugh Dykes, in 1966. This seems to suggest how early a pecking order developed between friends and rivals, so that direct contests were avoided. An example of this is found in Michael Howard's and Norman Lamont's successive tenure of the chair, although they were Political Officer and Research Secretary respectively in 1969–70. Good friends, they shared a flat on Harley Street. This brings us to a different side of the Group.

As was shown by Michael Heseltine's decision to take his future wife to a Bow Group meeting on an early date, the value of the Group to its members was complex. It is notable that so strong a reputation could develop and rub off on its members, given the Group's transient management. But the press was, for a time in the early 1960s, almost entranced by the Group, its function and the ambition of its members. As a result, the Group could attract the very best graduates arriving to work in

London, many of whom had not been involved in university politics at all. To this day, as when the Archbishop of Canterbury, Dr George Carey, addressed the Group in October 1999, the Group has had an ability to rise above politics and attract members for its research and publishing functions alone. It is hard to imagine the Archbishop of Canterbury addressing any other Conservative group.

Although lofty at times, the Group has often been quick to spot opportunities to make its mark. It was one of the earliest groups to realise the potential of the Party Conference fringe, both as a way of gaining exposure when the national media were present in force, and because it was – and remains – the only time of year when Government Ministers escape their civil servants and can be tempted to be more forth-right than usual in the intoxicating atmosphere political conferences can generate. By 1965 the Bow Group's Conference cocktail party attracted over 300 people, most of them not members of the Group. In 1969, at its first formal fringe meeting, a debate on the worsening situation in Northern Ireland, the Group recognised that by providing free speech in an otherwise tightly stage-managed environment, it could cause a real stir. This explains the attraction, based on the slightly heterodox reputa-tion the Group's fringe meeting had acquired, of the Group for a number of dissident speakers in the 1980s. Bringing Michael Portillo in from the political wilderness in 1999 to speak on education fell firmly in this tradition: the former Defence Secretary talking about a clearly social issue.

The willingness of the Group to court controversy deliberately and the political aspirations of its leading lights are obviously linked. At times, Chairmen of the Group shied away from publicity which they felt might raise questions about their loyalty to the Conservative Party. Greater centralisation of the Party's apparatus for selecting candidates over the years has heightened this concern. But the Party has been remarkably tolerant of the Group, whose value as a constructive critic has tended to be recognised by the Party hierarchy, if not by all its activists. The Group would have had little colour had it always been slavish to Central Office concerns. One of its earliest desires, to have 'no orthodoxy, so no heresies', is an almost evergreen mantra on which the health of the Group has most surely been based. That said, if allowed to flourish, the innate urge of many of the Group's most active members to gain publicity for themselves should make it hard for the Group ever to suffer a fatal excess of orthodoxy.

NOTES

1   For a fictional representation of the Group's members, see the 1970s BBC programme *The Doctors*, a twice-weekly drama in which Dr Liz McNeal had fallen in love with a married Bow Grouper who was also a Catholic, or David Walder's thinly veiled novel *The Shortlist*, which featured the 'Stepney Group'.

2   *Journal of Economic Affairs*, Spring 1983.

3   MacKenzie, letter.

4   *Crossbow*, Summer 1980. This was *Crossbow*'s 84th issue.

APPENDIX I

Principal Officers of the Bow Group and Editors of *Crossbow*

Officers: <u>Underlined</u> – MP/MEP, *Italics* – Cabinet Minister

YEAR	CHAIRMAN	SECRETARY	LIBRARIAN	TREASURER
1951–52	Griffiths	<u>Emery</u>	<u>Freeth</u>	Lemkin
1952–53	Lemkin	Bankes	Williams	*<u>Jenkin</u>*
1953–54	Stone	Cooper	Williams	Lewis
1954–55	Williams	Buck	Howe	Jones
1955–56	*<u>Howe</u>*	<u>Buck</u>	Lines	Jones
1956–57	Lemkin	Anderson	Lines	Pears
1957–58	Lemkin	Anderson	Lines	Pears
1958–59	Lewis	<u>Tuckman</u>	Fox	Walton/Hennessy
1959–60	Hennessy	Needs	Fox	Hooson
1960–61	<u>Hooson</u>	Needs	Howell	M. Wheaton
1961–62	*<u>Howell</u>*	Needs	*<u>Biffen</u>*	M. Wheaton
1962–63	*Hennessy*	Newton	MacGregor	Turner
1963–64	*<u>MacGregor</u>*	Newton	Brittan	A Wheaton

YEAR	CHAIRMAN	RESEARCH SECRETARY	POLITICAL OFFICER	SECRETARY	TREASURER
1964–65	*<u>Brittan</u>*	*<u>Newton</u>*	Bosch	Bing	Campbell
1965–66	Bosch	<u>Dykes</u>	Critchley	Bing	Campbell
1966–67	<u>Critchley</u>	Nelson-Jones	Watts	Brocklebank-Fowler	*Freeman*
1967–68	Watts	Nelson-Jones	<u>Sainsbury</u>	Brocklebank-Fowler	*Freeman*
1968–69	<u>Brocklebank-Fowler</u>	Lamont	Bland	Howard	Butcher
1969–70	Bland	Lamont	Howard	Watherston	Butcher

cont'd

YEAR	CHAIRMAN	RESEARCH SECRETARY	POLITICAL OFFICER	SECRETARY	TREASURER
1970–71	*Howard*	Lloyd	Lamont	Baker	Koops
1971–72	*Lamont*	Lloyd	Baker	Lilley	Koops
1972–73	Lloyd	Lilley	Craig	Dyas	Stern
1973–74	Lilley	Hodgson	Dyas	Clarke	Stern
1974–75	*Lilley*	Hodgson	*Butcher*	Clarke	Bradley
1975–76	Hodgson	Mahony	Stern	French	Bradley
1976–77	Clarke	Bradley	Stern	French	Simmons
1977–78	Stern	French	Dalton	Barber	Simmons
1978–79	French	Barber	Young	Egerton	Simmons
1979–80	Barber	Simmons	Deva	Egerton	Coulson-Thomas
1980–81	Simmons	Egerton	Deva	Shaw	Coulson-Thomas
1981–82	Deva	Coulson-Thomas	Shaw	Howard	Mabey
1982–83	Coulson-Thomas	Mabey	Lingens	Taylor/Hearn	Jenkins
1983–84	Shaw	Perry	Lingens	Hearn	Jenkins
1984–85	Lingens	Perry	Waterson	Donaldson	Porter/Rossi
1985–86	Perry	Paterson	Waterson	Donaldson	Rossi
1986–87	Waterson	Paterson	Rossi	Gillan	Lavy
1987–88	Gillan	Donaldson	Rossi	Potter	Pender
1988–89	Rossi	Donaldson	Harvey	Kochanski	Fernyhough
1989–90	Donaldson	Kochanski	Harvey	Clark	Fernyhough
1990–91	Harvey	Hawkins	Jerome-Smith	Exten-Wright	Castle
1991–92	Jerome-Smith	Toner	Campbell Bannerman	Roberts	Jones
1992–93	Hawkins	Roche	Toner	Langford	Coburn
1993–94	Campbell Bannerman	Nicoll	Ive	Langford	T. Buxton
1994–95	Nicoll	Fox	Elliott	Bowes	Walker
1995–96	Button	F. Buxton	Hoare	T Buxton	Walker
1996–97	Bradshaw	F. Buxton	Green	Patient	T. Buxton

YEAR	CHAIRMAN	RESEARCH SECRETARY	POLITICAL OFFICER	SECRETARY	TREASURER
1997–98	Green	Calderbank	Edgar	Jones	Meggitt
1998–99	Edgar	Penrose	Jones	Anderson	Haver
1999–2000	Jones	Strafford	Greening	Moore	Bird
2000–01	Strafford	Hinds	Morgan	Roper	Ellwood

Editors of *Crossbow* 1957–2001

Autumn 1957–New Year 1958 Colin Jones (2 issues)

Spring 1958–Spring 1960 Tim Raison (9 issues)

Summer 1960–New Year 1962 Geoffrey Howe (6 issues)

Spring 1962–June 1964 David Howell (8 issues)

July 1964–September 1966 Michael Wolff (9 issues)

October 1966–December 1968 Leon Brittan (9 issues)

January 1969–December 1970 Simon Jenkins (7 issues)

January 1971–June 1972 Christopher Bland (6 issues)

August 1972–June 1974 Leith McGrandle (8 issues)

December 1974–Summer 1976 Peter Lloyd (6 issues)

Autumn 1976–Summer 1980 Patricia Hodgson (10 issues)

Autumn 1980–Spring 1983 Richard Barber (4 issues)

October 1983–Autumn 1985 Nirj Deva (7 issues)

Summer 1986–Autumn 1988 Nicholas Perry (10 issues)

Spring 1989–Winter 1989 Joanna Bogle (4 issues)

Spring 1990–Summer 1991 Julian Samways (3 issues)

Autumn 1991–Autumn 1992 David Harvey, Mark Field (2 issues)

October 1993   Amanda Slater (1 issue)

February 1994–October 1994 Fiona Buxton, Andrew Hicks

BIBLIOGRAPHY

PRIMARY SOURCES

BOW GROUP RECORDS::

Termcards 1953–2000

Bow Group Confidential File

Bow Group newspaper cuttings archive

Bow Group, Council Minutes, four volumes: 1959–66, 1966–70, 1971–81, 1981–87

Bow Publications, Board Minutes, one volume: 1957–80

Correspondence files in the Bow Group's archive: Tom Hooson 1960–61; David Howell 1961–62; Henry Bosch 1964–64

BOW GROUP PUBLICATIONS:

Crossbow, 1957–99

Pamphlets 1952–2000 [see Appendix II]

CONSERVATIVE PARTY ARCHIVE

CCO 3/2/62; CCO 3/3/48; CCO 3/4/32; CCO 3/4/38; CCO 3/6/38; CCO 3/7/4; CCO 20/43/2; CCO 20/6/1; CCO 20/29/1; CCO 140/4/1/1; CCO 140/4/1/6; CCO 140/4/3/11; CCO 140/2/1/7; CCO 140/2/3/4; CCO 140/2/3/6; KJ/2/1

PRIVATE PAPERS

Fiona Buxton, David Campbell Bannerman, Nicholas Perry, The Rt Hon. Lord Jenkin of Roding, The Rt Hon. Lord Howe of Aberavon, Bruce Griffiths

LETTERS AND EMAILS

The Rt Hon. Sir Tim Sainsbury, Alan Bennett, Katherine Bowes, Fred Kellogg, Michael Lingens, Henry Bosch

INTERVIEWS

The Rt Hon. Lord Jenkin of Roding, 2 March 1999; The Rt Hon. Lord Howell of Guildford, 24 March 1999; Nirj Deva, 8 April and 24 September 1999; The Rt Hon.

Michael Howard MP, 13 April 1999; The Rt Hon. Peter Lilley MP, 13 April 1999; Pamela Thomas, 24 April 1999; Jeremy Bradshaw, 29 April 1999; James Lemkin, 4 May 1999; The Rt Hon. Sir Peter Emery MP, 6 May 1999; Nigel Waterson MP, 19 May 1999; Stuart Jackson, May 1999; Patricia Hodgson, 14 June 1999; Russell Lewis, 30 June 1999; Simon Jenkins, 19 October 1999; Michael Stephen, 24 October 1999; Nick Hawkins MP, 27 October 1999; David Shaw, 24 November 1999; The Rt Hon. Lord Howe of Aberavon, 8 December 1999; Douglas French, 21 December 1999; The Rt Hon. Sir Leon Brittan, 14 January 2000; Nicholas Perry, 28 January 2000; David Campbell Bannerman, 14 February 2000; David Harvey, 9 March 2000, Marie-Louise Rossi, 29 March 2000; The Rt Hon. Sir Peter Lloyd MP, 17 October 2000; Guy Strafford, 13 December 2000; Maurice Button, 14 December 2000.

BOOKS, ARTICLES, THESES

Nigel Ashford, *The Conservative Party and European Integration 1954–1974*, unpublished PhD Thesis, Warwick University, 1983.

Clement Attlee, *As it Happened*, London 1954

Robert Blake, *The Conservative Party from Peel to Major*, London 1997

David Butler and Richard Rose, *The General Election of 1959*, London 1960

Alan Clark, *Diaries: Into Politics*, London 2000

Peter Clarke, *Hope and Glory*, London 1996

Richard Cockett, *Thinking the Unthinkable*, London 1994

Ivor Crewe and Anthony King, *SDP: the Birth, Life and Death of the Social Democratic Party*, Oxford 1994

Michael Crick, *Michael Heseltine: A Biography*, London 1997

Julian Critchley, *A Bag of Boiled Sweets*, London 1994

Richard Crossman, *Diaries of a Cabinet Minister*, London 1977

Martin Francis and Ina Zweineger-Bargelowska, eds, *The Conservatives and British Society*, Cardiff 1996

Morrison Halcrow, *Keith Joseph: A Single Mind*, London 1989

Denis Healey, *The Time of My Life*, London 1989

Edward Heath, *The Course of My Life*, London 1998

Nicholas Henderson, *Channels and Tunnels*, London 1987

Nicholas Henderson, *Mandarin: The Diaries of an Ambassador 1969–82*, London 1994

Judy Hillman and Peter Clarke, *Geoffrey Howe: A Quiet Revolutionary*, London 1988

Michael Heseltine, *Life in the Jungle*, London 2000

Quintin Hogg, *The Case for Conservatism*, London 1959

J. O. Holroyd-Doveton, *Young Conservatives*, London 1996

Geoffrey Howe, *Conflict of Loyalty*, London 1994

Richard Lamb, *The Macmillan Years, 1957–1963*, London 1994

Philip Murphy, *Party Politics and Decolonization: The Conservative Party and British Colonial Policy in Tropical Africa 1951–1964*, Oxford 1994

Gordon Pepper, *Inside Thatcher's Monetarist Revolution*, London 1998

John Ramsden, *The Making of Conservative Party Policy*, London 1980

John Ramsden, *The Winds of Change: Macmillan to Heath 1957–1974* (Longman History of the Conservative Party, Vol. 6), London 1996

John Ramsden, *An Appetite for Power*, London 1998

Robert Rhodes James, *Ambitions and Realities*, London 1972

Peter Riddell, *Honest Opportunism*, 2nd edn, London 1996

Richard Rose, 'The Bow Group's Role in British Politics', *Western Political Quarterly*, Vol. XIV, No. 4, December 1961, pp. 864–78

Andrew Roth, *Parliamentary Profiles*, London 1994

Anthony Sampson, *The Anatomy of Britain*, London 1962

Anthony Seldon and Stuart Ball, eds, *The Conservative Century*, Oxford 1994

Robert Shepherd, *Iain Macleod*, London 1994

Nicholas Timmins, *The Five Giants: A Biography of the Welfare State*, London 1994

David Walder, *The Short List*, London 1964

Admiral Sandy Woodward, *One Hundred Days*, London 1990

Hugo Young, *This Blessed Plot*, London 1998

INDEX